Ellen Ebralidze
Rising employment flexibility and young
workers' economic insecurity

Ellen Ebralidze

Rising employment flexibility and young workers' economic insecurity
A comparative analysis of the Danish model of flexicurity

Budrich UniPress Ltd.
Opladen, Berlin & Farmington Hills, MI 2012

All rights reserved. No part of this publication may be reproduced, stored in or introduced into a retrieval system, or transmitted, in any form, or by any means (electronic, mechanical, photocopying, recording or otherwise) without the prior written permission of Barbara Budrich Publishers. Any person who does any unauthorized act in relation to this publication may be liable to criminal prosecution and civil claims for damages.

You must not circulate this book in any other binding or cover and you must impose this same condition on any acquirer.

A CIP catalogue record for this book is available from
Die Deutsche Bibliothek (The German Library)

© 2012 by Budrich UniPress Ltd. Opladen & Farmington Hills
www.budrich-unipress.eu

ISBN 978-3-940755-96-4

Das Werk einschließlich aller seiner Teile ist urheberrechtlich geschützt. Jede Verwertung außerhalb der engen Grenzen des Urheberrechtsgesetzes ist ohne Zustimmung des Verlages unzulässig und strafbar. Das gilt insbesondere für Vervielfältigungen, Übersetzungen, Mikroverfilmungen und die Einspeicherung und Verarbeitung in elektronischen Systemen.

Die Deutsche Bibliothek – CIP-Einheitsaufnahme
Ein Titeldatensatz für die Publikation ist bei Der Deutschen Bibliothek erhältlich.

Budrich UniPress Ltd.
Stauffenbergstr. 7. D-51379 Leverkusen Opladen, Germany

28347 Ridgebrook. Farmington Hills, MI 48334. USA
www.budrich-unipress.eu

Jacket illustration by disegno, Wuppertal, Germany – www.disenjo.de
Printed in Europe on acid-free paper by Paper & Tinta, Warsaw.

Acknowledgements

Throughout my work on this dissertation, I have benefited from the support of different institutions and people, and I want to take this opportunity to thank them here. The institutions to which I am indebted for support in one form or another are the *Otto-Friedrich-University Bamberg*, the *German Research Foundation* (DFG), the *European Science Foundation* (ESF), *Statistics Denmark*, and the *National Center For Register-Based Research* at Aarhus University, Denmark.

Among the persons I am grateful to, I first want to thank my supervisor, Professor Hans-Peter Blossfeld, for his guidance and continuous support throughout the last few years. Among my colleagues at Bamberg University, especially two people encouraged me throughout my work on this thesis: Sandra Buchholz and Dirk Hofäcker who always found time for me when I had questions or wanted to discuss things with them. Sandra warmly welcomed me when I was a new member of the Bamberg working group; she also patiently taught me how to apply event history analysis. Dirk discussed my project ideas with me and provided me with valuable comments on earlier drafts. I am also indebted to Søren Leth-Sørensen not only for providing access to the Danish data set and deeper insights into the Danish labor market context; but also for his great hospitality. Furthermore, I sincerely thank Daniela Grunow, Karin Kurz and Thorsten Schneider for their generous help in various ways. For professional discussions, I would like to thank my former *flexCAREER* colleagues and the members of the research colloquium at the *Chair of Sociology I*, Bamberg University, who gave me much valuable advice that greatly improved my work. Moreover, in the final stage of this dissertation, I very much appreciated the help of Jonathan Harrow with the language editing of the text and Julia Unfried for checking the references. I would also like to express my gratitude to Professor Johannes Schwarze and Professor Gerhard Schulze for kindly agreeing to join my doctoral committee.

I also thank my parents for believing in me and my husband for all his love, moral support, and help. Finally, I thank our daughter Emma for continuously reminding me of what really matters in life—my memories of the time working on this dissertation will forever be linked to images of her early childhood.

Bamberg, March 2010   Ellen Ebralidze

Preface

Today's first-time labor market entrants are particularly exposed to the risks of employment flexibility in most industrialized societies. However, the majority of comparative studies tell us rather little about the variation of young workers' employment dynamics between countries. In particular, available research ignores the subjective side of the related insecurities: Do young people themselves *perceive* their jobs as being more insecure, and do they *worry* about potential job losses, or do they even appreciate being more flexible and mobile than their parents? Above all, we do not know much about how national institutions shape young people's insecurity experiences and perceptions—despite their immense individual and social impacts on, for example, family formation and fertility behavior.

Ellen Ebralidze's study on young people's objective and subjective economic insecurity is the first one to close this gap. Considering national concepts of labor market regulation, it compares not only labor market entry processes across nine countries but also the individual responses of young people to survey questions about their insecurity perception. The reference society for Ebralidze's study is Denmark, often internationally praised for its successful combination of flexibility and individual security. One of Ebralidze's central questions is therefore whether the Danish flexicurity policy is able to minimize young people's labor market risks and worries.

Her findings indicate that Denmark does indeed stand out in terms of low labor market risks and low individual job-loss worries. However, in all nine countries included in the study, flexible and precarious forms of employment and employment instability have become increasingly frequent at labor market entry; and entry in a 'bad' job raises the risk of unemployment in the later career. Surprisingly, the degree of individual job-loss worry among young workers in the liberal labor market institutions of the United States seems to be just as low as that in Denmark's flexicurity system—of course, this was all before the financial crisis of 2008.

Ebralidze delivers an excellent discussion and explanation of these partly surprising results. She also provides interesting policy suggestions. All in all, this is a convincing comparative study with compelling conclusions. Her book is excellent in both theory and methodology, and an essential reference for both labor market researchers and policymakers that highlights the severe consequences of the employment flexibilization that European insider-outsider labor markets are systematically imposing on their young generations.

Bamberg, May 2011   Hans-Peter Blossfeld

Contents

Introduction 11
1. Studying the economic insecurity of labor market entrants in Denmark from a cross-national perspective 15
   1.1. Preliminary note 15
   1.2. Employment flexibilization and increasing economic insecurity at labor market entry 18
   1.3. The role of institutional settings for shaping school-to-work transitions 29
   1.4. Danish flexicurity as a framework for labor market entry processes 39
   1.5. How to study objective and subjective insecurities at the beginning of the employment career from a cross-national perspective 46
2. Insecurity experiences: The development of employment risks at labor market entry since the 1980s 54
   2.1. Preliminary note 54
   2.2. Labor market entries and early careers in Denmark 1981–2003 58
      2.2.1. Introduction 58
      2.2.2. Research design 60
      2.2.3. Hypotheses 61
      2.2.4. Data and Methods 66
      2.2.5. Empirical findings 68
      2.2.6. Conclusions on the country study of Denmark ... 82
   2.3. Comparison with labor market entries in other OECD countries 84
   2.4. Preliminary conclusion on the development of objective economic insecurity in Denmark and the other countries ... 98
3. Insecurity perception: The translation of unemployment risks into job-loss worry in times of flexible employment 104
   3.1. Preliminary note 104
   3.2. A cross-national comparison of young worker's job-loss worry 106
      3.2.1. Introduction 106
      3.2.2. The meaning of 'unemployment' and the importance of job security for young people in different national contexts 108
      3.2.3. Research design 119
      3.2.4. Hypotheses 124

	3.2.5. Data and methods	128
	3.2.6. Empirical findings	131
	3.2.7. Preliminary conclusion on subjective economic insecurity in Denmark and the other countries	142
4.	Summary and discussion	146
References		160
Appendix		174

List of Figures

Figure 1.1: OECD summary indicators of the overall strictness of employment protection legislation: Late 1980s and late 1990s 30

Figure 1.2: OECD summary indicators of the strictness of employment protection legislation for temporary and regular employment: Late 1980s and late 1990s 31

Figure 1.3: Public spending on active labor market programs and on unemployment compensation, both in percentage of GDP, 1997 33

Figure 1.4: Average tenure with the same employer (in years) in the countries under study in 2000 41

Figure 1.5: The qualification effect and the motivational effect of activation measures in Denmark 43

Figure 1.6: The four labor market entry regimes 48

Figure 2.1: Schematic representation of the longitudinal design 55

Figure 2.2: Denmark: Registered unemployment per year as a percentage of the labor force, 1980-2002 64

Figure 3.1: Short- and long-term youth unemployment for both sexes, percentage shares: 1985–2005 109

Figure 3.2: Early-, mid-, and late-career employees: Importance of job security, 1997 and 2005 118

Figure 3.3: Basic model of job-loss worry 120

Figure 3.4: The determinants of young workers' job-loss worry 123

Figure 3.5: Percentage shares of early-career employees who perceived job insecurity, 1997 and 2005 132

Figure 3.6: Percentage shares of early-career employees who perceive employment insecurity, 1997 and 2005 135

Figure 3.7: Percentage shares of early-career employees who worry about job-loss, 1997 and 2005 138
Figure 4.1: Percentage shares of early-career employees worrying about job loss and national total fertility rates, 1997.................159
Figure A.1: Scatterplot of the countries' positions within the four labor market entry regimes, 1997 174
Figure A.2: Schematic representation of the career phase definition...........176

List of Tables

Table 1.1: Institutional characteristics of education systems......................37
Table 1.2: Comparison of research design in both empirical studies..........50
Table 2.1: Denmark: Transition into first employment after leaving the education system (discrete-time logistic regression) 69
Table 2.2: Denmark: Low-wage job in the first year of employment after leaving the education system (logit models) 72
Table 2.3: Denmark: Transition into first unemployment after first labor market entry (discrete-time logistic regression) 74
Table 2.4: Denmark: First wage mobility between firms (discrete-time logistic regression) 77
Table 2.5: Labor market entry regimes and their expected impacts on school-to-work transitions and early career trajectories 86
Table 2.6: Summary: Labor market entry regimes and changes in school-to-work transitions and early career trajectories since the 1980s 99
Table 3.1: Employed and unemployed persons between 18 and 65: Very important job attributes in 1997 and 2005 (in parentheses)...117
Table 3.2: Expected labor market entry regime-specific insecurity perception patterns 125
Table 3.3: High job insecurity perception of early-career employees (logit models) 133
Table 3.4: High employment insecurity perception of early-career employees (logit models) 136
Table 3.5: High job-loss worry of early-career employees (logit models) 140

Table A.1: Total unemployment rates of 15- to 24- and 25- to 54-
year-olds of both sexes, 1985-2005 175
Table A.2: Typical graduation ages and subsample age ranges used in
this study 178
Table A.3: Explanatory variables used in the Danish country study 180
Table A.4: OECD indices on labor market conditions and policies
used in the present study 182
Table A.5: Explanatory variables used in the cross-national study on
job-loss worry 183

Introduction

The present study traces how globalization and the accompanying rise in employment flexibility relate to young people's labor market risks and economic insecurity. It takes a cross-national perspective while focusing on Denmark, the "darling of flexicurity literature" (Madsen 2006: 14), famous for its successful combination of flexibility and individual security. The empirical analyses will go beyond the usual conceptualization of economic insecurity as an objective phenomenon linked to specific labor market risks and also include an investigation of young people's perceptions of economic insecurity.

Starting point and research interests

The notion of *economic insecurity* refers to the security of having stable access to sufficient and regular income. For today's young labor market entrants, this security is threatened by the volatility of global markets, the diffusion of precarious forms of work, and a rising risk of unemployment.

These developments have serious consequences for the young, because the dynamics of labor market entry and the first years of the employment career determine how far young people are able to build up and secure a certain standard of living, establish and maintain their social status, attain and retain social relationships, and develop a personal identity (Münch 2001). Moreover, as a prerequisite for gaining economic independence, entering the labor market and attaining economic security represent an important step toward adulthood.

The transition to adulthood can be characterized as a stepwise process in which young people adopt specific roles (Mills and Blossfeld 2005). It involves the following four main transitions: (1) leaving school, (2) getting the first job, (3) forming a serious partnership, and (4) entering parenthood. In his comparative study on Italy, Great Britain, and Sweden, Schizzeretto (2001: 112 ff.) has found empirical indications for the "persistence of normative clocks" regulating the expected sequence of these steps. These normative clocks demand that family formation "should take place when education has been completed and a secure job has been found that guarantees minimum economic independence." This underlines the central role of a successful labor market entry and the related attainment of economic security for young people at the threshold to adulthood.

In recent years, long-term full-time work has declined in modern societies in favor of so-called 'nonstandard' employment forms such as part-time, fixed-term, and own-account self-employment (i.e., without employees). As recent research has shown, these trends are most pronounced at labor market entry, leading to a longer entry process and increasing difficulties for education system leavers to establish themselves in the labor market (e.g., Blossfeld et al. 2005; Müller and Gangl 2003).

As Mills et al. (2005) have worked out, specific national institutions filter the impact of global macroeconomic developments and channel specific forms of economic insecurity toward young people. These, in turn, affect their individual behavior. The timing of labor market entry, marriage, and family formation is influenced not only by social norms or "normative clocks" (Schizzeretto 2001) but also by rational decision-making, which is deeply embedded in country-specific structural contexts (Esser 1991; Lindenberg 1983; Regini 2000a). As Regini (2000a: 8) puts it: "The institutional context, in fact, provides actors with a set of resources and constraints that they must necessarily take into account when choosing among different alternatives and consequently shapes their actions." This also means that young people take into account structural factors when thinking about their risk of experiencing economic insecurity (e.g., in terms of unemployment) and when drawing their personal conclusions on this risk. Within a given institutional context, decisions like forgoing parenthood until having obtained economic security and adequate certainty over one's future life path may well be a rational choice for young people. When trying to explain such possible behavioral outcomes of economic insecurity, it makes sense to look not just at the 'objective' experiences individuals make within their institutional contexts; empirical research should also consider the individual country-specific *perception* of insecurity.

Denmark makes an interesting case for such an investigation because of its long tradition of combining a considerable level of labor market flexibility with high levels of social security within a highly organized labor market (Grunow 2006). Compared to many other modern societies, the central changes on the Danish labor market have not been associated with increasing employment flexibility, but with the activation reforms of the mid-1990s and a coinciding economic boom leading to a tremendous decrease in unemployment. On the other hand, the mid-1990s also saw the decentralization of wage setting, increasing the scope for Danish employers to adjust to changed labor market conditions via wages. In a country study on Denmark, I shall describe how these developments have affected labor market entry processes and young people's economic security.

A good way to acquire knowledge about one case is to compare it to other ones. Consequently, this study takes a comparative view of Denmark. This makes it possible to put the changes in labor market entry processes in Denmark into perspective, revealing how the empirical transition patterns, economic risks, and insecurity perceptions of labor market entrants in the Danish labor market differ from those in other countries, and showing whether the Danish flexicurity concept helps to minimize young people's labor market risks.

Overall, with a focus on the situation of young people on the highly flexible Danish labor market, the present study investigates 'Insecurity experiences: The development of employment risks at labor market entry since the 1980s' (Chapter 2) as well as 'Insecurity perception: The translation of unemployment risks into job-loss worry in times of flexible employment' (Chapter 3). Important labor market transitions and responses to survey questions on perceived insecurity from young people in Denmark are compared to those of their contemporaries in France, Germany, Italy, the Netherlands, Spain, Sweden, the United Kingdom, and the United States.

Structure of the book

In *Chapter 1*, I develop the conceptual framework for this study by explaining what has to be taken into account when analyzing the economic insecurity of young people at labor market entry from a cross-national perspective. Here I shall describe the mechanisms behind the flexibilization of young people's employment relationships and explain the role of institutional settings in shaping labor market entry processes. The chapter ends with a description of Danish flexicurity as a framework for this important life-course transition.

Chapter 2 conceptualizes economic insecurity as an objective phenomenon (Näswall and De Witte 2003b). The aim is to find out how the immediate school-to-work transition and the early career have changed since the early 1980s, and how this life-course transition varies across the different labor market entry regimes. In particular, I am interested in whether changes in labor market entry processes in Denmark have a distinctive pattern compared to other OECD countries. These questions are examined with a comparative cross-national study design: I compare a case study on Denmark to other country studies conducted for the same research project (the German Research Foundation [DFG] project 'Flexibility forms on the labor market – a cross national comparison of the development of social inequality,' *flexCAREER*). These country studies are based mainly on longitudinal panel surveys or retrospective studies collected in the 1990s and the early 2000s (Kurz et al. 2008). For the study on Denmark, I used a sample of 15- to 36-year-old persons living in Denmark extracted from the IDA, the *Integrated Database for Labor Market Research*. All the country studies cover the period from the 1980s until the first years of the new millennium, and all applied a longitudinal, school-leaver cohort design; that is, different cohorts were followed from leaving the education system until the end of their early career (defined as the first 5 years after entering the first job), making it possible to study changes in labor market entry processes and the related insecurities over the course of rising employment flexibility.

In *Chapter 3*, I focus on one of the core dimensions of young people's economic insecurity: the risk of unemployment (Osberg 1998: 31), and present the first cross-national quantitative study on young worker's perceptions of economic insecurity that encompasses more dimensions than just job insecurity. In particular, I shall analyze the following dimensions of individual insecurity perception in early-career employees: (1) the perception of the risk of job insecurity (i.e., the individual's estimate of the probability that she or he will lose her job), (2) the perception of the risk of employment insecurity (i.e., the individual's estimated probability of not finding another—more or less equivalent—job), (3) the perception of the risk of income insecurity (i.e., the individual's estimated probability of an income loss due to unemployment), and (4) the overall risk of job-loss worry (i.e., the extent to which a person worries about losing her or his job) which is equated with the employees' overall extent of economic insecurity perception. The main research questions are: How do institutional frameworks differ with regard to insecurity perception? Does the specific Danish combination translate into less job-loss worry when comparing young workers in Denmark to those in other OECD countries? In contrast to the empirical study on objective insecurity (Chapter 2), an integrated cross-national study design is applied here: Using data from one international data set, the countries are represented in the models by dummy variables and Denmark is taken as the reference country; that is, the perceived job insecurities of respondents from the other countries are compared to the insecurities of their counterparts within this classic flexicurity regime. The data comes from a subsample of early-career employees extracted from pooled international survey data conducted in 1997 and 2005 as part of the *Work Orientations* studies by the *International Social Survey Program* (ISSP). The subsample has been created by selecting respondents in the first 6 years after graduation, with the graduation time proxied by using country- and education-specific *typical graduation ages*. This design allows an analysis of the insecurity perception of early-career employees during a time when all the countries under study had already undergone major flexibilization processes.

The book ends with a concluding *Chapter 4* that not only summarizes the theoretical arguments from Chapter 1 and the most important findings of the studies presented in Chapters 2 and 3, but also discusses what policymakers might learn from the Danish case while outlining an agenda for further research.

1. Studying the economic insecurity of labor market entrants in Denmark from a cross-national perspective

1.1. Preliminary note

Is it justified to assume growing economic insecurity due to the diffusion of flexible and precarious forms of work? Some researchers reject any increase in insecure employment. For instance, in a paper entitled "Employment Insecurity and Social Theory: The Power of Nightmares," Fevre (2007) states that

During the 1990s, social theorists popularized the idea that the affluent societies of the West were entering a new age of insecure employment in which more and more people would be forced to stitch together patchwork careers consisting of short-term spells of work. More and more of us were going to be working on fixed-term contracts, finding work through temporary agencies or relying on casual work. Continuity of employment would be a fond memory and, for many, brief spells in work would be interspersed with unemployment. Even those few who were lucky enough to remain in permanent jobs would always be fearful of losing them. Hindsight makes this view seem overly pessimistic but it is important to realize that the evidence for it was never strong (Fevre 2007: 517 f.).

Indeed, empirical findings are to be found that contradict the idea of a disappearance of long-term employment relationships. In fact, employment stability, measured by average tenure, has hardly changed since the 1990s in OECD countries (Auer 2006; Doogan 2005, 2001). Hence, Doogan (2001) speaks of the "pervasive sense of insecurity" arguing that, because the length of job tenure has been stable, the evidence for job insecurity is weak.

However, relying on job tenure as a measure of insecurity is problematic, because increased job tenure and high levels of temporary employment can exist side by side in the same labor market. Conley (2008) points to the example of Spain that, on the one hand, shows one of the greatest increases in job tenure between 1992 and 2002 (see Doogan 2005), but, on the other hand, the highest share of fixed-term contracts in its labor market. Therefore, in this labor market, obviously "job tenure increases for some and only temporary employment is available to others" (Conley 2008: 732). Indeed, while overall employment patterns may have remained relatively stable for the working population as a whole, many modern countries reveal a substantial increase in fixed-term jobs, unemployment experience, and labor market difficulties for young people entering the labor market (Blossfeld et al. 2005).

In the present chapter, I develop the conceptual framework for this study by explaining what has to be taken into account when studying the economic insecurity of young people at labor market entry from a cross-national perspective. First of all, I find it important to distinguish the concepts of *insecurity* and *uncertainty* and to clarify which dimensions of economic insecurity are relevant for labor market entrants and early-career employees. Furthermore, I shall describe the mechanisms behind the flexibilization of young people's employment relationships and point to its social consequences. When explaining the role of institutional settings for shaping labor market entry processes and describing the Danish flexicurity as a framework for this important life-course transition, it will become clear why Denmark makes such an interesting case as a reference country.

I shall argue that increased global competition and the related employment flexibilization have changed young people's school-to-work transitions and early careers. As employers in modern societies respond to the volatility of global markets by transferring market risks to their workers, and as first-time jobseekers who usually lack work experience and relevant networks are a particularly vulnerable outsider group on the labor market, it seems a logical consequence that flexible and precarious entry jobs must have become more frequent, and that unemployment risks in the early career have risen across successive cohorts. Thus, the primary thesis of this study is that earlier cohorts of school-leavers face increasing economic insecurity and uncertainty at labor market entry.

However, these transformations are filtered by different, historically grown and country-specific institutional arrangements such as the national level of employment protection, the focus of labor market policies, and the organization of general and vocational education, and these channel rising economic insecurity toward specific social groups within countries. In a cross-national comparison, this leads to divergent path-dependent developments and different responses at the microlevel.

Especially in the insider-outsider labor markets with closed employment relations, employers will try to implement numerical flexibility in the form of fixed-term contracts for new labor market entrants. Denmark, in contrast, is a special case for applying the *flexibilization hypothesis*, because of its long tradition of combining a high level of labor market flexibility with high levels of social security. Compared to most of the other countries considered in the present study, the central changes in the Danish labor market are *not* associated with increasing employment flexibility, but with the turn toward activation in the 1994 labor market reforms and a coinciding economic boom that led to a tremendous decrease in unemployment—especially for youth. However, the mid-1990s also brought the decentralization of wage setting down to the level of firms in Denmark, widening the scope for employers to adjust to changing labor market conditions via wages. Furthermore, there are some hints that compulsory activation has the negative side effect that some people who are pushed by job-search requirements to find work end up in jobs with lower wages than might otherwise be the case.

When the main issue for labor market entrants in insider-outsider labor markets is to get a first foothold in the labor market, then in countries with weak employment protection (as in liberal market economies and in Denmark), their main risk could be to start and remain stuck in bad entry positions that restrict upward mobility. Therefore, one of the main research questions in this study is whether changes in the immediate school-to-work transition and the early career in Denmark reveal a distinctive pattern in contrast to other OECD countries when comparing labor market entry cohorts from the early 1980s to the beginning of this millennium. The countries chosen for the cross-national comparisons of this study are typical representatives of the classic welfare state (Esping-Andersen 1990) and labor market regime typologies (e.g., Hall and Soskice 2001; Soskice 1999): Denmark, France, Germany, Italy, the Netherlands, Spain, Sweden, the United Kingdom, and the United States.

In this first part of this book, I shall also point to the social consequences of increasing the economic insecurity of young people. The most relevant one is probably the postponement or forgoing of parenthood. However, this argumentation only makes sense when looking at how the young perceive the different forms of economic insecurity—and whether their perceptions actually correspond to their objectively given situation. Therefore, the empirical part consists of two chapters with different conceptualizations of insecurity: In Chapter 2, I present an empirical study that treats insecurity as an objective phenomenon, whereas the study presented in Chapter 3 conceptualizes it as a subjective phenomenon, seeking answers to the question how institutional frameworks differ with regard to perceptions of insecurity, and whether the specific Danish combination translates into less perceived economic insecurity when comparing young workers in Denmark to those in the other OECD countries since the major flexibilization processes the insider-outsider labor markets have gone through. These two conceptualizations result in different data requirements and two separate research designs, which will be introduced at the end of this chapter.

The remaining part of this chapter is structured as follows: In Section 1.2, I shall discuss the reasons behind the increase in labor market flexibility and economic insecurity along with the consequences of this for young people at the beginning of their careers. Section 1.3 explains the role of institutional settings for shaping school-to-work transitions. This is followed by a detailed description of the Danish institutional setting as a framework for labor market entry processes (Section 1.4). Based on these considerations, Section 1.5 will describe the research designs of the two empirical studies on 'objective' and subjective—or: perceived—insecurities at labor market entry to be presented in the two empirical chapters of this book.

1.2. Employment flexibilization and increasing economic insecurity at labor market entry

Increasing global competition and the related employment flexibilization have changed young people's school-to-work transitions and early careers. It can be assumed that flexible and precarious entry jobs have become more frequent, and that unemployment risks in the early career have risen across successive cohorts. Although young people do develop context-specific strategies to respond to this rising economic insecurity (Mills and Blossfeld 2005), some of them face a higher risk than others of not only starting their career in a precarious job but also facing high degrees of economic insecurity throughout their whole employment career.

Before discussing in more detail the reasons underlying the increase in labor market flexibility and the consequences this has for young people at the beginning of their careers, I shall explain what I mean by the notion *economic insecurity*.

Economic insecurity and economic uncertainty - a distinction

In this study, *economic security* refers to the security of having stable access to sufficient and regular income.[1] This definition assumes that individuals are either able to provide for their income on their own, or, "if this is not the case, [for it to be] secured by some kind of social security provided by the state or private actors" (Werthes et al. 2009: 19).

It can be assumed that most young people who have finished their general education do not want to be dependent on social welfare or the financial support of parents. Gaining economic independence is part of the transition to adulthood. Thus, the economic security of young people is linked closely to having sufficient and regular work.

The economic security of today's young labor market entrants is threatened by the volatility of global markets, the diffusion of precarious forms of work, and a rising unemployment risk. The fact that unemployment benefit entitlements normally require long, continuous employment histories certainly adds to young people's economic insecurity (Grimshaw and Rubery 1997).

Insecurity and *uncertainty* are sometimes used synonymously, definitions of the two in the literature are ambiguous, and the range of partly overlapping

---

1   The meaning of 'sufficient,' however, depends on the individual context. The general, admittedly still imprecise meaning is high enough "to provide a minimum standard of living" (Werthes et al. 2009: 19) for oneself and one's dependents.

meanings associated with them can be confusing. I suggest the following distinction (Altvater 2003): *Insecurity* refers to a certain external risk or hazard; it describes a lack of safety and protection and is related to individual anxieties. Uncertainty refers to the psychological reaction to unknown and unpredictable future developments. *Uncertainty* does not necessarily cause anxieties, but it always causes a more or less diffuse feeling of disorientation.

In that sense, *economic uncertainty* can be defined as the uncertainty about whether one will have sufficient employment-related or alternative resources over time. The unknown and unpredictable future momentum is if and when the income flow will stop.[2]

I have made the distinction between economic insecurity and economic uncertainty, because it is the uncertainty that is often the causal mechanism for a specific individual behavior. However, I assume that economic uncertainty is triggered by the prevalence of economic insecurity, and thus, to simplify matters, I shall often limit myself to the use of the notion *economic insecurity*.

The shift of global market risks to labor market entrants

The analysis of employment tenure data and separation rates by destination over the 1980s and 1990s does not show any dramatic changes in job stability in most of the industrialized countries under review. [...] However, labour markets are better described as being segmented than generally "flexibilized." Numerical flexibility (of an involuntary nature) is still very much concentrated on young workers (Auer and Cazes 2003: 53 f.).

Continuous full-time work is becoming less frequent in modern societies. Instead, nonstandard forms of employment such as part-time work, fixed-term contracts, and self-employment without employees are gaining importance (Bukodi et al. 2006). These trends are supposed to be more pronounced at labor market entry, leading to a longer entry process, increasing difficulties in becoming established in the labor market, and, thus, to economic insecurity (Blossfeld et al. 2005). What are the mechanisms behind all this?

When trying to understand the acceleration of social and economic processes in modern societies in general and the rapid changes in the employment forms in particular, journalists, policymakers and scientists have often referred to the term *globalization* (Waters 2001). For example, Castells (2000) considers globalization as a major force demanding more employment flexibility and thus inducing a weakening of dismissal protection. However,

---

2   To use a metaphor, the threat of having no sufficient income is like the sword of Damocles. *Economic insecurity* addresses the question whether it hangs over young peoples' heads or not, whereas *economic uncertainty* concerns the (unanswerable) question, if and when it might eventually fall down on them.

as mentioned above, there is also empirical evidence contradicting the idea that globalization is leading to the disappearance of long-term employment relationships. In fact, employment stability, measured by average tenure, has hardly changed since the 1990s in OECD countries (Auer 2006; Doogan 2005). Nonetheless, while employment patterns may have remained relatively unchanged for the working population as a whole, many countries reveal a substantial increase in fixed-term jobs for people entering the labor market (Blossfeld et al. 2005). An explanation for this is that employers pass down their risks and uncertainties to their employees, especially to those who lack work experience and are thus in an inferior bargaining position.

Globalization generates uncertainty for organizations; it requires rapid and flexible reactions based on a restricted amount of information. Breen (1997) argues that for employers in modern societies, the attraction of long-term commitments is declining due to the volatility of global markets. They respond to this phenomenon by transferring market risks to their employees. Breen uses the notion of *recommodification of risks* to describe these processes. He speaks of *contingent asymmetric commitment*, in which employers have the option to withdraw from employment contracts at any time (and so remain flexible), while employees have no other choice than to accept this decision. This is one of the reasons behind the rise in employment flexibility in many industrialized countries.

Via flexible forms of employment, companies are able to adapt their workforce promptly to changing demands. They can choose between different types of flexibility strategies (e.g., Atkinson 1984; Bruhnes 1989; Regini 2000b). The most relevant ones applied toward labor market entrants are (1) *numerical flexibility*, that is, the possibility of adjusting the number of employees, for example, by using fixed-term contracts, layoffs, or outsourcing certain tasks (e.g., by subcontracting self-employed people who do not receive an employment contract); (2) *wage flexibility*, that is, the possibility of adjusting wages or job-related benefits to changing market conditions; and, (3) *temporal flexibility*, that is, the possibility of adjusting working times, for instance, by increasing or decreasing the working hours of employees to fit a company's current situation (e.g., by using part-time contracts).

However, not all employees are exposed to flexible forms of employment. Companies do not spread their market risks evenly among their workers. Doeringer and Piore's (1971) theory of the dual labor market distinguishes between a primary and a secondary segment. The employees in the primary segment are relatively unaffected by employment flexibility and may enjoy long-term, stable employment with structured and predictable career opportunities. It is those in the secondary labor market who serve as a buffer against their employer's economic uncertainties. Generally, jobs in the secondary segment of the labor market involve lower skill requirements, lower wages, fewer career prospects, and less attractive employment trajectories (Capelli and Neumark 2004). These jobs are usually relatively low paid and without any guarantee of social security and can thus be considered to be precarious (Kim and Kurz 2003; Kurz and Steinhage 2001; Mills and Blossfeld 2003).

There are two main reasons why labor market entrants and young employees are more likely to be in a flexible form of employment (Bukodi et al. 2006): In contrast to the more experienced, established employees, entrants are outsiders to the labor market. Their lack of work experience, seniority, a lobby, and relevant networks makes it difficult for them to access the employment system. To get a first job, school leavers are often forced to accept more flexible employment contracts. Especially in the so-called *insider-outsider labor markets* with closed employment relations (e.g., France, Germany, Italy, the Netherlands, Spain, and Sweden), employers will try to impose numerical flexibility in the form of fixed-term contracts on them, whereas in countries with more deregulated open labor markets (such as Denmark, the United Kingdom, and the United States), the majority of employees face labor market flexibility, irrespective of their seniority or experience.

An additional explanation is given when employers offer labor market entrants temporary jobs in order to screen their work potential. This argument is stronger for countries with on-the-job training systems (as the United Kingdom and the United States) but, nevertheless, also true in general. It is costly to dismiss employees who are on permanent contracts. In this context, young people in their early career are more likely to be exposed to numerical flexibility—'last hired, first fired'—especially during periods of economic recession.

Different dimensions of economic insecurity and the importance of analyzing insecurity perception

For education system leavers who are entering the labor market for the first time, economic insecurity is mainly related to the question of gaining access to the labor market and finding a first job. This is a special form of *employment insecurity*, defined as the insecurity over being able to find a new job. For early-career employees, namely, those who successfully made the transition into paid work, economic insecurity can be decomposed into three dimensions: (1) *job insecurity*, that is, the insecurity over keeping the current job; (2) *employment insecurity* (as defined above); and (3) *income insecurity*, that is, the insecurity over maintaining a sufficient and stable income in case of unemployment, sickness, or accident. Job insecurity relates to the risk of unemployment, whereas employment and income insecurity relate to its possible consequences (Anderson and Pontusson 2007; Bredgaard et al. 2005).

Accordingly, for young people at the beginning of their employment careers, economic insecurity comes in many shapes: young education system leavers having difficulties in finding a first job, early-career employees being at risk of losing theirs, or young unemployed having no reemployment opportunities while simultaneously failing to meet the entitlement criteria for unemployment benefits.

All dimensions of economic insecurity can be conceptualized in two ways: as 'objective' and as subjective—or perceived—insecurities. The *objective conceptualization* focuses on the objective context in which the employees work, for example, in terms of an "objective threat of unemployment" (Näswall and De Witte 2003b: 191). Standard objective measures of job insecurity are tenure or labor market turnover (e.g., Burchell 2005; Doogan 2005; OECD 1997a) as well as fixed-term employment (e.g., Fevre 2007; Muñoz de Bustillo and de Pedraza 2007) which, however, is problematic when making international comparisons (Campbell and Burgess 2001; Meulders et al. 1994).[3]

The *subjective conceptualization* is regarded as an important complement to such objective measures, because it is not their objectively given situation, but rather "the way individuals interpret their environment [that] affects how they react to it" (Näswall and De Witte 2003b: 191). Of course, individuals take objective factors into account when thinking about the risk of losing their job (Anderson and Pontusson 2007); however, their interpretation of their situation may well differ from that of an independent observer. This is because they frame their situation within a particular social environment and in relation to *significant others* such as family members, peers, or colleagues rather than taking an 'objective' cross-national point of view.[4]

Consequently, the analysis of insecurity perception serves as a useful analytical strategy for linking macrolevel changes, like globalization and rising employment flexibility, with the microlevel of the individual perception of job-loss risk, economic insecurity, and the associated behavioral outcomes.

---

3   In countries with an overall high level of employment protection, having a fixed-term contract is very likely to be related to additional insecurity, whereas this is not necessarily the case in countries with overall low dismissal protection.
4   The moderating effects of this 'country-specific relative insecurity perception' in different institutional settings will be discussed in Chapter 3 (Section 3.2.3).

Increasing economic insecurity, uncertainty, and the postponement of long-term binding life-course decisions

How does economic uncertainty at labor market entry and in the early career affect young people's life-course decisions? Usually, individual choices are led by reliable distinctions, for example, reasonable versus silly, useful versus useless, profitable versus harmful, and so forth. These guiding principles help individuals to make the right decisions based on what they expect will happen in the future (Baumann 1999). If future developments become uncertain, these guiding principles are hard to attribute to different options.

An effective technique to reduce the choice complexity of long-term courses of action under uncertainty is committing oneself to specific actions in the future. This so-called *self-binding* makes one's promises to significant others more credible; it enhances the trust that actors have in each other and enables them to interact and cooperate more effectively (Elster 1979). So, on the one hand, self-binding is a prerequisite for creating certainty as well as credibility and trust in one's interactions with others. However, on the other hand, it diminishes the ability to adapt to changing conditions, and this is exactly what young people in flexible forms of employment have to be prepared for, because, for instance, the termination of a fixed-term contract may necessitate a move from one city to another for a new job.

When young people working in a flexible job try to plan their future, they sometimes do not know what is the right thing to do in order to achieve their personal goals—or even, what these goals should be: Would it be mad to get married before gaining a foothold in the labor market, or would it be wise, because one partner could support the other if one became unemployed? Would it be silly to have a child under such circumstances, or would it be sensible, because having a baby would make it necessary to interrupt the employment career anyway?

Higher levels of economic uncertainty increase the difficulties for young people to make choices and long-term binding life-course decisions, and this may translate into reactions such as opting for cohabitation instead of marriage or forgoing parenthood until they feel they have obtained adequate certainty for their future life path (Blossfeld 1995; Kurz et al. 2005; Mills and Blossfeld 2005; Oppenheimer 1988, 2003; Oppenheimer et. al 1997).

McDonald (2006) offers an additional explanation for why flexibilization has led to delayed family formation. One of the key changes caused by labor market deregulation is "the rise of risk aversion among young people of both sexes in an increasingly competitive labor market" (McDonald 2006: 492). Their engagement in deregulated labor markets involves increased risks, and young people react to that rationally by trying to follow pathways with lower risk. At the same time, "[globalization] and sharply rising education levels have created high economic aspirations among young people" (McDonald 2006: 493). Consequently, the most important way of avoiding economic risk for them is to invest in their own human capital: in education as well as in work experience. As a result, family formation is put on hold while human capital is accumulated.

Hence, in some country contexts, young people react to economic insecurity by remaining in the education system longer or combining school and work.

Rising labor market risks and the extension of education

When comparing cohort-specific attendance rates across various levels of education for different countries, Klijzing (2005) has found a prolonged extension of school participation over time. This trend is related to educational expansion; however, for some countries, it is also linked to the uncertainties young people are facing in today's labor market. For some youth, the education system may seem a safe resort from an unreceptive labor market. Two different trends emerge from this.

The first one is to remain in full-time education longer. The option to take the *alternative role* (Offe 1977) of being a student depends on the existence and nature of national support systems for young adults who prefer to stay in (higher) education. Some countries such as Denmark, Germany, the Netherlands, and Sweden have a more generous system of education grants or loans, which may be, in contrast, limited (as in the United Kingdom and France), highly insufficient (as in the United States), or virtually nonexistent in other countries (such as Italy and Spain). However, the existence or nonexistence of tuition fees also has to be taken into account, and even seems to be more important. For example, in spite of a lack of education grants or loans, attendance rates in tertiary education are increasing strongly in southern European countries such as Italy and Spain (Guerrero 1995) that do not charge tuition fees. In these countries, university students are either supported by their parents or they have to work while still in education.

This points to the second trend responsible for the observed extension of school participation over time: the strategy of combining school and work (Mills et al. 2005)—either by doing both at the same time (part-time education combined with part-time work) or alternating between phases of (full-time) education and work. There are various reasons why young people may decide to combine both. These may relate not only to different support systems but also to the costs of living—in some countries, young people simply have to work in order to finance their studies. However, acquiring work experience while still in education may also be a wise tactic in order to gain a foothold in the labor market. It signals to employers that a person has the talent to organize herself and is able to juggle multiple tasks and cope with a heavy workload. Above that, it gives the young employee an opportunity to acquire experience and connections, thereby helping to build up a network in the labor market—with one foot still in the safe resort of the education system.

In their study on "Globalization, Uncertainty and Youth in Society," Blossfeld et al. (2005) revealed that particularly in liberal countries, youth follow the strategy "to take on multiple roles such as combining school and work" (Mills et al. 2005: 439). They explain this finding by referring to the education systems in these countries. However, many youth working while still in education could also be observed in Hungary and the Netherlands as well as in Spain, where this behavior "served as a protective strategy […], with those who combined education and work being significantly less likely to fall into unemployment" (Mills et al. 2005: 439). In these countries, the combination of school and work may be a way for more highly educated youth to cope with increasing employment flexibility and the difficulties in becoming established in the labor market.

There is probably also a comforting psychological effect of still keeping one's options open, especially if the first working experiences are deflating. However, whether combining school and work is a real option for young people depends strongly on the openness and flexibility of a country's education system. Sweden and Denmark, for example, offer very good conditions for doing so: Their school systems are almost free of educational dead ends, and students completing vocational training are, in principle, eligible for studies at higher levels, although additional qualifications must sometimes be obtained. These can be acquired in the comprehensive systems of adult education (Bygren et al.2002; Cort 2002; Statistics Denmark 2004).

The issue of remaining in education longer is more relevant in some country contexts than in others, and it is hard to disentangle attendance rates that have risen solely because of educational expansion from ones in which, at least partly, young people opt to remain in education in order to avoid unemployment. However, not all young people have this option, and some face a higher risk of not only starting their career in a precarious job but also facing high degrees of economic insecurity throughout their whole employment career. This will be discussed in the next two subsections.

Reinforcing social inequalities

A popular view states that in a globalized economy with rising insecurity, the risk of job loss and unemployment is no longer confined to individuals in certain class positions (based on the differentiation of employment relations), but has become a widespread phenomenon affecting all people alike. In the past, this risk was limited mainly to the unskilled working class. However, in the global economy, professionals, managers, and administrative employees might become similarly exposed to higher levels of insecurity. The threats of job loss and unemployment may "correspond less and less to class stereotypes" (Beck 2000: 153). Likewise, it has frequently been claimed that full-time employment in a specific occupation as well as the traditional, predictable career patterns during the life course are vanishing, and new types of employment trajectories are emerging without permanent attachment to any particular occupation or organization (see, e.g., Castells 2000).

Social stratification and mobility research literature offer an opposing point of view. A number of studies published since the early 1980s emphasize the persistence of social class as a predictor of inequality or, in a broader sense, the continuing influence of individuals' resources in structuring the opportunities and constraints of the different aspects of the life course (e.g., Breen 2004; Erikson and Goldthorpe 1992; Shavit and Blossfeld 1993). Empirical findings seem to confirm this perspective. The strength of association between social class and the risk of job loss has scarcely changed over the last decade, particularly in countries with insider–outsider employment regimes (e.g., Bernardi 2006; Goldthorpe and McKnight 2006; Kurz et al. 2006; Luijkx et al. 2006). Likewise, evidence indicates a strong persistence of managerial and professional career structures, at least in Great Britain (Taylor 2002).

Considering these opposed perspectives, one important question addresses the dynamics of inequality: Have social inequalities related to educational qualification and occupational class been weakened, stabilized, or even reinforced through the rising flexibilization of young people's labor market entry? Due to their lack of employment experience or networks, school-leavers who enter the labor market as unskilled (industrial or service) workers probably face a much higher risk of experiencing job loss than their counterparts in more advantaged class positions. Employers tend to dismiss unskilled workers more quickly, because the dismissal costs are quite low for employees who do not possess specific job-related knowledge, expertise, or skills that are important for the employing organizations.

Moreover, as a growing share of young workers start their labor market careers in flexible jobs, the question emerges whether these positions have different implications for people with different educational levels and different entry class positions. There is some evidence that professionals in fixed-term jobs are in a much better situation than unskilled laborers or routine service workers with temporary contracts (Gallie et al. 1998). Thus, one can expect that nonstandard work may serve as a 'bridge' to a permanent, secure 'career-type' job for labor market entrants in the professional class, whereas a temporary job might become a trap for young people in unskilled laborer positions (see Bernardi and Nazio 2005; Layte et al. 2005).

Bad entry jobs: Stepping stones or traps?

Consequently, another central question is whether a 'bad entry' with precarious employment such as a fixed-term or low-paid job has a long-lasting and negative impact on the subsequent employment opportunities, or whether it has only a transitory character leading to a 'normal' career later on. There are two major theoretical approaches to this issue: the stepping-stone and the entrapment hypothesis. The former emphasizes the temporary character of a first job and assumes upward mobility, especially during the first phase of the career. The latter asserts that a bad labor market entry has salient negative consequences for later employment trajectories.

With respect to fixed-term employment, the *stepping-stone hypothesis* rests on the screening theory. In this theory, a job with a temporary contract can be viewed as an extended probation period (Wang and Weiss 1998). In order to reduce risks caused by the limited amount of information about potential employees, employers tend to hire young workers on a fixed-term basis. Especially in highly regulated labor markets with strict dismissal protection, temporary contracts are used as a screening tool. If the employer judges the worker's performance positively, the contract may be turned into a permanent one. If not, dismissal costs are saved.

In countries with little employment protection (i.e., where employers can hire and fire employees relatively easily), fixed-term contracts do not offer the advantage of additional flexibility. Hence, other precarious entry jobs exist, which are likewise low-priced in terms of labor costs for the employers, and can serve as stepping-stones to better positions for the employees. For example, in the United States, stopgap jobs are common. These are highly flexible part-time jobs with low skill requirements, no social protection (e.g., no health insurance), low pay, and few prospects for career advancement. This kind of job is typically used by young people as a way to get an initial foothold on the labor market (Oppenheimer and Kalmijn 1995). The situation is similar in the United Kingdom, where part-time jobs and seasonal or casual work are the most important forms of precarious work (Schmelzer 2008).

In contrast to the stepping-stone hypothesis, the *entrapment hypothesis* assumes that a bad labor market entry will not be overcome by upward mobility, but, instead, will have negative consequences on the whole employment career. A theoretical justification for this hypothesis is that bad positions, especially for labor market entrants, are found in the *peripheral segment* of the labor market rather than among the *core positions* (see Capelli and Neumark 2004). Moreover, exchanges between the two segments are limited, resulting in possible entrapment in the periphery of bad entry jobs. Furthermore, potential employers may consider bad employment positions as a signal of an applicant's lack of skills, abilities, and qualifications, because these jobs are not accompanied by the same opportunities for further (general and specific) training as 'normal' positions (Goudswaard and Andries 2002). Low-level jobs might thus have a *scar effect*, that is, an enduring negative effect on the worker's career in terms of employment stability and future earnings (e.g., Booth et al. 2002; Gangl 2006; Muffels 2008). Overall, the entrapment hypothesis predicts a lower accumulation of human capital among employees who entered the labor market in a nonoptimal job leading to lower chances for further career development and, thus, to higher job, employment, and income insecurity.

In summary, the point of this section has been to show that globalization generates uncertainty for organizations, that they respond to this by transferring market risks to their employees via flexible forms of employment, and that young people at the beginning of their employment career are more likely to start in flexible and precarious entry jobs. As their lack of work experience and relevant networks makes it difficult for them to gain access to the employment system, they have to put up with employers dictating the conditions of their employment contracts. Consequently, under rising employment flexibility, younger cohorts of school-leavers can be assumed to be exposed increasingly to labor market risks and economic insecurity, which I have defined as a lack of stable access to sufficient and regular income. Whereas education system leavers first have to gain access to the labor market, early-career employees can experience economic insecurity on three dimensions: first, job insecurity (i.e., insecurity over keeping the current job); second, employment insecurity (i.e., insecurity over being able to find a new job); and third, income insecurity (i.e., insecurity over having a sufficient and stable income in case of unemployment). Economic insecurity causes economic uncertainty, and this may lead to reactions such as the postponement of labor market entry, marriage, and family formation. In order to link the macrolevel changes of globalization and rising employment flexibility with the microlevel of individual behavior, one useful analytical strategy is to study both 'objective' and perceived insecurities. Both kinds of analyses have to consider that employers do not spread their risks evenly across their employees, but that young people with low investments in education face a higher risk of starting their employment career in more precarious, flexible forms of employment. But not only the distribution of risk re-forms along already established lines of social inequality. Some individuals will accept or even opt for the risks, knowing that they will be able to use bad entry positions as stepping-stones, while especially unskilled labor market entrants have no other choice than to accept the risks and may become entrapped in the labor market periphery of bad entry jobs.

In the following section, I shall show that whether nonoptimal entry positions can serve as stepping-stones or may lead to entrapment also depends on the institutional framework, especially with regard to differences in employment protection, the use of employment sustaining policies, and the organization of vocational training.

1.3. The role of institutional settings for shaping school-to-work transitions

As Mills et al. (2005) have shown, specific national institutions filter the impact of globalization and channel economic insecurity and uncertainty toward young people and specific social groups in various countries.

Increasing uncertainty does not impact all regions, states, organizations or individuals in the same way. There are institutional settings and social structures, historically grown and country-specific, that determine the degree to which people are affected by rising uncertainty [...]. These institutions have a certain inertial tendency to persist [...] and act as a sort of intervening variable between global macro forces and the responses at the micro level [...]. Thus, [...] we claim that there are path-dependent developments within countries (Mills et al. 2005: 6).

The institutions with the most impact on young people's labor market entry processes are national employment protection legislation, labor market policies, and educational and training systems. This section describes how these regulations affect school-to-work transitions and early-career trajectories and concludes by summarizing the role of these institutional features for young people's possibilities to use nonoptimal entry positions as stepping-stones.

Employment protection legislation

The rigidity of employment protection legislation impacts on individual job and employment insecurity, because it defines opportunities and sets limits for firms regarding the implementation of different types of flexibility (Bukodi et al. 2008). Briefly, employment protection legislation consists of a set of rules governing the processes of hiring and firing (OECD 2004a); it restricts the ability of employers to dismiss workers and imposes costs on them if they do so (Anderson and Pontusson 2007). The strictness of employment protection legislation has consequences for labor market entry in terms of the duration of search for the first employment as well as in terms of the quality of the first job (Scherer 2005). Regarding the early career, strict employment protection legislation impedes job mobility because it reduces the labor market turnover and thus results in low external vacancy levels (Gangl 2003a).

Whereas, initially, employment protection legislation had been introduced in order to improve working conditions in terms of job security, from the employers' point of view, strict employment protection hinders the adjustment of companies to changing economic conditions. Consequently, rapidly changing global markets have induced many advanced societies to reduce the strictness of their employment protection legislation (Bukodi et al. 2008; OECD 2004a).

The OECD's *Employment Protection Legislation Index*, a summary standard indicator measuring the overall level of employment protection, encompasses three main components: protection of regular workers against dismissal, regulation of temporary forms of employment, and requirements for collective dismissals (OECD 2004a).

Looking at the distribution of index scores in Figure 1.1, there appear to be two opposite 'poles' of employment protection among OECD countries: On the left-hand side of the figure, we find a group of countries with very low or low strictness of protection of employees, namely the liberal countries and Denmark (DK); on the right-hand side, there are countries with relatively strict employment protection that tends to separate labor market insiders from outsiders: the Netherlands (NL), France (F), Germany (D), Sweden (S), Italy (I), and Spain (E).

Figure 1.1: OECD summary indicators of the overall strictness of employment protection legislation: Late 1980s and late 1990s

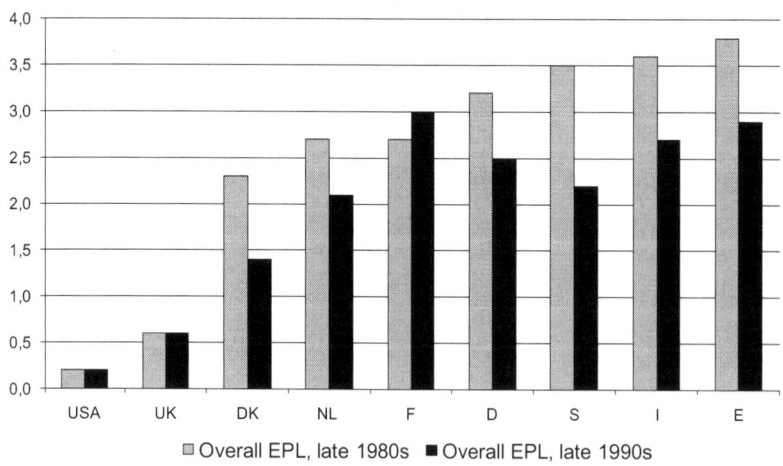

Source: OECD 2004a (index version 1).

In these *insider-protection countries*, established employees benefit from the outcomes of negotiations between unions and employers, whereas 'outsiders,' who often have less work experience and are seeking access to the labor market, rarely have strong ties to work organizations.

Figure 1.1 also reveals that over the course of two decades, most of these countries with relatively rigid employment relations gradually flexibilized their labor markets. Nearly all of them achieved this by weakening the protection for temporary forms of employment alone while leaving the protection for regular employment largely unchanged (OECD 2004a).

Figure 1.2 shows the changes in protection of temporary and regular employment from the late 1980s to the late 1990s.

Figure 1.2: OECD summary indicators of the strictness of employment protection legislation for temporary and regular employment: Late 1980s and late 1990s

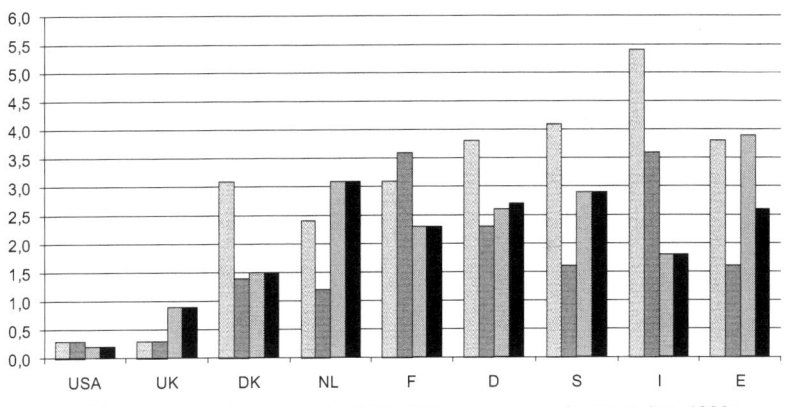

□ Temporary employment, late 1980s ■ Temporary employment, late 1990s
□ Regular employment, late 1980s ■ Regular employment, late 1990s

Source: OECD 2004a (index version 1).

As the graph shows, except for the two liberal countries under study, almost all countries introduced legislative changes reducing work regulations for fixed-term employment.[5] However, despite these flexibilization processes, separation is still a distinctive feature of the insider–outsider labor markets: Fixed-term jobs may foster young people's initial labor market entry and offer them a possibility to gain useful work experience, but although temporary employees have entered the labor market in formal terms, they cannot yet be

---

5 A notable exception is France that has increased the regulations for temporary forms of employment.

regarded as established insiders. Often, they face a high risk of becoming unemployed when their contracts expire. Furthermore, as postulated by the entrapment hypothesis, starting the career in a fixed-term job mostly has a negative impact on career advancement, because the still relatively strict overall employment protection legislation in the respective labor markets reduces job turnover and future mobility chances (Gangl 2003a).

While globalization has led many countries to reduce their employment protection, the United States, the United Kingdom, and Denmark have a long history of overall weak employment protection, which allows companies to transfer market risks directly to their employees. At first sight, this seems advantageous for labor market entrants, as all employees face the same risk of job loss, regardless of their labor force experience. Compared to strict protection, weak employment protection should result in a shorter duration of job search and more upward-mobility chances, because the hire-and-fire principle leads to a relatively high level of external vacancies, thus fostering job mobility (Gangl 2003a; Mills and Blossfeld 2005). However, in an increasingly globalized world, companies might implement flexible forms of work even more rigorously than before, and this could affect the speed of labor market entries, the quality of entry jobs, and early career trajectories. In countries with relatively low employment protection, individuals' labor market resources, such as qualifications and labor force experience, might become crucial for securing a rewarding employment position (DiPrete et al. 1997).

Labor market policies and flexicurity

Modern states apply two kinds of policies to buffer the insecurities of those affected by unemployment: passive and active labor market policies. *Passive labor market policies* buffer income insecurity by redistributing from the employed to the unemployed via unemployment and cash benefit systems. However, entitlement to unemployment benefits typically depends on making a certain number of contributory payments over a specified period, and first-time job seekers and early-career employees often will not be able to meet these entitlement conditions. Furthermore, in some southern European countries, including Italy and Spain, the two countries with the highest rates of youth unemployment[6], young people are generally not even eligible for unemployment benefits (Howell 2005; OECD 2002).

Active labor market policies are targeted at motivating the unemployed to actively seek work, while, at the same time, they aim to upgrade the qualifications and employability of those who are unable to find their own

---

6 See Table A.1 in the appendix.

way back into the labor market (Bredgaard et al. 2005). These policies are therefore directed toward reducing employment insecurity. They intervene in spells of unemployment by requiring unemployed people to participate in activation programs such as education and training measures as well as public job placement. After a certain time of 'passive unemployment' (i.e., benefit reception without obligation), the unemployed person gets a job or training offer that she or he has to accept in order to remain eligible in the unemployment insurance system.[7]

A comparison of the public expenditures on labor market policy measures by the countries included in this study (expressed as a percentage of their gross domestic product, GDP) reveals considerable differences (see Figure 1.3).

Figure 1.3: Public spending on active labor market programs and on unemployment compensation, both in percentage of GDP, 1997

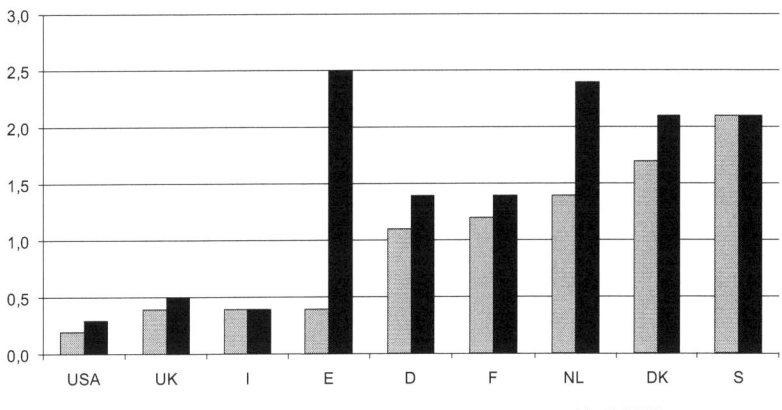

Source: OECD 2009b.

In general, the northern European countries (Denmark, Germany, France, the Netherlands, and Sweden) spend relatively high shares of their GDP on labor market policies, whereas the southern European countries (Italy and Spain) and the liberal market economies (the United Kingdom and the United States) offer rather low support for those who are not employed. However, it is important to note that expenditures on labor market policies depend on the

---

7   In the majority of OECD countries, this intervention does not happen prior to 6 months of unemployment, because, during the early stages of an unemployment spell, the rate of independent job finding is relatively high (OECD 2001).

given unemployment rate. A good example is Spain, which, in Figure 1.3, appears to spend the highest GDP share on unemployment compensation, because its unemployment rate in 1997 was at over 20 percent (OECD 2009a)—the highest level among the nine countries compared. Furthermore, spending on unemployment benefits, measured as a percentage of a country's GDP, ignores cross-national variation in the coverage of unemployment insurance (entitlement and eligibility criteria) as well as the duration of benefit reception (Anderson and Pontusson 2007).

One successful labor market concept combining weak employment protection with high public spending on both active labor market policies and unemployment benefits is called *flexicurity* (OECD 2004a). It has become very fashionable in recent years (Kronauer and Linne 2005) because its fundamental idea is that flexibility and security are not contradictory, but rather mutually supportive. The increased use of active labor market policies involves a shift from job security toward employment security (Bredgaard et al. 2005): The idea of protecting the workforce from job loss (by strict employment protection) is abandoned in favor of the idea of offering them opportunities to find new jobs by promoting labor market mobility and individual employability. At the same time, a comprehensive social safety net ensures income security for the duration of unemployment. Flexicurity is probably the best labor market concept currently available for maximizing employment opportunities while simultaneously minimizing the labor market risks of young people. However, there are differences between individual flexicurity countries.

Denmark and the Netherlands are regarded as the two original flexicurity countries. The *Danish model of flexicurity* is well-known for its successful combination of labor market flexibility and individual security. Low dismissal protection is combined with generous unemployment benefits and—since the labor market reforms of the mid-1990s—extensive active labor market programs to help the unemployed find their way back into paid work (Bredgaard et al. 2005). Barbier (2008), who has compared the meaning of *employment precariousness* in different European countries, concludes that this is an unknown notion in Denmark.

An important feature for the labor market chances of young people in Denmark is that, due to the low protection for permanent work, employment chances are less closely related to labor force experience, tenure, and seniority than in other coordinated market economies like the Netherlands where closed employment relations protect labor market insiders. Although the Netherlands have had a strong flexicurity element in their employment legislation since 1999 (Bredgaard et al. 2005; Wilthagen 1998), the overall level of deregulation has remained comparatively moderate (OECD 2004a), and this undermines the labor market opportunities for school-leavers, among other things, because of strong seniority principles that safeguard against dismissal (Wolbers 2008).

Compared to the two flexicurity countries and Sweden, which has now been spending a considerable percentage of its GPD on active labor market policies for a long time, France and Germany, the two remaining northern European countries covered by this study, traditionally have spent a lower share of their GDP on active labor market policies (OECD 2009b). Being more transfer-oriented, their labor market policies focus on protecting the living standards of those who are not active members of the labor force instead of increasing their reemployment chances. Therefore, these countries guarantee support for relatively long durations of unemployment. This means that workers can afford to search more selectively for adequate employment in terms of income, rather than being forced to accept the next available, but less rewarding job offer. This might lead to a relatively low rate of job and occupational mobility (Gangl 2004).

With respect to the integration and reintegration of young people into the labor market, southern European countries like Italy and Spain offer youth only moderate support in case of unemployment. However, in contrast to the liberal countries in which the state gives way to the rules of the market, kinship networks are of a particular relevance here, especially in helping young people to integrate into the labor market (e.g., Biggart 2005). This family-oriented welfare model owes its informal institutional character to the deeply rooted cultural view of morally reciprocal attitudes (Mills et al. 2005).

In the liberal countries, relatively low-level and means-tested unemployment benefits coerce many young people into employment, forcing them to take less attractive job offers at the beginning as well (Gangl 2004). Following the laissez-faire principle, neither the state nor employers feel obligated to support the (re-)qualification of the workers, which especially affects poorly educated young people's employment opportunities.

Labor legislation and employment policies frame the flexibility strategies applied to young people in a given country as well as the related insecurities. However, the nature of the education system, especially the degree of occupational specificity in vocational education, is also relevant for shaping labor market entry processes and early careers.

Educational and training systems

The organization of educational and vocational systems influences the duration of young people's job searches, the quality of their first job, and the mobility processes during their early careers (Shavit and Müller 1998). Additionally, the type of education system has consequences for how well companies cope with economic changes and how well employees adjust to different forms of flexibility (CEDEFOP 1993). Allmendinger (1989) has introduced a widely used typology for classifying educational regimes that meets the requirements of an internationally comparative approach (see also Blossfeld 1992; Shavit and Müller 1998). It focuses on two dimensions of qualification systems: standardization and stratification. *Standardization* denotes "the degree to which the quality of education meets the same standards nationwide" (Allmendinger 1989: 46). *Stratification* refers to the number and type of transitions to the next educational level.

Regarding labor market entries and early careers, in *standardized systems*, certificates provide employers with reliable information on the suitability of employees (Allmendinger 1989; Breen 2005; Müller et al. 2002; Tuma 1985). This results in smooth transitions between the educational and the occupational systems. *Stratified systems* provide firms with preselections of people based on their performance at school. In countries with such systems, for example, Germany and the Netherlands, educational opportunities of youth are stratified because they are streamed into specific educational tracks at a younger age. In the unstratified systems, in contrast, all children have the opportunity to attend a school that may lead to postsecondary education until the age of 18, providing the same range of options (theoretically) to all students. In these countries, a larger proportion of a cohort completes the maximum number of school years provided by the general education system (Mills et al. 2005). Countries with more unstratified systems include the United States, the United Kingdom, and Sweden. Countries like France, Italy, and Spain show a medium level of stratification.

The extent of standardization and stratification affects the matching process between education and work, and crucially influences upward and downward mobility throughout careers. Mismatches between individuals and jobs, as well as high rates of occupational mobility, are to be expected in nonstratified and nonstandardized systems (e.g., in the United States). In contrast, stratified and standardized educational regimes (e.g., the three-track education system in Germany) might reduce entries into inadequate positions and inhibit the chances and risks of upward and downward job mobility (Scherer 2005). Systems with a combination of both characteristics lie in between these two extremes.

Table 1.1 clusters the education systems of the nine countries under study by their levels of standardization and stratification. It is based on a well-known study of education systems by Müller and Shavit (1998) with an extension of the countries classified by Hofäcker (2010).

Table 1.1: Institutional characteristics of education systems

		Stratification of secondary education		
		Low	Medium	High
Standardization	Medium / High	Sweden** Denmark***	France** Italy** Spain**	Germany*** Netherlands***
	Low	United Kingdom** United States*		

Source: Hofäcker 2010.
Note: * little / ** moderate / *** strong occupational specificity in vocational education.

Apart from their general education system, we can differentiate countries on the basis of the organization of vocational training (Blossfeld and Stockmann 1998/99; Shavit and Müller 1998). This can be, first, theoretical vocational training, mainly in schools; second, a dual system encompassing both school training and gaining work experience at the workplace; or third, on-the-job training. These types of vocational training all have different levels of occupational specificity. The notion *occupational specificity* refers to the degree to which secondary school leavers exit education with occupationally specific skills. Table 1.1 also includes information on the occupational specificity of each country's vocational education system. Countries displaying a high degree of educational specificity usually rely on developed apprenticeship programs with training in detailed occupations. In contrast, in countries with a low degree of educational specificity, training curricula are rather general and occupation- or firm-specific training largely takes place 'on the job.' Thus, differences in the organization of vocational training might have a different impact on the duration of job search, matching quality, and mobility processes.

In countries in which training is limited to merely theoretical learning in *vocational schools* (e.g., France and Sweden), labor market entrants lack practical experience and networks; this puts them in a disadvantageous position compared with more experienced workers. Thus, they may have to deal with relatively long phases of job search before achieving the transition from vocational training to employment.[8] On the other hand, theoretical vocational training promotes a broader understanding of tasks in different jobs and provides general skills, enabling labor market entrants to start in more rewarding positions. Furthermore, theory-oriented vocational training makes it easier for young employees to switch between firms within the same economic or industrial segment.

In contrast, the highly specialized vocational training in *dual systems* (e.g., in Denmark and Germany) enables a large number of apprentices to make a smooth transition to the labor market with only a short duration of job search (Müller et al. 2002). Additionally, through being supervised by national institutions, the dual system provides highly regulated qualification and curriculum standards drawn up partly in accordance with companies' requirements. Employers refer to certificates as signals for the employees' key qualifications, whereas employees use them as a basis for negotiation. Thus, high standardization of vocational certificates might reduce the risk of mismatches between qualification and occupation. However, it leads to a labor market that is segmented by occupational skills. Thus, a strong association between vocational skills and occupational opportunities in these systems may confine career mobility and be disadvantageous for those whose vocational skills have become obsolete in the labor market. Those completely lacking vocational education are disadvantaged even more strongly.

Nonstandardized *on-the-job training* (e.g., in Italy, Spain, the United Kingdom, and the United States) might be regarded as advantageous insofar as employees are not restricted to narrowly defined occupational fields (Mills and Blossfeld 2005). The apparent disadvantage of this system is that neither employers nor employees can rely on certificates, resulting in a higher risk of mismatches between qualification and occupation. Therefore, becoming established in the labor market might be prolonged in terms of attaining an adequate job match. However, employment protection may play an important role for the behavior of employers and employees in countries with extensive on-the-job training. In countries where existing employment relationships are less protected (e.g., the United Kingdom and the United States), employers are fairly keen to create new job offers or to fill existing vacancies. This might result in school-leavers finding employment in a relatively short period, as well as a relatively high rate of occupational mobility during their early working lives. In countries where employment protection legislation is rather strict (as in Italy and Spain), in contrast, employers are reluctant to create new positions. This probably prolongs the duration of search for the first

---

8   An exception among the countries under study is the Netherlands where "vocational education has a clear, occupation-specific character [...], despite the fact that the provision of vocational skills is primarily school-based" (Wolbers 2008: 78).

employment and inhibits further career advancement (Breen 2005; Scherer 2005).

In this section, I have discussed the influence of labor market legislation, employment policies, and educational and training systems on labor market entry processes and early employment careers. Whether early-career employees are generally able to use nonoptimal entry positions as stepping-stones or are more likely to be trapped in them depends strongly on these institutional arrangements. In regimes with strict employment protection, a nonoptimal entry is more likely to have a scar effect on subsequent career chances, whereas in countries with weak employment protection and a more flexible labor market, bad entry jobs might serve as a stepping-stone to a better, more secure labor market position. Furthermore, active labor market policies foster young people's labor market integration in case of unemployment and may thus (at least) prevent an entrapment in unemployment. Flexicurity countries combine both weak employment protection with high public spending on active labor market policies and therefore manage to link employment flexibility with individual employment security. These countries expose their employed workforce to high job insecurity, but, in the figurative sense, offer them more stepping-stones. With regard to education systems, a high standardization and vocational specificity of secondary education may ease transitions out of flexible entry positions like fixed-term jobs—but only for those who have obtained the right skills. In countries with low standardization and specificity in vocational education in which occupation and firm specific training mostly takes place on the job, all individuals who started their career in 'bad' jobs theoretically have the chance to use these jobs as stepping-stones to better ones. This, however, requires the availability of external vacancies, which, in turn depends on weak employment protection. All the above-mentioned institutional regulations are intertwined, and thus commonly affect the dimensions of individual economic security.

1.4. Danish flexicurity as a framework for labor market entry processes

Being a flexicurity country, Denmark's institutional system has already been mentioned in the previous section. This section describes the main components of the Danish model of flexicurity in more detail in order to outline the framework for labor market entry processes in Denmark since the early 1980s.

The Danish employment system, the activation reforms of the mid-1990s, and the decentralization of wage setting

The Danish employment system has a long tradition of combining low dismissal protection with a strong and close-knit social safety net. Way back in their General Agreement of 1899, Danish unions and employers decided to regulate the labor market on their own with collective agreements (Bredgaard et al. 2005; Madsen 1999). As part of the agreement, the trade unions accepted the employers' right to hire and fire their employees. Since then, the social partners have negotiated agreements on wages and work conditions that, to a large extent, represent the labor constitution (Steffensen 2005). State intervention in the negotiation process is an exception restricted to cases in which no agreement can be reached (Madsen 1999).

Today, in an international comparison, Denmark is characterized by high employment and low marginalization of the workforce. It is widely assumed that these favorable results are due to the particular Danish mix of flexibility and security (Bredgaard et al. 2005). The Danish model of flexicurity rests on three pillars: a high degree of mobility between firms, a comprehensive social safety net for the unemployed, and active labor market policies, including rights and duties of education and job placement.

Compared to other countries, the Danish labor market exhibits a high numerical flexibility. Figure 1.4 shows the average tenure with the same employer, the standard indicator for numerical flexibility, in the countries under study.

As the graph shows, there are pronounced cross-national differences in average firm tenure among the labor forces, ranging from 7 years in the United States to 12 years in Italy. With an average of 8 years of employment tenure, Denmark is among a group of countries with a rather high degree of numerical flexibility that is comparable to the United Kingdom. These differences are, of course, the product of a number of causes, for example, variations in national unemployment rates. But it still seems that the most likely explanation for the variations in tenure is the ease with which employers can hire and fire employees (Bredgaard et al. 2005).

Figure 1.4: Average tenure with the same employer (in years) in the countries under study in 2000

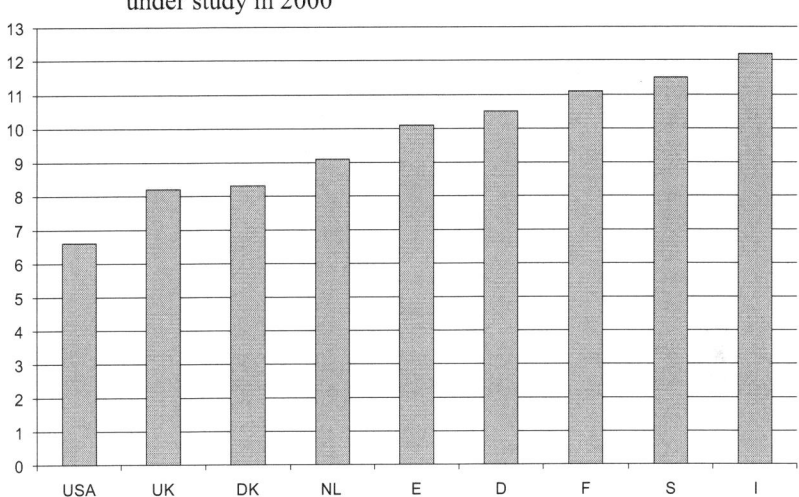

Source: Auer and Cazes 2003.

The OECD's aggregate measure for employment protection places Denmark in the group of countries with the overall lowest level of employment protection (OECD 2004a), mainly due to the low protection for permanent work (see Figure 1.2 in the previous section). Related to this low employment protection, one feature of the Danish employment system is the high interfirm mobility: Each year, up to 35 percent of the Danish workforce changes its employers (Bredgaard et al. 2005). Some of the job moves between firms involve spells of unemployment, and almost a quarter of the labor force receives unemployment or social benefits each year (Bredgaard et al. 2005). This high share is also due to the low dismissal protection in Denmark. Both the high mobility and the low dismissal protection are related to the Danish industry structure, which is dominated by small and medium-sized enterprises (Bredgaard et al. 2005).

The high job insecurity in Denmark is counterbalanced by a public unemployment benefit system, supplemented with social welfare for noninsured unemployed (Bredgaard et al. 2005). This social safety net has been characteristic of the Danish labor market for many decades. Benefits are mainly tax financed and organized around private unemployment insurance funds; they create an income guarantee of up to 90 percent for low-income groups (Pedersen 2005). Membership of an unemployment insurance fund is voluntary, but since these funds are highly subsidized by the state, there is a very high coverage of unemployment insurance for low-skilled workers facing a high unemployment risk. On average, 80 percent of the Danish labor force belongs to unemployment insurance funds (Pedersen 2005). Since 1999, the maximum duration of unemployment benefit reception has been 4 years.[9] However, in order to be entitled to benefits, an unemployed individual must have been employed for 12 of the last 30 months (e.g., Bredgaard et al. 2009; Pedersen 2005); this also includes employment on the basis of a vocational training contract (Pedersen 2005). Nevertheless, first-time job seekers and early-career employees who lost their jobs before they could gain a full year of work history are unable to meet these entitlement conditions; they can only apply for social assistance.

The addition of the unemployment benefit system can be regarded as the "basic trade-off between flexibility and security" in the Danish employment system (Bredgaard et al. 2005: 25). In this sense, Denmark already combined flexibility with security before the notion of *flexicurity* was invented. However, it is the active labor market policies stressing the upgrading of skills and job training that finally completed what is now known as the Danish concept of flexicurity.

The labor market reforms launched in 1994 were a reaction to soaring unemployment and completed the Danish concept of flexicurity: Low dismissal protection and the unemployment insurance system were supplemented by activation programs, giving the unemployed not only a right but also a duty to participate in activation measures. The active labor market policies involve individual action plans, including education and training or public job placement. After a certain period of 'passive unemployment,' an unemployed person will get a job or activation offer that she or he has to accept in order to remain eligible in the unemployment insurance system. The period until activation is 12 months for unemployed people over 25 years and 6 months for younger ones (Madsen 1999).[10] Young people who go to the local authorities and ask for social assistance immediately get a job offer. These jobs are usually (not very attractive) communal jobs. This policy is called *Instant Activation*. It has brought a sharp decline in the number of youths asking for social welfare (Jacobsen 2005).

Instant Activation was introduced in 1996 together with another change in labor legislation regarding young unemployed: The *Youth Unemployment Program* is directed toward unemployed, low-educated youth and contains incentives to resume education or to find a job (Jensen et al. 2003). The program was implemented even though youth unemployment was already on its way down as a consequence of increased public spending on labor market measures for youth since 1992 (Drøpping et al. 1999; OECD 1994). In addition, the emphasis on individual tutoring was increased (Wallin 2006). Since 1996, the Danes have managed to turn around the negative trend for

---

9   It used to be 5 years after 1996, 7 years after 1994, and even longer before.
10 Before 1999, this used to be 2 years for those over 25.

young people—not least because the *Youth Unemployment Program* helped to raise the transition rate from unemployment to schooling (Jensen et al. 2003). However, not all young people on the margins of the Danish labor market profit from the positive effects of these measures.

Ideally, the activation measures should help the unemployed to become integrated into the labor market via skills upgrades. Apart from this *qualification effect*, measures can also have a *motivational effect* in that unemployed persons who are approaching the time when they are due for activation and view activation a negative prospect may well intensify their own job search (Bredgaard et al. 2005). Figure 1.5 illustrates both effects.

Figure 1.5: The qualification effect and the motivational effect of activation measures in Denmark

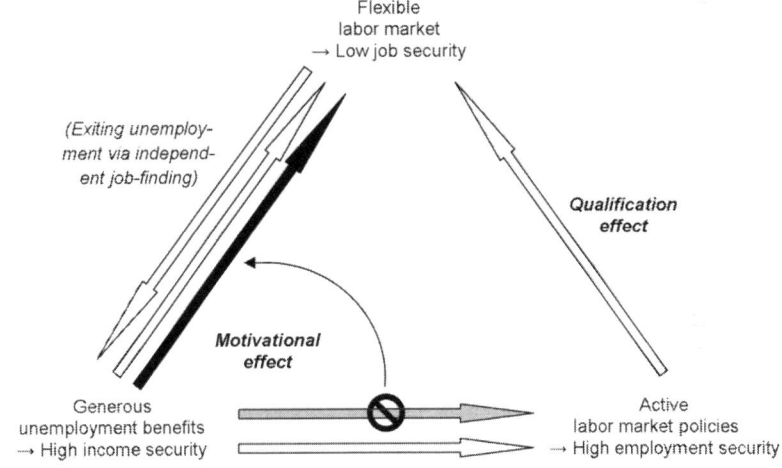

Source: Own illustration; modified version of Figure 1.1 in Bredgaard et al. 2005.

The motivational effect can result in making some peoples' situation worse in the long run, because they may end up in a *casual work trap*: The jobs these people get in order to avoid activation are usually low paid and may involve bad working conditions. At the same time, these people no longer count as unemployed; hence, labor market integration measures focusing on getting unemployed people into further education do not reach this group.

Nonetheless, for the majority of youth, Denmark provides good employment opportunities. The so-called *employment miracle* after 1994 attracted international attention. It broke the pattern of high unemployment that had held since the mid-1970s, with unemployment dropping from 12 percent (1993) to 5.5 percent (1999) (Westergaard-Nielsen 2001). However, two aspects should be mentioned regarding this success story: (1) the large number of persons in active labor market programs would more than double the unemployment figure if these groups were included in the unemployment statistics (Madsen 1999). (2) The decline in unemployment cannot be attributed solely to the labor market reforms; an economic upswing starting in the mid-1990s also contributed. Because both changes occurred in the same period, it is difficult to disentangle policy effects on unemployment from the effects of the economic cycle (Grunow and Leth-Sørensen 2006a; 2006b).

Since the 1980s, there has been a tendency toward greater decentralization of wage bargaining, which also promoted the positive trend on the labor market. Traditionally, wages were set in central tariff agreements. This left only limited scope for employers to adjust to changed labor market conditions via wages, and resulted in a very compressed wage structure (Eriksson and Westergaard-Nielsen 2004). Particularly unskilled labor benefited from this practice (Emmerich et al. 2000). However, in the mid-1980s, fixed wages and the low level of wage segregation were regarded as the major cause for continuously high unemployment rates (Grunow and Leth-Sørensen 2006b). In the following years, the policy of central wage setting was abandoned. In 1987, wage bargaining was moved down to the level of industries; from 1994 to 1995, further down to the level of firms. As a result, wage gaps between firms increased, and the Danish labor market is now characterized by high wage mobility (Eriksson and Westergaard-Nielsen 2004).

The Danish education system: Closely linked to the labor market and demanding constant skills upgrading

Denmark is an *occupational labor market system* (Marsden 1999) in which education and training systems are geared toward the skills required on the labor market. This leads to an immediate and close match between qualifications and job-specific skill demands upon labor market entry. As in Germany (Buchholz and Kurz 2008), labor market institutions and the state cooperate in defining curricula and leaving certificates. The standardization of certificates is a prerequisite for the high level of interfirm mobility, because vocational titles guarantee occupation-specific knowledge that can be transferred between firms (Grunow and Leth-Sørensen 2006b; Allmendinger 1989).

The usual path through the Danish education system is to finish general schooling and then to start vocational training or enroll in higher education. Stratification between different educational tracks starts relatively late: For the first 3 years of secondary education (until age 15), Danish students attend comprehensive schools. It is only with the beginning of upper secondary education that those on the academic route and those on different vocational routes start to attend separate schools (Cort 2002). In 2004, a total of 40 percent of 30- to 60-year-olds had completed an apprenticeship in the dual system (Statistics Denmark 2004), a combination of theoretical vocational education in schools and practical vocational training in firms. For those in higher education, Denmark offers generous educational grants. Colleges and universities charge no tuition fees, and students receive high income support (Cort 2002; OECD 1998b).

The Danish school system is, in principle, free of educational dead ends; students finishing vocational training are theoretically eligible for studies at higher levels, although additional qualifications must sometimes be obtained. These can be acquired in the comprehensive system of adult education. A fairly large percentage of all university students in Denmark does not enter directly from secondary school, but first works for some time before enrolling in higher education (Cort 2002; Statistics Denmark 2004).

The system of adult education and labor market training plays an important role within the Danish flexicurity concept, offering various programs for both the employed and unemployed. The public provision of these programs is related to the Danish firm size structure: Small firms often cannot afford to invest in training their employees. Furthermore, due to the high probability that employees will not stay in the firm, the individual enterprise has little incentive to develop their competences. Especially investments in the more general qualifications do not seem to be profitable. However, a well-educated labor force is important to maintain and enhance the competitiveness and adaptability of the labor market. In this regard, from an economic point of view, the existence of a comprehensive public training and education system "corrects the 'market failure'" (Bredgaard et al. 2005: 12).

High investments in education and life-long learning can be seen as Denmark's answer to the challenges of globalization:

There seems to be widespread agreement among both the political parties and the parties of the labour market that the solution to the challenges of globalisation is not to increase employment protection or to introduce restrictions on the free movement of goods, services and labour. Denmark cannot and should not compete on the price of products or labour, but on the quality. This means that education will be the resounding answer to the challenge, which means a strengthening of both ordinary education, and adult vocational training (Bredgaard et al. 2005: 30).

This has positive effects on the level of employment and reduces individual employment insecurity. It also means that, for the individual, being able to compete on the Danish labor market is inseparably connected to regular skills upgrading.

However, this does imply that the workforce is constantly being productivity tested and thus exposed to a permanent selection process;

unskilled people are therefore one of the groups at risk of being gradually excluded from the labor market (Bredgaard et al. 2005). Some of them may be located in the 'gray area' of the labor market related to the casual work trap described above; others probably shift between work, unemployment, and activation.

In sum, compared to other employment regimes, the Danish flexicurity framework offers almost everything theoretically possible to reduce the labor market risks of young people and to minimize their economic insecurity and uncertainty. On the other hand, even in Denmark there are still groups at the margins of the labor market.

1.5. How to study objective and subjective insecurities at the beginning of the employment career from a cross-national perspective

Based on the descriptions in the previous sections, this study will seek answers to the following main research questions:

- *How have the immediate school-to-work transition and the early career changed in different labor market entry regimes since the early 1980s?*
- *Do changes in this life-course transition have a distinctive pattern in Denmark compared to other OECD countries?*
- *How do institutional frameworks differ with regard to insecurity perception?*
- *Does the specific Danish combination translate into less job-loss worry when comparing young workers in Denmark to those in other OECD countries?*

In this section, I develop an employment regime typology based on a country's employment protection and its active labor market policies. I assume these to be important institutional determinants of labor market entrants' economic insecurity, and I shall use them to answer the above questions. Furthermore, I shall describe the research designs of the studies presented in Chapter 2 and 3 that form the empirical part of this book.

A regime typology for international comparisons of the situation of labor market entrants

As noted, during recent decades, globalization has caused a more rapid rise in the demand for employment flexibility in almost all modern societies. Whereas Denmark and the two liberal countries under study (i.e., the United States and the United Kingdom) already had flexible labor markets, other countries (e.g., Germany and Spain) have just started to introduce new flexibility forms. For a systematic comparison of Denmark with the other countries covered by this study, I clustered the countries by the main flexibility forms applied toward labor market entrants, the strictness of their employment protection, and their supply of active labor market policies (see Figure 1.6).

The horizontal axis of Figure 1.6 represents the countries' level of employment protection; the vertical axis represents their relative expenditures on active labor market policies. The country clusters positioned on the right-/left-hand side of the vertical axis have relatively strict/weak overall employment protection (OECD 2004a), and the regimes positioned above/below the horizontal axis spend a relatively high/low share of their gross domestic product (GDP) on active labor market policies (OECD 2009b).

Consequently, four labor market entry regimes can be distinguished, representing specific combinations of employment protection strictness and the supply of active labor market policies that frame young peoples' economic insecurity at labor market entry and in their early careers: (1) The upper left-hand quadrant of Figure 1.6 contains the *Danish flexicurity regime* with relatively weak employment protection (i.e., high labor market flexibility via generally low dismissal protection) and high government spending on active labor market policies; (2) the country cluster in the lower left-hand quadrant represents the *liberal regime* which includes countries with weak employment protection and low government spending on active labor market policies, namely, the United Kingdom and the United States of America; (3) the country cluster in the upper right-hand quadrant of Figure 1.6 represents the *Northern European insider-protection regime* which includes countries with relatively strict employment protection (i.e., low labor market flexibility for labor market 'insiders' and high flexibility for 'outsiders' mainly via fixed-term employment) and a relatively high supply of active labor market policies, namely, Germany, France, the Netherlands, and Sweden; (4) and the country cluster in the lower right-hand quadrant represents the *Southern European insider-protection regime* which includes countries with strict employment protection accompanied by low government spending on active labor market policies, namely Italy and Spain.

Figure 1.6: The four labor market entry regimes

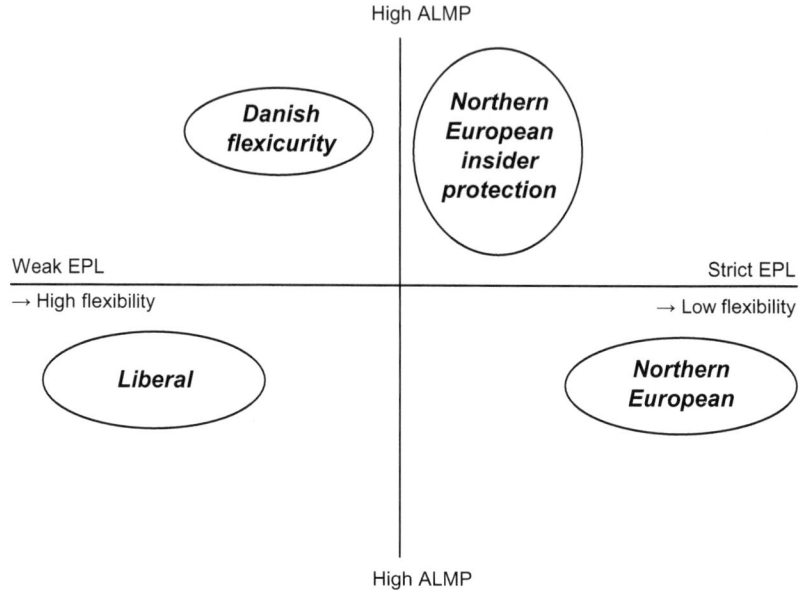

Source: Own illustration; modified version of Figure 1.1 in Bukodi et al. 2008.
Notes: The figure reflects the countries' positions in the late 1990s (for the exact position of the single countries in 1997, see the scatter plot in Figure A.1 in the appendix). However, the relative position of nations across the overall spectrum of employment protection legislation (EPL) strictness did not change much between the late 1980s and the early 2000s (OECD 2004a). Likewise, changes in public spending on active labor market policies (ALMP) since the 1980s affected only some of the countries' positions *within* the four regimes (OECD 2009b).

This regime typology is the basis for the empirical analyses comparing the economic insecurity of labor market entrants and early-career employees in the nine OECD countries in this study.

Two empirical studies and two research designs

Focusing always on the comparison with Denmark, the empirical part of this book is split into two chapters with different research designs (see Table 1.2) in order to tackle the research questions with appropriate theoretical concepts while simultaneously using the most suitable data available.

In both chapters, I apply an individual-level approach to identify cross-national differences (Leung 1989) between Denmark (respectively the *Danish flexicurity regime*) and the following countries: the United Kingdom[11] and the United States (representing the *liberal regime*); Germany, France, the Netherlands, and Sweden (representing the *Northern European insider-protection regime*); and Italy and Spain (representing the *Southern European insider-protection regime*).

In *Chapter 2*, I present the empirical study on 'Insecurity experiences: The development of employment risks at labor market entry since the 1980s.' Here, insecurity is conceptualized as an objective phenomenon (Näswall and De Witte 2003b). The aim is to find out how the immediate school-to-work transition and the early career have changed since the early 1980s, and how this life-course transition varies across the different labor market entry regimes. In particular, I am interested in the question whether changes in labor market entry processes in Denmark have a distinctive pattern compared to other OECD countries.

When trying to find answers to these main research questions, I shall not focus simply on the risk of being exposed to one of the dimensions of economic insecurity defined at the beginning of this book (see Section 1.2). Instead, two of these dimensions, namely, employment insecurity (i.e., insecurity over being able to find a new job) and job insecurity (i.e., insecurity over keeping the current job), will be analyzed within the dynamics of labor market entry and establishment processes at the beginning of young people's working lives.

The idea is, that during the course of rising employment flexibility, it has probably become more likely that all young people will start their careers in precarious jobs, but—depending on individual factors and institutional contexts—some may be able to use these jobs as stepping-stones to positions that protect against job insecurity and offer better career prospects, whereas for others, a bad career entry will prove to be a trap.

---

11 Or, in Chapter 3, Great Britain, because the ISSP interviews were conducted in Great Britain (i.e., the United Kingdom without Northern Ireland).

Table 1.2: Comparison of research design in both empirical studies

Chapter 2. Insecurity experiences: The development of employment risks at labor market entry since the 1980s	Chapter 3. Insecurity perception: The translation of unemployment risks into job-loss worry in times of flexible employment
Objective conceptualization of insecurity	*Subjective conceptualization of insecurity (perceived insecurity)*
Main research questions:	Main research questions:
• How have the immediate school-to-work transition and the early career changed in different labor market entry regimes since the early 1980s? • Do changes in this life-course transition in Denmark have a distinctive pattern compared to other OECD countries?	• How do institutional frameworks differ with regard to insecurity perception? • Does the specific Danish combination translate into less job-loss worry for young workers in Denmark compared to those in other OECD countries?
Relevant processes and aspects under study:	*Relevant aspects under study:*

• Labor market entry:
    - Duration of job search until first employment (→ employment insecurity)
    - Quality of job at employment entry
 • Early career development (taking the characteristics of the first job into account):
    - Risk of unemployment (→ job insecurity)
    - Risk of downward mobility
    - Chance of upward mobility
	• Different dimensions of the individual perception of insecurity in early-career employees:
	    - Perception of risk of job insecurity
	    - Perception of risk of employment insecurity
	    - Perception of risk of income insecurity
	    - Risk of job-loss worry (→ overall economic insecurity)

Comparative cross-national study design comparing a case study on Denmark to eight other country studies conducted for the same research project (*flex*CAREER)	*Integrated cross-national study design* analyzing one international data set (ISSP), using dummy variables for the nine different countries, and taking Denmark as the reference country
Data:	*Data:*
• Subsamples of different national data sets (for the Danish study, a sample of 15- to 36-year-old persons living in Denmark, extracted from the IDA, the *Integrated Database for Labor Market Research*) • Observation window: country-specific, from the 1980s until the first years of the new millennium (for Denmark: from 1980 to 2003)	• A subsample of early-career employees extracted from pooled international survey data collected in 1997 and 2005 as part of the *Work Orientations* studies by the International Social Survey Program (ISSP) • Subsample definition: employees in the first 6 years after graduation, selected by using country- and education-specific 'typical graduation ages' (resulting age span: 18 to 32 years)
Longitudinal, school-leaver cohort design:	*Cross-sectional design:*
• Different cohorts are followed from leaving the education system until the end of their early career (defined as the first 5 years after entering the first job) • Allows the study of changes in labor market entry processes during the course of rising employment flexibility	• Allows the study of insecurity perception at a time when all countries studied have already undergone major flexibilization processes

Source: Own illustration.

Based on this consideration and the institutional descriptions in the previous sections, the first study analyzes the following processes and aspects in order to learn about the effects of increasing labor market flexibility on young people's objective insecurity experiences in the countries under study. Regarding initial labor market entry, the important characteristics to look at are (1) the duration of job search until first employment (as an indicator of individual employment insecurity) and (2) the quality of the first job. Regarding the further development of the employment career, the most interesting question is whether labor market entrants, especially those working in flexible forms of employment, are able to establish themselves in the labor market. Therefore it makes sense to control for the characteristics of the first job and to analyze early-career employees' (3) risk of unemployment (i.e., their job insecurity), (4) their risk of downward mobility, and (5) their chances of upward mobility in the different countries.

These processes are analyzed in a comparative cross-national study design: I compare a case study on Denmark to other studies on other countries conducted for the same research project, namely, the German Research Foundation (DFG) project 'Flexibility forms on the labor market – a cross national comparison of the development of social inequality' (*flexCAREER*). This project has studied flexibility strategies on the labor market and their impact on social inequality structures in 11 industrial countries. The first phase of the project concentrated on labor market entry and early careers (Blossfeld et al. 2008).

The majority of data used for the single country studies in the *flexCAREER* project came from longitudinal panel surveys or retrospective studies collected in the 1990s and the early 2000s (Bukodi et al. 2008). For the Danish country study, I used a sample of 15- to 36-year-old persons living in Denmark extracted from the IDA, the *Integrated Database for Labor Market Research*.[12] The observation window for the Danish study opens in 1980 and closes in 2003; those of most of the other country studies also open sometime in the 1980s and close in one of first years of the new millennium.

All the country studies applied a longitudinal, school-leaver cohort design; that is, different cohorts were followed from leaving the education system until the end of their early career (defined as the first 5 years after entering the first job). In comparison to cross-sectional study designs, this longitudinal comparative cross-national design allows much more effective causal analyses. In particular, it can "illuminate age and cohort effects, specific historical processes, varying national 'clocks' for the timing of life events, and contextual effects." (Blossfeld 2009: 286). Hence, this design permits the study of changes in labor market entry processes during the

---

12 For a more detailed description of the data used and of the construction of the subsample for the study on Denmark, see the data and methods section 2.2.4.

course of rising employment flexibility, which is the general focus of the empirical study presented in Chapter 2.

In *Chapter 3*, I focus on one of the core dimensions of young people's economic insecurity: the risk of unemployment (Osberg 1998: 31) and present the empirical study on 'Insecurity perception: The translation of unemployment risks into job-loss worry in times of flexible employment.' Consequently, this study conceptualizes insecurity as a subjective phenomenon (Näswall and De Witte 2003b) in order to seek answers to the following main research questions: How do institutional frameworks differ with regard to insecurity perception? Does the specific Danish combination translate into less job-loss worry when comparing young workers in Denmark to those in other OECD countries?

In particular, it analyzes the following dimensions of individual insecurity perception in early-career employees: (1) the perception of the risk of job insecurity (i.e., the individual's estimate of the probability that she or he will lose her or his job), (2) the perception of the risk of employment insecurity (i.e., the individual's estimated probability of not finding another—more or less equivalent—job), (3) the perception of the risk of income insecurity (i.e., the individual's estimated probability of an income loss due to unemployment),[13] and (4) the overall risk of job-loss worry (i.e., the extent to which a person worries about losing their job), which is equated with the employees' overall perception of the extent of economic insecurity.

In contrast to the first empirical study presented in Chapter 2, this study applies an integrated cross-national design. Using data from one international data set, the countries are represented in the models by dummy variables and Denmark is taken as the reference country; that is, perceived job insecurities in respondents from the other countries are compared to the perceived insecurities of their counterparts in this classic flexicurity regime.

The data come from a subsample of early-career employees extracted from pooled international survey data conducted in 1997 and 2005 as part of the *Work Orientations* studies by the *International Social Survey Program* (ISSP). The subsample has been created by selecting respondents in the first 6 years after graduation, with the graduation time defined by using country- and education-specific *typical graduation ages*. The resulting age span is 18 to 32.[14]

Compared to the longitudinal comparative cross-national design used in Chapter 2, this cross-sectional design has a series of inferential limitations for

---

13 Unfortunately, the data set used here does not allow a direct measurement of income insecurity; proxies for nonmarket support within the models on job-loss worry were used instead.
14 For a more detailed description of the data used and of the construction of the early-career employees subsample, see the data and methods section 3.2.5.

causal analysis (Blossfeld 2009). However, the chosen design permits the study of the insecurity perceptions of early-career employees during a time when all the countries under study had already undergone major flexibilization processes.

As a bridge to the following empirical part of this book, the reader should bear in mind that the study presented in Chapter 2 treats economic insecurity as an objective phenomenon, whereas the study presented in Chapter 3 conceptualizes it as a subjective phenomenon, because both 'objectively' observable insecurity experiences and personal perceptions of economic insecurity determine young people's further life courses.

2. Insecurity experiences: The development of employment risks at labor market entry since the 1980s

2.1. Preliminary note

This empirical part focuses on 'objective insecurities,' that is, events and experiences linked to an "objective threat of unemployment" (Näswall and De Witte 2003b: 191) and other forms of economic insecurity. As outlined in Chapter 1, economic insecurity comes in many shapes and sizes for young people at the beginning of their employment career, and these depend on the country context: First-time education system leavers may have difficulties in finding employment, and those who have made this transition successfully may be at risk of losing their job again because, for example, they are working on the basis of a fixed-term contract. At the same time, both school-leavers and early-career employees often fail to meet the entitlement criteria for unemployment benefits that, in most countries, require long, continuous employment histories (Grimshaw and Rubery 1997). All these problems threaten young people with insecurity over having stable access to sufficient and regular income.

In this chapter, I shall seek answers to the following research questions:

1. *How have the immediate school-to-work transition and the early career changed in different labor market entry regimes since the early 1980s?*
2. *Do changes in this life course transition in Denmark reveal a distinctive pattern compared to other OECD countries?*

When studying young people's objective insecurity experiences, I shall not simply look at the risk of being exposed to one of the dimensions of economic insecurity defined at the beginning of this dissertation (see Section 1.2). Instead, I shall analyze two of these dimensions, namely, employment insecurity (i.e., insecurity over being able to find a new job) and job insecurity (i.e., insecurity over keeping the current job) within the dynamics of labor market entry and establishment processes at the beginning of young people's working lives. The idea is that, during the course of rising employment flexibility, it will probably have become more likely that all young people start their careers in precarious jobs. However, depending on individual factors and institutional contexts, some may be able to use these jobs as stepping-stones into positions that protect against job insecurity and offer better career prospects, whereas others will find that a bad career entry has turned into a trap.

Consequently, the two global research questions posed above are decomposed into a set of more detailed research questions that will be addressed for Denmark and the other countries under study:

- *What can be regarded as a 'bad,' that is precarious, employment position for youth in different national contexts?*
- *Has the risk of a bad start to the employment career increased across cohorts?*
- *Is a bad career entry typically a trap, or can it serve as a stepping-stone toward more rewarding jobs?*
- *Do changes in youth employment trajectories lead to a persistence or even reinforcement of social inequalities related to educational qualification and occupational class?*

I shall address these questions by studying the following processes and aspects (see Figure 2.1): Regarding the initial labor market entry, the important characteristics to look at are (1) the duration of job search until first employment (as an indicator for individual employment insecurity) and (2) the quality of the first job. Regarding the further development of the employment career, the most interesting question is whether labor market entrants, especially those working in flexible forms of employment, are able to establish themselves in the labor market. Therefore, it makes sense to control for the characteristics of the first job and to analyze early-career employees' (3) risk of unemployment (i.e., their job insecurity), (4) risk of downward mobility, and (5) chances of upward mobility in the different countries.

Figure 2.1: Schematic representation of the longitudinal design

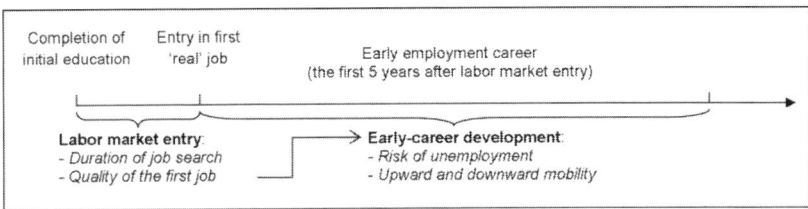

Source: Own illustration.

The first step will be to study these processes in Denmark. The second step will compare results on that country study to those from similar studies on France, Germany, Italy, the Netherlands, Sweden, Spain, the United Kingdom, and the United States of America carried out within the *flexCAREER* project.

Scientific contribution

Several studies have noted that the risks of employment flexibility (e.g., unemployment and fixed-term work) vary for different groups in the labor market. One group particularly exposed to these risks is first-time labor market entrants (e.g., Blossfeld et al. 2005; Müller and Gangl 2003) and, within this group, unskilled people. During the age of globalization, it is especially poorly qualified workers who face difficulties in the employment system, whereas the highly skilled can be regarded as the winners on *upgrading labor markets* (e.g., Dicken 2003; DiPrete and McManus 1996) in which certain businesses as well as the professional social services are characterized by a growing demand for highly educated personnel.

Within the countries covered by the comparison in this book, Denmark is a special case because of its long tradition of combining a considerable level of labor market flexibility with high levels of social security in a highly organized labor market (Grunow 2006). Compared to the other countries, the central changes in the Danish labor market were not associated with increasing flexibility, but with the labor market reforms of the mid-1990s and an accompanying economic boom that led to a tremendous decrease in unemployment. The country study on Denmark will describe how these developments have affected labor market entry processes. Special attention will be paid to the situation of unskilled people on this very flexible labor market.

As a good way to acquire knowledge about one case is to compare it with other ones, this study uses a comparative view of Denmark. It locates the changes in labor market entry processes in Denmark within a perspective revealing how the empirical transitions patterns, economic risks, and insecurity perceptions of labor market entrants in the Danish labor market differ from those in other countries, and whether the Danish flexicurity concept helps to minimize young people's labor market risks.

There are major differences in employment flexibility and individual economic insecurity between countries, because country-specific policies and historically grown institutional systems shape and filter the effects of globalization (Mills and Blossfeld 2005). They delineate the direction and the degree of possible innovations within the adaptive processes under globalization pressures, thereby producing strong national path dependencies that, in turn, affect national strategies of employment flexibilization.

We still know surprisingly little about the employment dynamics for labor market entrants during recent decades and their variation between countries with different institutional packages. Most studies have compared only a small number of countries (e.g., Brauns et al 1999; Gangl 2003a; Scherer 2004), and some have cross-sectional designs making them unable to capture employment dynamics (e.g., Bowers et al 1998; Breen 2005; OECD

1998a; Schömann et al. 1998; van der Velden and Wolbers 2003). An exception is Blossfeld et al.'s study on 'Globalization, Uncertainty and Youth in Society' (2005) that has applied longitudinal methods to a large range of countries. However, this project did not include Denmark, and its main goal was to understand how employment insecurities at labor market entry impact on partnership and family formation rather than to examine the full dynamics of the early employment career. In particular, it tells us nothing about how the early employment career depends on the smoothness of labor market entry.

Furthermore, most of the above-mentioned studies used birth cohorts to analyze cohort effects on transition processes into the labor market. If we want to explain how the growing global demand for employment flexibility and other developments on the macrolevel affect young people's employment careers, it makes more sense to refer to education leaver cohorts or labor market entry cohorts, because when leaving the education system and entering the labor market, members of the same birth cohort are confronted with very different labor market conditions depending on the level and duration of their education (Buchholz 2008; Kurz 2005; Scherer 2004). As Buchholz (2008: 45) has illustrated for Germany, a university graduate may enter the labor market up to 10 years later than a person of the same birth cohort who has not acquired any vocational education qualifications.[15] The situation of the university graduate then needs to be compared with that of an unskilled person from a younger birth cohort. Consequently, the analyses I am going to introduce in following sections are based on education system leaver cohorts.

Applying a longitudinal design, this first empirical part of this book investigates how the immediate school-to-work transition and the early career have changed in Denmark as a result of the rising globalization pressures since the 1980s. This country study has been designed as a contribution to the *flexCAREER* project (Blossfeld et al. 2008). This makes it possible to perform the second step that compares findings on Denmark with those of other country studies conducted within the same project, because they all apply a common conceptual framework and similar research designs to examine the early careers of recent school-leaver cohorts via different labor market entry transitions. This should reveal cross-national differences in labor market establishment processes and cohort-specific dominant experiences of the transition process. However, this empirical study goes beyond this rather descriptive perspective and also addresses the mechanisms behind observable transition experiences.

The international comparison in this study starts from the assumption that national contexts continue to shape young people's objective and subjective

---

15 A look at the respective *typical graduation ages* confirms this (see Table A.2 in the appendix).

economic insecurity during the course of rising flexibility. In particular, I argue that national contexts determine individual labor market risks and perceived economic insecurity through the strictness of employment protection legislation, the focus of labor market policies, and the nature of education and training systems. I assume that these national institutional arrangements do not simply coexist, but are interwoven; and I shall explain how the interplay of these institutional features determines the level and pattern of individual economic insecurity in different countries. Consequently, the countries within this comparison can be clustered into different labor market entry regimes according to their combinations of institutional characteristics. This will enable me to explain both the basic mechanisms behind and the contextual conditions affecting labor market entry processes. It will also help to understand how employment risks are borne by certain groups of labor market entrants in the different countries under study.

The following section sheds light on labor market entry trends in Denmark between 1981 and 2003. Section 2.3 will compare these trends to changes in labor market entry patterns in other OECD countries.

2.2. Labor market entries and early careers in Denmark 1981–2003[16]

2.2.1. Introduction

In many OECD countries, young people at labor market entry have been confronted increasingly with flexible forms of employment and periods of unemployment over the past two decades (e.g., Blossfeld et al. 2005).

Developments in Denmark have been different: Empirical findings point out that overall employment instabilities have not increased since the 1980s (Braun 2003; Döhrn et al. 1998; Madsen 1999). This is due initially to the country's long tradition of labor market flexibility dating back to 1899. When globalization started to provoke flexibilization processes in other employment systems, the Danish one had already reached a very high flexibility level. However, as the Danish labor market expert Per Kongshøj Madsen has put it,

---

16 Parts of this section draw on 'Weaker Entries – Lower Risk of Unemployment. Labor Market Entry Trends in Denmark between 1981 and 2003' published in Blossfeld et al. (2008). I would like to thank my coauthor on this chapter Søren Leth-Sørensen for making the Danish data set available for the analyses, supporting me in modeling the transition from education to work, and for his helpful comments on earlier versions. Furthermore, I sincerely thank Karin Kurz for her final revision of the book chapter.

the internationally praised Danish flexicurity model providing both flexibility and individual security is "more about luck" than a result of strategic planning (Steffensen 2005: 10). The Danish history of liberal employment protection legislation and high job mobility is closely related to an industry structure that has always been dominated by small businesses dependent on being able to dismiss workers in order to survive and adapt to the market. The state took over support for the unemployed via generous unemployment benefits. Furthermore, for the period under study here, two factors were counteracting possible globalization pressures on the Danish labor market: First, Denmark experienced two economic booms, one in the mid-1980s and one in the mid-1990s, that had a positive effect on the labor market (Madsen 1999). Second, in 1994, the Danes launched some labor market reforms including the introduction of extensive, active labor market programs (e.g., Bredgaard et al. 2005; Madsen 1999; Pedersen 2005). Since then, the country has experienced a tremendous decrease in unemployment, especially for youth.

This study investigates how these developments have affected labor market entry processes between 1981 and 2003. Despite the positive macroeconomic developments on the Danish labor market it is necessary to point out that the second economic upswing and the 1994 reforms were accompanied by a decentralization of wage setting down to the level of firms (Eriksson and Westergaard-Nielsen 2004). Furthermore, there are some hints that the practice of compulsory activation has a negative side effect in that some people who are pushed to find work by job-search requirements end up in jobs with lower wages than might otherwise be the case (Jacobsen 2005; Jochem 2009; OECD 2001). This probably impacts particularly on unskilled people.

After defining 'bad,' that is precarious, employment positions in the Danish context as low-wage jobs, the present country study will seek answers to the following research questions in order to shed light on changes in labor market entry processes and developments in social inequality structures since the early 1980s: (1) Has the risk of a bad start to the employment career increased across cohorts? (2) Is a bad career entry typically a trap, or can it serve as a stepping-stone toward more rewarding jobs? (3) Do changes in youth employment trajectories lead to a persistence, or even reinforcement of social inequalities related to educational qualification and occupational class? Four cohorts of education system leavers will be compared by studying labor market entry through event history analyses on the transition into first employment and logit models on the risk of starting in a low-paid job. The event history analyses will track the early career by plotting the transition into first unemployment and any upward and downward wage mobility linked to job moves between firms. Social inequalities will be examined in terms of gender, ethnic origin, and vocational qualification.

The remainder of this section is structured as follows: The next subsection introduces the research design of the country study and outlines which aspects need to be considered when studying labor market entry processes in Denmark. After deducing the research hypotheses and describing the data and methods used, I shall present the results of my empirical analyses. The section concludes with a summary of the most important findings and proposes answers to the four detailed research questions as a starting point for the subsequent international comparison.

2.2.2. Research design

Becoming established on the Danish labor market is anything but a well-defined process. Early careers are unstable. Many people return to education in the first years after labor market entry (Brzinsky-Fay 2007); others move to another firm or experience unemployment (Bredgaard et al. 2005). Still, in general, young labor market entrants face similar opportunities and risks to those of mid-career employees.[17]

Regarding labor market entries in Denmark, the first significant event to be investigated is the *transition into first employment* after leaving the education system. Although this is an unproblematic move for most young Danes, it makes sense to assume that in times of bad labor market conditions, education leavers face difficulties in making a smooth transition into a first job. On the other hand, the introduction of activation programs may have accelerated the entry process.

Another important issue is the *quality of the first job*. The low dismissal protection for all Danish employees makes it necessary to ask which jobs are related to higher insecurity in this country. Fixed-term jobs are as insecure as any other job in Denmark, because employers can easily adjust the number of their employees by layoffs. This results in high job mobility and high job turnover rates, so that "the ordinary workforce can be considered 'temporary workers'" (Bredgaard et al. 2009: 4), and the share of persons with fixed-term contracts is relatively low (Madsen 1999). Part-time work is mostly chosen voluntarily and regulated by the same collective agreements as full-time work (Madsen 1999).[18] Hence, instead of focusing on one of these employment

---

17 For example, Gangl (2003b) examined unemployment during the first 10 years of labor force experience and found that, at a given qualification level, unemployment rates are almost constant over time in the Danish labor force.
18 Bredgaard et al. (2009), who investigated the relationship between the Danish flexicurity and different forms of 'atypical employment' (part-time employment, fixed-term contracts, temporary agency work, self-employed, and so-called 'flex-jobs'), did not find that atypical employment is becoming more common or that it is unregulated and poorly protected. In

types, the quality of the first job will be evaluated by considering people's gross hourly wages. *Low-wage jobs* are jobs with earnings within the lowest decile of the wage distribution. Empirical studies have shown that the risk of starting in such a job has always been relatively high in Denmark. Young people tend to be hired at the bottom of the wage distribution within a firm and then move upwards as they gain experience (Bingley and Westergaard-Nielsen 1997; Eriksson and Westergaard-Nielsen 2004; OECD 1996a). However, it will be interesting to find out how the interaction between improved labor market conditions, activation reforms, and wage setting decentralization have influenced the risk of starting in a low-wage job, especially for unskilled labor market entrants. In summary, analyses of the initial labor market entry will include the transition into first employment after leaving the education system as well as the risk of starting in a low-wage job.

The longitudinal early-career analyses consider the first 5 years in the labor market and study the risk of first unemployment along with (the first) upward and downward wage mobility linked to firm changes. The focus is on interfirm mobility for two reasons: First, the available data do not adequately capture intrafirm moves; second, the most important moves occur between firms in Denmark. As mentioned in Section 1.4, up to 35 percent of the Danish workforce changes employer each year (Bredgaard et al. 2005). This observation is related to the low dismissal protection and dominance of small businesses. Small firms are generally more vulnerable to cyclical fluctuation and also offer fewer opportunities for internal career mobility compared to large firms. This, in turn, implies that moves are often either job moves across firms or into unemployment (Grunow and Leth-Sørensen 2006b).

Apart from the general trends, one particular interest of this study is the labor market chances of unskilled employees: Has their risk of unemployment declined considerably since 1994? Did chances of making an upward move increase or decrease for those entering the labor market since the reforms compared to earlier cohorts? In other words, could they profit from the positive effects of the welfare reforms and the economic boom of the mid-1990s as much as better educated persons can be expected to have done?

2.2.3. Hypotheses

Before proposing hypotheses referring directly to the main research questions, I shall present the expectations regarding the influence of

---

contrast, the authors concluded that Danish flexicurity seems to have been extended to include 'atypical' workers.

individual and firm characteristics on young people's chances on the Danish labor market.

Parameters of labor market success in Denmark

Individual characteristics

Persons with an immigration background, women, and unskilled people can be assumed to have a more problematic labor market entry in Denmark compared to native Danes, men, and people who have completed vocational education.

Immigrants have considerably lower employment rates than native Danes; this is partially related to human capital factors such as language skills and educational attainment (Zimmermann und Hinte 2005). Nevertheless, there might also be an unresolved discrimination problem (Hjarnø and Jensen 1997; Liebig 2007).[19] Consequently, immigrants can be expected to have a lower transition rate into first employment, a higher risk of starting in a low-wage job, a higher risk of unemployment, as well as lower chances of upward mobility in their early careers. It also makes sense to assume a higher risk of downward mobility when the starting position (which is typically already low) has been taken into account.

Another relatively disadvantaged group is *women*. The Danish labor market is characterized by an apparent gender wage gap (Ganßmann and Haas 2001; Statistics Denmark 2004). Furthermore, studies show that, due to statistical discrimination, making a transition into a first job within various occupational fields takes female education system leavers significantly longer than their male counterparts (Nielsen 2003; Nielsen et al. 2001). Thus, women are expected to have a lower transition rate into first employment, a higher risk of starting in a low-wage job, a higher risk of unemployment, and less upward and more downward mobility than men.

Unskilled persons face the most severe problems on the flexible Danish labor market (Bredgaard et al. 2005; Ganßmann and Haas 2001). Due to the low dismissal protection, the workforce is being tested constantly in terms of productivity. As a result, unskilled people are "more or less permanently balancing on the edge of the labour market or outside it" (Bredgaard et al. 2005: 29). The *motivational effect* (Bredgaard et al. 2005: 5) of the activation reforms could have pushed some of them into a *casual work trap* (Wallin

---

19 Persons with a migration background are less likely to be invited to a job interview (Hjarnø and Jensen 1997) and have more difficulties getting an apprenticeship contract with a firm (Liebig 2007). Furthermore, the average earnings prospects of immigrants are lower than those of native Danes (Roseveare and Jorgensen 2004).

2005): If unskilled youth find jobs themselves in order to avoid activation, these jobs are likely to be low-paid casual ones (Jacobsen 2005). Hence, this group can be expected to have the lowest transition rate into first employment, the highest risk of starting in a low-wage job, the highest risk of unemployment, only moderate upward mobility chances, and a high risk of downward mobility in relation to their starting position. Conversely, the best chances with regard to these aspects should be observed for persons who have finished vocational training in the dual system or completed higher vocational education.

Firm characteristics

According to the theory of labor market segmentation (Doeringer and Piore 1971), the labor market cannot be regarded as a homogeneous entity. Instead, it is composed of separate segments with different employment conditions and career prospects. Firm characteristics like size and industry can thus be expected to have an impact on an employee's further career outcomes: They influence upward and downward mobility chances and the risk of unemployment. With regard to *firm size*, the internal labor markets in large enterprises grant their employees better chances for promotion than those in small firms, that is, the former have better internal upward mobility opportunities. Thus, their external mobility rates—both upward and downward—are expected to be lower than those of people employed in smaller firms. Furthermore, they are expected to have a lower risk of unemployment, because large companies are not as vulnerable to cyclical fluctuation as small ones.

It would go beyond the scope of this study to formulate detailed hypotheses on a person's career prospects on an industry level. However, the effects of this variable will be controlled for in some models.

Changes over time: Hypotheses regarding the three research questions

First, has the risk of a bad start to the employment career increased across cohorts?

My analyses cover the period from 1981 to 2003. Figure 2.2 shows how the overall unemployment rate and the youth unemployment rate have developed since 1980.

Figure 2.2: Denmark: Registered unemployment per year as a percentage of the labor force, 1980-2002

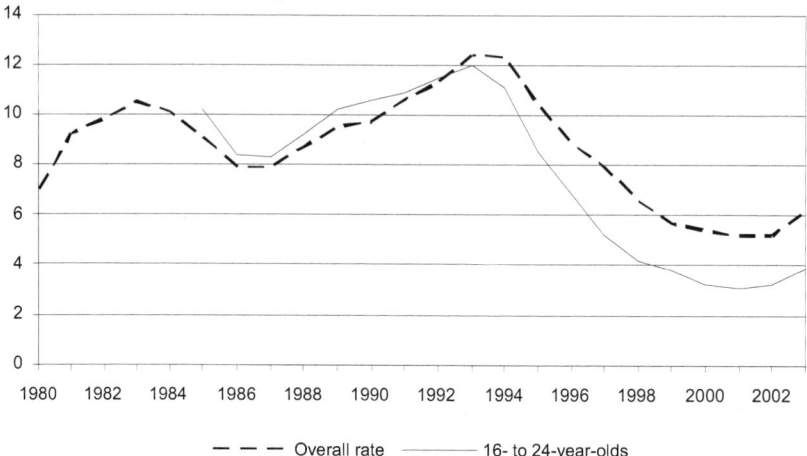

Source: Statistics Denmark.
Note: Data for the 16- to 24-year-old unemployed age group has only been available since 1985. Before that year, Statistics Denmark used different age groups in their unemployment statistics.

Before the launch of the labor market reforms in 1994, macroeconomic cycles created varying circumstances for labor market entrants, and individual labor market chances can be expected to have depended highly on the unemployment rate at the time of leaving the education system. After peaking in 1993, unemployment dropped considerably with the beginning of the activation reforms and the coinciding economic upswing. Consequently, it is unlikely that we shall find a general worsening of the situation of labor market entrants in Denmark. Instead, it can be expected that young people leaving education since 1994 have experienced an overall improvement in employment opportunities, a smoother transition into first employment, a lower risk of unemployment after their labor market entry, higher chances for upward mobility, and lower chances of downward mobility.

However, with regard to the quality of entry jobs in terms of wages, I expect a change for the worse for young people entering the labor market since 1994. This anticipation is linked to the decentralization of wage bargaining and the *motivational effect* of the activation reforms: Wage gaps between firms have increased, and some otherwise unemployed people may have preferred to take a poorly paid job instead of being 'activated.'

Second, is a bad career entry typically a trap, or can it serve as a stepping-stone toward more rewarding jobs?

In the present study, 'bad' entry positions in Denmark are defined as low-wage jobs, that is, jobs within the lowest earning decile of the wage distribution. The risk of starting in such a job has always been relatively high in Denmark, as young people tend to be hired at the bottom of the wage distribution and then move upward as they gain experience and establish careers (Bingley and Westergaard-Nielsen 1997; Eriksson and Westergaard-Nielsen 2004; OECD 1996a). However, it is hard to predict how interactions between improved labor market conditions, activation reforms, and wage-setting decentralization have influenced the labor market chances of early-career employees in low-wage jobs. There is empirical evidence for not only high upward-mobility rates but also high transition rates into unemployment (Bingley and Westergaard-Nielsen 1997). It makes sense to assume that education is the key variable responsible for the difference here.

Third, do changes in youth employment trajectories lead to a persistence or even reinforcement of social inequalities related to educational qualification?

This study labels persons as 'unskilled' if they have not completed any education beyond lower secondary schooling. According to this definition, the share of unskilled labor market entrants has decreased continuously over the four cohorts of education leavers in the sample: from 32 percent among those who left education between 1981 and 1983 to 18 percent among those who left education between 1994 and 2003. Concerning the risk of unemployment, I assume that unskilled people have been able to profit from the substantial unemployment decrease since 1994. Consequently, they can be expected to reveal an increase in the transition rate into first employment as well as a decrease in the transition rate into first unemployment.

On the other hand, if the activation reforms actually 'motivated' some otherwise unemployed unskilled youth to find themselves jobs to avoid activation, these are likely to be low-paid, casual jobs (Jacobsen 2005). Therefore an increase in the risk of starting their career in low-wage jobs can be expected. The question is, however, whether this is followed by increasing upward mobility rates. These hypotheses and open questions will be studied by introducing interaction effects between qualification and the period of education leave in the models.

2.2.4. Data and Methods

The above hypotheses were tested in a sample of 15- to 36-year-old persons living in Denmark extracted from the IDA, the *Integrated Database for Labor Market Research* (Leth-Sørensen 1997). This data set is based on administrative registers and allows education and employment sequences to be followed on the individual level. The data from 1980 to 2003 were collected each year on the last day of November. This causes a particular bias: It fails to register short episodes of any kind that started after November 30 of year x and ended before November 30 of the following year x + 1.

For the purpose of this study, I defined a subsample of 34,007 education leavers: persons who were out of education, but had been registered as being in general education, vocational training, or tertiary education in the preceding observation year. Besides waiting periods associated with compulsory military service, certain gaps between two education spells were closed: all one-year gaps between any kind of education (since they may be related to the yearly data structure) as well as gaps up to 4 years, if the individual was not registered as being unemployed in the preceding observation year[20] and if these gaps occurred between general and vocational education. Although this may surprise readers from other societies, a longer education interruption between general and vocational education is a frequently chosen option in Denmark, selected mostly by upper secondary graduates who take a sabbatical before entering university (Statistics Denmark 2005).[21] Some of them work in casual jobs for at least part of their break; others gain work experience in order to qualify for those kinds of vocational education in which this is required. Such activities during one of the above-mentioned gaps were treated as part of a person's first education spell; they were not considered to be their first 'real job.'

For the transition into first employment, I considered only moves into dependent full-time or part-time work by persons who had left the education system for the first time. I censored transitions into self-employment and episodes ending with a transition back into education or out of the labor force. Analyses on the quality of the first job were based on the first year of the first job spell. As an indicator for job quality, a variable was used to mark low-wage jobs. These were defined as jobs with gross hourly wages within the lowest 10 percent of the wage distribution (gross hourly wages, deflated)

---

20 In case of a prior unemployment spell, a return into education could have been part of an activation program.
21 "[Only] 24 per cent of students who graduated in 1988/1989 and 19 per cent of students who graduated in 2002/2003 continued their education immediately after completing their second-level education. [...] Many did not resume their studies until 3–4 years after graduation" (Statistics Denmark 2005).

of all employees between the ages of 15 and 59.[22] Using a relative measure based on gross earnings is in line with the OECD's definition of low-paid employment (OECD 1996). However, the OECD uses two-thirds of median earnings as the cut-off point for determining low pay—a commonly used mark in poverty research. The very low threshold of 10 percent was chosen here, because the wage distribution in Denmark is very compressed, which means that the difference between being in the lowest earnings decile and being in the highest is much smaller than in most other countries (Westergaard-Nielsen 2008).[23]

The risk set for the early-career analyses was restricted to individuals who entered first employment after having left the education system for the first time.[24] The early career was defined as the first 5 years following the transition into the first job. After this period of time, all episodes were censored. For the transition into first unemployment, only moves into registered unemployment were regarded. Employees who made a transition back into education, into self-employment, or out of the labor force were excluded from the risk set (i.e., the episodes were censored). Upward wage mobility was defined in terms of significant gains (10%) in (deflated) gross hourly wages after a firm change. Downward wage mobility was defined analogically. Only a person's first mobility event was considered. Transitions back into education, into self-employment, into unemployment, or out of the labor force were treated as right-censored.

Various explanatory variables were included in the models:[25] four dummies representing the singular cohorts of education system leavers to capture cohort effects; different sets of duration dummies (grouped in years) measuring the time since leaving education, the duration of first job search, and the duration of the first employment spell; furthermore, the yearly average unemployment rate to measure period effects; covariates for individual characteristics: sex, ethnic origin, and qualification; covariates for job characteristics: 'wage level' and the dummy variable 'low-wage job'; covariates for firm characteristics: firm size and industry; and finally, the

---

22 Originating from administrative registers, the IDA information on a person's hourly wage rate is constructed using information on earned income in a job from annual tax records divided by the number of hours worked during the year.
23 The particular choice of the 10 percent threshold was further inspired by a paper on individual wage mobility in Denmark in which Bingley and Westergaard-Nielsen (1997) used deciles as the wage concept and, in a subsection, analyzed moves out of Decile 1.
24 Those who were registered in a first employment in 2003, the last observation year, were excluded from the early-career analyses. Due to the yearly data structure, they could not be observed as having any further activity. For this reason, the starting population for the early-career analyses (29,544 persons) was smaller than the number of events for making a transition into first employment (31,292).
25 Table A.3 in the appendix provides an overview.

interaction between qualification and (education leavers') cohort to control for changes in the effect of the single qualification levels between the four education system leavers' cohorts (in line with the second research question, the interpretations of the interaction effects concentrated on the lowest educational level).

Discrete-time logistic regression models (Allison 1982) were computed for both the longitudinal analyses on the transition into first employment and for the early-career analyses (i.e., the analyses on the transition into first unemployment and on wage mobility). Logit models were estimated for the analyses on the quality of the first job (i.e., the risk of having a low-wage job in the first year of employment).

2.2.5. Empirical findings

Labor market entry and quality of first job

Transition into first employment after leaving the education system

Table 2.1 reports three discrete-time logistic regression models for the transition into first employment.

The transition rate was highest within the first year after leaving the education system (time since leaving education: up to 1 year) and decreased over time.

The youngest cohort of education system leavers (i.e., individuals who entered the labor market since 1994) was expected to have the highest transition rate into first employment. However, those who left education during the first economic upswing between 1984 and 1987 were more likely to quickly enter a first job. People who finished education in times of rising unemployment (between 1981 and 1983 or between 1988 and 1993) had lower chances of making a transition into a first job. Correspondingly, the average yearly unemployment rate had a negative effect on the transition into first employment (see Model 2).

Table 2.1: Denmark: Transition into first employment after leaving the education system (discrete-time logistic regression)

	1	2	3
Constant	2.63**	2.85**	2.86**
Time since leaving education			
Up to 1 year (ref.)	–	–	–
1–2 years	–0.97**	–0.95**	–0.95**
2–3 years	–1.39**	–1.38**	–1.37**
3 and more years	–1.90**	–1.87**	–1.89**
Education leavers cohort			
1981–83 (unemp. ↑)	–0.02		–0.28**
1984–87 (unemp. ↓)	0.28**		0.17+
1988–93 (unemp. ↑)	–0.06*		–0.55**
1994–2003 (unemp. ↓) (ref.)	–		–
Unemployment rate		–0.02**	
Sex			
Male (ref.)	–	–	–
Female	–0.25**	–0.25**	–0.25**
Ethnic origin			
Danish (ref.)	–	–	–
Non Danish	–0.50**	–0.56**	–0.48**
Qualification			
1: Lower secondary without voc. qualification (unskilled)	–2.44**	–2.44**	–2.86**
2: Upper secondary without voc. qualification	–1.77**	–1.78**	–1.78**
3: Lower secondary with dual voc. qualification (ref.)	–	–	–
4: Lower secondary with short/medium-cycle higher voc. education	0.03	0.02	0.04
5: College/university and any long-cycle higher tertiary voc. education	–0.53**	–0.54**	–0.94**
Interaction qualification*cohort			
Qualification 1*1981–83			0.47**
Qualification 2*1981–83			–0.16
Qualification 4*1981–83			–0.01
Qualification 5*1981–83			0.72**
Qualification 1*1984–87			0.27*
Qualification 2*1984–87			–0.27*
Qualification 4*1984–87			–0.04
Qualification 5*1984–87			0.50**
Qualification 1*1988–93			0.84**
Qualification 2*1988–93			0.02
Qualification 4*1988–93			0.13
Qualification 5*1988–93			0.76**

Table 2.1: continued

	1	2	3
No. of person-year-observations	49,183	49,183	49,183
No. of persons	34,007	34,007	34,007
No. of events	31,292	31,292	31,292
−2*diff (LogL)	28,885	28,796	29,109

Source: Own calculations based on a sample taken from the IDA Data Base (1980–2003).

Notes: ** significant at $p < 0.01$; * significant at $p < 0.05$; + significant at $p < 0.10$; controlled for missing values.

As expected, young women and immigrants had lower transition rates into first employment, when controlling for qualification. The results for qualification itself were also in line with the hypotheses: People who completed vocational training in the dual system after finishing lower secondary education (i.e., the reference group) had the best chances of quickly entering a first employment, whereas unskilled youth had the lowest transition rate into a first job. Compared to the reference group, college or university graduates needed a relatively long time to make the transition into first employment. This finding can be explained by the dual system's embedment in the employment system: It serves as an institutionalized bridge to the labor market. A second interpretation refers to the reservation wage theory: People with higher educational attainment might wait longer to find a job that pays more. Furthermore, some of these people take some time off between finishing their education and starting to work, for example, for traveling.

Model 3 included the interaction between qualification and (education leavers') cohort. The reference group consisted of individuals who finished lower secondary school and vocational training in the dual system and left education between 1994 and 2003. Compared to this group, earlier unskilled and earlier high skilled cohorts showed higher transition rates than those who left the education system after 1994, regardless of whether the earlier cohorts left education in times of rising unemployment (between 1981 and 1983 and between 1988 and 1993) or falling unemployment (between 1984 and 1987). This finding contradicted the expected increase in the transition rate into first employment for unskilled persons because of the improved economic situation and welfare reforms. Instead, it was especially skilled individuals with a medium education level who profited in the youngest cohort; unskilled individuals as well as college and university graduates profited less.

The risk of starting in a low-wage job

Table 2.2 shows logit models on the risk of having entered a low-wage job after leaving the education system.

The reservation wage theory explains why the risk of starting in a low-paid job decreases with the duration of job search: Those who aim at a higher entry wage wait until they find a job that meets their expectations. However, it should be borne in mind that, due to the yearly data structure, short employment spells were not registered; those who are observed in a relatively high-paid 'first' job 2 years after leaving the education system might well have worked in some kind of short-term job before.

Concerning the education leavers' cohorts, people who left education between 1988 and 1993 faced the highest risk of starting their careers in a low-wage job. Furthermore, people who finished their education before 1988 had a lower risk of starting in a low-paid job, regardless of whether they entered the labor market in times of rising (between 1981 and 1983) or falling (between 1984 and 1987) unemployment. There are two possible explanations for the relatively high risk that the youngest cohort of education system leavers will start in a low-paid job: First, the *motivational effect* (Bredgaard et al. 2005: 5) of the labor market reforms—when approaching the time when they are due for activation, some people may have preferred to find a low-paid job. Second, this outcome is probably also linked to the accompanying decentralization of wage setting (Eriksson and Westergaard-Nielsen 2004).

The unemployment rate had a positive effect on the risk of starting in a low-wage job. The results for the influence of gender confirmed the respective hypothesis: Women had a higher risk of starting their career in a low-wage job. For immigrants and their descendants, the result was contrary to expectations, because they had a lower risk of beginning in a low-wage job. This might reflect a change in the group composition since 1980. Up until 1990, most immigrants were from western countries. Immigrants and their descendants from these countries are known to have better paid jobs than Danes (Nielsen 2001).

Looking at qualification, it became clear that education pays. As in other countries, wages in Denmark are linked closely to qualification (Bingley and Westergaard-Nielsen 1997; Eriksson and Westergaard-Nielsen 2004): the higher the level of vocational qualification, the lower the risk of starting in a badly paid job after leaving education.

Table 2.2: Denmark: Low-wage job in the first year of employment after leaving the education system (logit models)

	1	2	3
Constant	−0.59**	−0.82**	−0.58**
Duration of job search			
Up to 1 year (ref.)	–	–	–
1–2 years	−1.08**	−1.10**	−1.09**
2 and more years	−1.45**	−1.47**	−1.46**
Education leavers cohort			
1981–83 (unemp. ↑)	−0.17**		−0.24**
1984–87 (unemp. ↓)	−0.17**		−0.24**
1988–93 (unemp. ↑)	0.11**		0.15**
1994–2003 (unemp. ↓) (ref.)	–		–
Unemployment rate		0.02**	
Sex			
Male (ref.)	–	–	–
Female	0.84**	0.83**	0.84**
Ethnic origin			
Danish (ref.)	–	–	–
Non Danish	−0.24*	−0.19+	−0.25*
Qualification			
1: Lower secondary without voc. qualification (unskilled)	1.09**	1.07**	1.15**
2: Upper secondary without voc. qualification	0.33**	0.34**	0.25**
3: Lower secondary with dual voc. qualification (ref.)	–	–	–
4: Lower secondary with short/medium-cycle higher voc. education	−1.96**	−1.95**	−2.08**
5: College/university and any long-cycle higher tertiary voc. education	−3.10**	−3.08**	−3.03**
Interaction: qualification*cohort			
Qualification 1*1981–83			0.14
Qualification 2*1981–83			0.29*
Qualification 4*1981–83			−0.15
Qualification 5*1981–83			−1.76+
Qualification 1*1984–87			−0.17
Qualification 2*1984–87			0.40**
Qualification 4*1984–87			0.85**
Qualification 5*1984–87			0.38
Qualification 1*1988–93			−0.13
Qualification 2*1988–93			−0.17
Qualification 4*1988–93			−0.02
Qualification 5*1988–93			−0.27

Table 2.2: continued

	1	2	3
No. of cases	24,097	24,097	24,097
–2*diff (LogL)	6,983	6,937	7,059

Source: Own calculations based on a sample taken from the IDA Data Base (1980–2003).
Notes: ** significant at $p < 0.01$; * significant at $p < 0.05$; + significant at $p < 0.10$; controlled for missing values.

For unskilled school leavers, there were no significant interaction effects between qualification and (education leavers') cohort (see Model 3). Compared to the reference group (i.e., persons who finished lower secondary school and vocational training in the dual system), their risk of entering a low-paid job did not change over time; it has always been high.

The early career

The transition into first unemployment

Table 2.3 includes discrete-time logistic regression models on the risk of making a first transition into unemployment during the first 5 years after labor market entry. The risk of making such a transition decreased with the duration of the first employment spell.

As expected, the lowest transition rate into unemployment was found for people who left the education system between 1994 and 2002, that is, since the implementation of the welfare reforms and the beginning of the Danish employment boom. Compared to this youngest cohort of education system leavers, all other cohorts had a higher transition rate into unemployment. However, it should be mentioned that unemployed people who were placed in a supported job as part of the activation measures are recorded as employed in the official labor market statistics.

Results on the influence of gender and ethnic origin were also in line with the hypotheses: Women and immigrants had a significantly higher risk of becoming unemployed. Furthermore, findings suggested that the lower the level of vocational qualification, the higher the risk of becoming unemployed. Models 3 to 5 controlled for job quality in terms of wages and compared the transition rates of employees in low-wage jobs to the risk of employees in more highly paid jobs. The former had a significantly higher risk of making a transition into unemployment.

Table 2.3: Denmark: Transition into first unemployment after first labor market entry (discrete-time logistic regression)

	1	2	3	4	5
Constant	−3.39**	−3.17**	−3.35**	−3.90**	−3.32**
Duration of first employment spell					
1–2 years (ref.)	−	−	−	−	−
2–3 years	−0.36**	−0.33**	−0.25**	−0.24**	−0.25**
3–4 years	−0.67**	−0.64**	−0.53**	−0.50**	−0.53**
4–5 years	−1.53**	−1.50**	−1.37**	−1.29**	−1.36**
Education leavers cohort					
1981–83 (unemp. ↑)	0.57**	0.61**	0.64**		0.50**
1984–87 (unemp. ↓)	0.62**	0.63**	0.65**		0.59**
1988–93 (unemp. ↑)	0.77**	0.76**	0.76**		0.78**
1994–2002 (unemp. ↓) (ref.)	−	−	−		−
Unemployment rate				0.11**	
Sex					
Male (ref.)	−	−	−	−	−
Female	0.22**	0.24**	0.20**	0.21**	0.19**
Ethnic origin					
Danish (ref.)	−	−	−	−	−
Not Danish	0.56**	0.56**	0.56**	0.50**	0.60**
Qualification					
1: Lower secondary without voc. qualification (unskilled)	0.63**	0.66**	0.53**	0.56**	0.37**
2: Upper secondary without voc. qualification	0.05	0.10+	−0.00	−0.02	−0.21+
3: Lower secondary with dual voc. qualification (ref.)	−	−	−	−	−
4: Lower secondary with short/medium-cycle higher voc. education	−0.61**	−0.59**	−0.55**	−0.57**	−0.37**
5: College/university and any long-cycle higher tertiary voc. education	−0.80**	−0.69**	−0.65**	−0.69**	−0.31+
Job quality					
Low-wage job			0.31**	0.29**	0.31**
Higher-paid job (ref.)			−	−	−
Firm size (no. of employees)					
1–10 (ref.)		−	−	−	−
11–50		−0.05	−0.02	−0.03	−0.02
51–500		−0.11*	−0.05	−0.06	−0.05
Over 500		−0.26**	−0.18**	−0.17**	−0.18**

Table 2.3: continued

	1	2	3	4	5
Industry					
Extractive sector		–0.74**	–0.81**	–0.84**	–0.81**
Transformative sector (ref.)		–	–	–	–
Producer services		–0.58**	–0.63**	–0.63**	–0.63**
Distributive services		–0.22**	–0.28**	–0.29**	–0.27**
Personal services		–0.06	–0.03	–0.06	–0.02
Social services		–0.13**	–0.21**	–0.21**	–0.20**
Interaction: qualification*cohort					
Qualification 1*1981–83					0.36**
Qualification 2*1981–83					0.39
Qualification 4*1981–83					–0.10
Qualification 5*1981–83					–0.35
Qualification 1*1984–87					0.26*
Qualification 2*1984–87					0.21
Qualification 4*1984–87					–0.25
Qualification 5*1984–87					–0.81**
Qualification 1*1988–93					0.05*
Qualification 2*1988–93					0.24
Qualification 4*1988–93					–0.33*
Qualification 5*1988–93					–0.45*
No. of person-year-observations	106,863	106,863	106,863	106,863	106,863
No. of persons	29,544	29,544	29,544	29,544	29,544
No. of events	4,144	4,144	4,144	4,144	4,144
–2*diff (LogL)	2,400	2,649	2,800	2,675	2,837

Source: Own calculations based on a sample taken from the IDA Data Base (1980–2003).

Notes: ** significant at $p < 0.01$; * significant at $p < 0.05$; + significant at $p < 0.10$; controlled for missing values.

Expectations on firm size were also confirmed: Employees in bigger firms faced a lower risk of becoming unemployed—at least when comparing very small firms to those with more than 500 employees.

Model 5 controlled for the interaction between qualification and cohort. When focusing on education leavers with the lowest educational level, earlier cohorts had higher transition rates into first unemployment than those who left the education system after 1994 (compared to the reference group of lower secondary graduates who completed a vocational training in the dual system and left education between 1994 and 2002). The relative decrease in transitions to first unemployment is probably related to three factors: (1) improvements on the labor market that provided more employment opportunities; (2) the activation tool of job placement, due to which some of the otherwise unemployed unskilled people are placed in supported jobs (officially classified as being 'employed'); (3) the *motivational effect* (Bredgaard et al. 2005: 5) prompting unemployed persons who consider activation a negative prospect to intensify their job search efforts when approaching the time when they become due for activation.

The first upward and downward wage mobility between firms

Table 2.4 presents the results of analyses on external job mobility in the early career. Upward mobility was defined as a significant (at least 10%) gain; downward mobility, as a significant loss in hourly gross wages linked to a firm change.

Models 1–4 show the results of analyses on upward mobility; Models 5–8, on downward mobility. In contrast to upward mobility, such kinds of moves should mostly be involuntary. Both kinds of mobility decreased with the duration of the first employment spell, probably because the majority of people with longer firm tenure were employed in larger firms offering higher job security and internal labor markets with upward mobility possibilities within the firm.

When turning to the education leavers' cohorts, those who left education during the first economic upswing between 1984 and 1987 had the highest upward mobility (see Models 1–4) and, at the same time, the lowest downward mobility rates (see Models 5–8). These favorable early career developments were expected to be experienced by the reference group, that is, by people who left education between 1994 and 2003.

This result is meaningful when related to the findings on the risk of starting the employment career in a low-wage job: Not only did people who left the education system after the implementation of the welfare reforms and the beginning of the Danish employment miracle have a relatively high risk of starting their career at the bottom of the wage distribution—they also did not have the best upward mobility prospects. Furthermore, their downward mobility rate did not differ significantly from those of the two earlier cohorts who left education in times of rising unemployment (i.e., between 1981 and 1983 or between 1988 and 1993). In all these respects, the 1984 to 1987 cohort had better labor market outcomes.

Table 2.4: Denmark: First wage mobility between firms (discrete-time logistic regression)

	Models 1-4: Upward mobility				Models 5-8: Downward mobility			
	1	2	3	4	5	6	7	8
Constant	−2.04**	−1.85**	−1.67**	−1.84**	−2.40**	−2.41**	−2.47**	−2.36**
Duration of first employment spell								
1–2 years (ref.)	–	–	–	–	–	–	–	–
2–3 years	−0.18**	−0.18**	−0.18**	−0.18**	−0.46**	−0.46**	−0.45**	−0.46**
3–4 years	−0.25**	−0.23**	−0.24**	−0.23**	−0.70**	−0.69**	−0.69**	−0.69**
4–5 years	−1.02**	−1.00**	−1.01**	−1.00**	−1.37**	−1.35**	−1.36**	−1.36**
Education leavers cohort								
1981–83 (unemp. ↑)	−0.07*	−0.06		−0.02	−0.08	−0.06		−0.13
1984–87 (unemp. ↓)	0.13**	0.14**		0.10*	−0.25**	−0.23**		−0.41**
1988–93 (unemp. ↑)	−0.14**	−0.14**		−0.20**	−0.09+	−0.08		−0.10
1994–2002 (unemp. ↓) (ref.)	–	–		–	–	–		–
Unemployment rate			−0.02**				−0.00	
Sex								
Male (ref.)	–	–	–	–	–	–	–	–
Female	−0.56**	−0.47**	−0.47**	−0.48**	0.34**	0.39**	0.38**	0.38**
Ethnic origin								
Danish (ref.)	–	–	–	–	–	–	–	–
Non Danish	−0.25*	−0.24*	−0.25*	−0.23+	−0.59*	−0.56**	−0.53**	−0.57**

Table 2.4: continued

	Models 1–4: Upward mobility				Models 5–8: Downward mobility			
	1	2	3	4	5	6	7	8
Qualification								
1: Lower secondary without voc. qualification (unskilled)	−0.35**	−0.40**	−0.39**	−0.48**	0.35**	0.32**	0.30**	0.35**
2: Upper secondary without voc. qualification	−0.33**	−0.29**	−0.28**	−0.38**	0.13+	0.17*	0.18*	−0.01
3: Lower secondary with dual voc. qualification (ref.)	–	–	–	–	–	–	–	–
4: Lower secondary with short/ medium-cycle higher voc. educ.	−0.04	0.12**	0.11*	0.13+	−0.38**	−0.32**	−0.30**	−0.50**
5: College/university and any long-cycle higher tertiary voc. educ.	0.44**	0.55**	0.54**	0.54**	−0.85**	−0.73**	−0.71**	−0.75**
Wage level								
1: Very low	1.29**	1.25**	1.24**	1.25**	−1.94**	−2.01**	−2.01**	−2.03**
2: Low	0.63**	0.63**	0.63**	0.63**	−0.97**	−1.01**	−1.01**	−1.01**
3: Medium (ref.)	–	–	–	–	–	–	–	–
4: High	−0.56**	−0.58**	−0.58**	−0.58**	0.90**	0.92**	0.92**	0.93**
5: Very High	−1.14**	−1.16**	−1.15**	−1.15**	1.38**	1.40**	1.38**	1.41**
Firm size (no. of employees)								
1–10 (ref.)		–	–	–		–	–	–
11–50		−0.20**	−0.20**	−0.20**		0.01	0.01	0.01
51–500		−0.22**	−0.22**	−0.22**		−0.09	−0.09	−0.09
Over 500		−0.31**	−0.31**	−0.31**		−0.24**	−0.24**	−0.24**

Table 2.4: continued

	Models 1–4: Upward mobility				Models 5–8: Downward mobility			
	1	2	3	4	5	6	7	8
Industry								
Extractive sector		0.26**	0.26**	0.26**		0.52**	0.54**	0.52**
Transformative sector (ref.)		–	–	–		–	–	–
Producer services		−0.01	−0.01	−0.01		−0.35**	−0.34**	−0.34**
Distributive services		−0.04	−0.04	−0.03		0.17**	0.18**	0.18**
Personal services		0.02	0.01	0.03		0.16	0.17+	0.17+
Social services		−0.34**	−0.34**	−0.32**		0.01	0.01	0.02
Interaction: qualification*cohort								
Qualification 1*1981–83				0.10				−0.03
Qualification 2*1981–83				0.08				0.39+
Qualification 4*1981–83				−0.34**				0.22
Qualification 5*1981–83				−0.29+				−0.11
Qualification 1*1984–87				0.08				0.06
Qualification 2*1984–87				0.16				0.60**
Qualification 4*1984–87				0.10				0.54**
Qualification 5*1984–87				0.06				0.20
Qualification 1*1988–93				0.12				−0.10
Qualification 2*1988–93				0.15				0.00
Qualification 4*1988–93				0.08				0.19
Qualification 5*1988–93				0.12				−0.01

Table 2.4: continued

	Models 1–4: Upward mobility				Models 5–8: Downward mobility			
	1	2	3	4	5	6	7	8
No. of person year-observations	79,395	79,395	79,395	79,395	79,395	79,395	79,395	79,395
No. of persons	29,544	29,544	29,544	29,544	29,544	29,544	29,544	29,544
No. of events	6,959	6,959	6,959	6,959	2,758	2,758	2,758	2,758
–2*diff (LogL)	5,955	6,183	6,136	6,205	2,706	2,797	2,781	2,820

Source: Own calculations based on a sample taken from the IDA Data Base (1980–2003).
Notes: ** significant at $p < 0.01$; * significant at $p < 0.05$; + significant at $p < 0.10$; controlled for missing values.

One possible explanation for the high downward interfirm mobility of the youngest education leavers cohort (see Models 5–8) is the *motivational effect* (Bredgaard et al. 2005: 5) of the labor market reforms that prompts some people to seek a low-paid job themselves rather than having to participate in an activation program.[26] This is also probably associated with the decentralization of wage setting that was shifted to the firm level from 1994 to 1995 (Eriksson and Westergaard-Nielsen 2004) and the fact that job applicants who are either unemployed or threatened by unemployment have only low bargaining power.

Not surprisingly, the average yearly unemployment rate had a negative effect on the chances of making an upward move. However, its effect on downward mobility was not significant. As expected, women had not only lower upward mobility (see Models 1–4) but also higher downward mobility rates (see Models 5–8) than men. Compared to native Danes, immigrants were less mobile—both upwardly and downwardly. This might be the result of a tendency of immigrants to find jobs of a specific type (industry, job level, etc.). These jobs could also be characterized by having a higher level of horizontal mobility—fewer chances of upward and less risk of downward moves.

There was a clear relation between an employee's highest level of qualification and wage mobility: the higher the level of vocational qualification, the higher the transition rate into a better paid job (see Models 1–4), and the lower the transition rate into a lower paid job with a new employer (see Models 5–8). Apparently, any kind of vocational qualification (i.e., any degree beyond upper secondary without vocational qualification) promotes upward mobility and shelters from downward mobility in terms of income loss.

All mobility models took the wage level of origin into account when estimating the transition rates into a higher (lower) paid job with a new employer, that is, when considering the employee's position in the wage distribution before an upward (downward) move. The wage level of origin had a significant effect in both mobility directions: the higher the wage level, the lower the chances of making an upward move (see Models 1–4), and the higher the risk of making a downward move (see Models 5–8). These findings were related to bottom and ceiling effects: Those in the lowest decile of the wage distribution could not move much further down (although a 10% income loss was possible for them), whereas those in the highest decile of the

---

26 Due to the yearly data structure, information about status changes in the months between each November is missing; short unemployament spells occurring in this period are not registered, and a labor market re-entry into a lower paid job is interpreted as downward interfirm mobility.

wage distribution could not move much further up (although a 10% income gain was possible for them).

Employees in low-wage jobs, that is, those in the lowest decile of the wage distribution (Wage level 1: very low), seemed to have relatively good upward mobility prospects. However, as Bingley and Westergaard-Nielsen (1997) point out, it is also more common for them to make a transition into unemployment, which is in line with the findings of the present study (see Table 2.3, Models 3–5).

As expected, the results for firm size showed that employees in larger firms were less mobile—either upward (see Models 1 to 4) or downward (see Models 5–8). Since we were looking at interfirm mobility, this result could be explained by bigger firms offering internal labor markets with good upward mobility chances as well as lower job insecurity. However, only employees in firms with more than 500 employees were relatively well shielded against downward mobility.

When the interaction between qualification and (education leavers) cohort was included (see Model 4), no significant effect was found for unskilled employees. This result is analogous to the finding on their risk of starting the employment career in a low-wage job: Compared to the reference group (i.e., persons who completed lower secondary school and a vocational training in the dual system and left education between 1994 and 2002), no improvement could be found in either their low chances of making an upward move (see Models 1–4) or their high risk of making a downward move (see Models 5–8) in the wage distribution.

2.2.6. Conclusions on the country study of Denmark

The aim of this study has been to investigate labor market entry processes in Denmark in the context of the macroeconomic and legislative changes occurring between 1981 and 2003. In contrast to the situation in many other countries, the Danish labor market was already highly flexible before the 1980s. A turning point for the general labor market situation occurred in 1994 with the launch of labor market reforms focusing on active labor market policies. Also due to a coinciding economic upswing, the country experienced a major drop in unemployment in the subsequent years. Therefore, a general trend toward more difficult labor market entry and a more flexible and instable career for the younger cohorts of education system leavers was not expected in Denmark. However, wage setting was further decentralized, increasing the scope for employers to adjust to changed labor market conditions via wages.

With regard to these changes, the present country study asks three specific questions: (1) Has the risk of a bad start to the employment career increased across cohorts? (2) Is a bad career entry typically a trap, or can it serve as a stepping-stone toward more rewarding jobs? (3) Do changes in youth employment trajectories lead to a persistence or even reinforcement of social inequalities related to educational qualification and occupational class? Comparing different cohorts of education system leavers, I first studied the transition into first employment and the risk of starting in a low-paid job, and then examined the early career in terms of the risk of unemployment and of upward and downward wage mobility linked to job moves between firms.

Before answering the research questions, I first have to recapitulate what can be regarded as a 'bad,' that is precarious, employment position for youth in the highly flexible Danish labor market in which fixed-term jobs are as insecure as any other job, and part-time work is mostly chosen voluntarily and regulated by the same collective agreements as full-time work. Instead of focusing on one of these employment types, I identified bad jobs in Denmark as *low-wage jobs*, that is, jobs with earnings within the lowest decile of the wage distribution.

As expected, I have not found a general worsening of the situation of youth. However, neither have I found that young people who left education after 1994 are generally better off than members of earlier school-leaver cohorts. Instead, the results of the cohort comparison are mixed: With regard to the process of labor market entry, some of the earlier cohorts of education leavers achieve better labor market outcomes: They not only have higher transition rates into first employment (i.e., they are exposed to lower employment insecurity), but also a lower risk of starting in a low-paid job. Investigating the early career development, the findings suggest that those who have left education since 1994 are in a better position with regard to the risk of unemployment (i.e., they are exposed to lower job insecurity). However, with regard to their upward and downward mobility chances, they have fared worse than the earlier 'upswing cohort' who left the education system between 1984 and 1987.

Results on the three research questions can be summarized as follows: First, *has the risk of a bad start to the employment career increased across cohorts?* The answer is yes, even though the 1994 labor market reform in Denmark was accompanied by an economic upswing with a strong decrease in unemployment rates, members of the relevant educational cohort reveal a lower transition rate into first employment than those leaving education during the earlier economic upswing between 1984 and 1987. Furthermore, individuals entering the labor market since 1994 face a high risk of starting their career in a low-wage job. There are two possible explanations for this last result: On the one hand, the activation policy for unemployed people introduced in Denmark in this period probably motivates some people to take up even a low paid job in order to avoid participation in activation programs.

On the other hand, wage setting was decentralized in the mid-1990s, leading to a reduction of wage levels.

Second, *is a bad career entry typically a trap, or can it serve as a stepping-stone toward more rewarding jobs?* The findings for Denmark suggest that employees in low-wage jobs seem to have relatively good upward mobility prospects and to be shielded against downward mobility when considering the employee's position in the wage distribution before a move. However, these findings may be partially explained by bottom effects. Furthermore, low-wage employees have a significantly higher risk of making a transition into unemployment than employees in more highly paid jobs.

Finally, *do changes in youth employment trajectories lead to a persistence or even reinforcement of social inequalities related to educational qualification?* For Denmark, I have found a persistence of social inequalities among labor market entrants with different educational levels. The empirical results show that unskilled people still are clearly disadvantaged. The activation reforms have improved their chances only with regard to the reduced transition rate into registered unemployment. At the same time, earlier cohorts of unskilled employees reveal higher transition rates into a first employment. Furthermore, unskilled persons in the youngest cohort still face the highest risk of starting in a low-paid job as well as low upward and high downward mobility rates even when taking their low current wage level into account.

These findings offer valuable clues regarding the changes in the labor market entry process in Denmark since the early 1980s. However, a comparison with other countries is necessary to put these changes into perspective, and find out whether labor market entry processes in Denmark follow a distinctive, country-specific pattern or whether we are looking at some global, cross-national trends.

2.3. Comparison with labor market entries in other OECD countries

Following the country study on labor market entry trends in Denmark, the next step is to compare the findings from the Danish study to those from other country studies conducted for the *flexCAREER* project in order to test the generality of findings and the role of institutional contexts (Blossfeld 2009; Kohn 1987).

What can this country comparison be expected to show? Changes in labor market entry transitions related to globalization and rising employment flexibility have occurred within very different institutional frameworks. For instance, in insider-protection countries, the main issue for labor market entrants is to gain a first foothold in the labor market, whereas in countries with weak employment protection, it is to use bad entry positions as stepping-stones into better jobs. However, alongside employment protection legislation, other institutional characteristics also play a role.

In the following subsection, I shall describe the mechanisms behind the findings for the Danish case and postulate hypotheses on developments in both liberal and insider-protection regimes. Then, I shall outline the methodological challenges of cross-national studies like the *flexCAREER* project and give an overview of the country-specific analyses that I shall use for the comparison of changes at labor market entry.

Changing labor market entry patterns: Institutional mechanisms behind the results on Denmark and expectations for the other regime types

The interaction of the given level of labor market flexibility with the 'institutional package' of each country evolves a particular influence for both the labor market entries and early careers of young people. Table 2.5 shows the institutional features of the nine countries to be compared—the level of employment protection, the related strategies of numerical flexibility, the national expenditures on active labor market policies, and the organization of vocational training—and the associated patterns of labor market entry processes arising from these.

After outlining the institutional mechanisms behind the findings for the Danish case, I shall present hypotheses on the changes in labor market entry processes and early career trajectories in the other regimes types, including my expectations on the development of social inequalities related to educational qualification.

Denmark is a highly coordinated market economy with a strong linkage between the education system and the labor market. At the same time, it has a long tradition of numerical flexibility and one of the lowest levels of employment protection for permanent work among OECD countries today (OECD 2004). The interplay between the standardized education and vocational system and the high degree of labor market flexibility allows a relatively smooth employment entry for young people (Müller et al. 2002) leading to low employment insecurity. The younger cohort's relatively high likelihood of starting in a low-wage job and the high job insecurity in Denmark are counterbalanced by high job mobility and a high supply of active labor market policies that prevent long-term unemployment. Compared to countries with other institutional arrangements, economic insecurity and social inequality are probably low among labor market entrants in Denmark.

Table 2.5: Labor market entry regimes and their expected impacts on school-to-work transitions and early career trajectories

Labor market entry regime:	Danish flexicurity	Liberal	N. European insider protection	S. European insider protection
Countries under comparison:	Denmark	United Kingdom, United States	France, Germany, Netherlands, Sweden	Italy, Spain
Strictness of employment protection:	Low	Very low	High	Very high
Strategies of numerical flexibility:	Low dismissal protection	Low dismissal protection	Fixed-term employment	Fixed-term employment
Expenditures on active labor market policies:	Very high	Low	High (very high in Sweden)	Low
Vocational training systems:	Dual system	On-the-job training	Germany: dual system; other countries: vocational schools	On-the-job training
General patterns of labor market entry processes:				
Labor market entry:	Smooth, short duration of job search → low employment insecurity	Smooth, short duration of job search → low employment insecurity	Relatively smooth (for those with occupation-specific voc. education) → medium level of employment insecurity	Very difficult, with very long durations of job search → high employment insecurity
Early career:	Unstable, high job mobility, high job loss-risk → high job insecurity	Unstable, high job mobility, high job loss-risk → high job insecurity	Stable, low job mobility, high job loss-risk for fixed-term employees → high job insecurity for them	Stable, low job mobility, high job loss-risk for fixed-term employees → high job insecurity for them

Source: Own illustration.

Still, although this flexicurity country is well equipped to meet the flexibility demands of global markets while simultaneously reducing employment insecurity, labor market risks for certain groups of young people have remained stable since the 1980s. As the Danish country study shows, especially unskilled people have a high risk of being confronted with disadvantageous employment forms in Denmark, chiefly because training programs or job placements do not reach all the unemployed. Those who regard such measures as a negative prospect increase their efforts to find a job (Bredgaard et al. 2005), even when this is a low-paid, casual job. Particularly unskilled youth are at risk of ending up in this 'gray area' of the labor market (Jacobsen 2005).

Both *liberal countries* included in this comparison are uncoordinated market economies with weak employment protection, low public spending on active labor market policies, a weak linkage between the education and the employment system, and with only a secondary relevance of certificated vocational skills. It is the low employment protection and the related mobility on these labor markets that promote young people's labor market entry and thus lead to low employment insecurity. However, like the rest of the workforce, early-career employees face high levels of job insecurity. Liberal countries have already been providing companies with all the flexibility tools, and earlier studies have shown that labor market entrants are exposed to all kinds of disadvantageous flexibility strategies (e.g., Blossfeld et al. 2005; Müller et al. 2002; Scherer 2005): numerical flexibility, temporal flexibility, wage flexibility, and externalization. However, the growing dynamics and volatility of global markets have probably forced companies to apply these flexibility strategies even more rigorously in recent years. Hence, I anticipate that entry-level employees will have started their first jobs increasingly in under-qualified and precarious positions that might lead to increasing economic insecurity. Furthermore, I expect early careers in liberal countries to have become even more unstable (rising job insecurity) and the establishing phase to have become prolonged, because binding commitments of employers toward entrants might well be declining under the new economic conditions. Due to the lack of valid and perceivable signals of the quality of education, companies screen the abilities of employees on the job; the fear of poaching intensifies the reluctance of employers to invest in occupational training.

On the other hand, binding commitments depend strongly on the human capital of labor market entrants. Since employers are particularly reluctant to invest in vocational education for less educated persons, I expect especially labor market entrants with lower education to have been progressively more exposed to all disadvantageous flexibility forms, because, unlike Denmark, a public system of adult education is missing. By the same token, I expect that the employment careers of low qualified persons have gained an increasingly 'entrapment' character depriving them of the chances of becoming established on the labor market. Instead, I anticipate much higher job and employment insecurity for them compared to people with better qualifications.

Though most countries described as *insider-protection countries* introduced legislation to deregulate temporary contracts over the last decades, the overall employment protection index is still higher than in Denmark and in the liberal countries (OECD 2004). In insider-protection countries, labor market policies focus more on sustaining the status quo than on promoting integration into the labor market. In these countries, the exigency for flexibilization splits the labor force into two groups: well-qualified labor market insiders whose jobs are relatively well protected versus outsiders (labor market entrants and especially low educated entrants) who lack both experience and strong ties to work organizations or relevant networks. Due to their lack of bargaining power, these outsiders have to put up with employers dictating the conditions of their work contracts. Thus for entrants, it has probably been increasingly difficult to gain access to the labor market, and they are likely to be exposed to numerical flexibility in the form of fixed-term contracts.

Though the insider-protection countries' deregulation of employment protection for temporary contracts might have facilitated access to the labor market, achieving an insider status has probably become increasingly more difficult. Many entrants can be expected to have faced a prolonged establishing process. Especially the lower qualified entrants are likely to have been confronted increasingly with high levels of employment insecurity and to have rarely become insiders because employers are unwilling to invest in human capital for them—viewing them as a cheap and easily replaceable workforce. They probably have experienced increasingly precarious employment with high job insecurity, leading to higher levels of economic insecurity. For two reasons, I expect these problems to be more severe in the southern European variant of this regime type.

The first argument addresses the institutional linkage between occupational qualifications and employment that plays an important role for the transition from an outsider to an insider status: Whereas the southern European countries (Italy and Spain) are semicoordinated market economies, the northern European countries (Germany, the Netherlands, and Sweden) are coordinated market economies with more highly standardized education and vocational systems that guarantee solid occupational skills and provide employers with reliable signals reducing the risk of mismatches.[27] As in

---

27 An exception is France. Its education system "places a strong emphasis on general and theoretical education [...]. All in all, a clear-cut match between school and work does not exist in France. Employers have to screen job candidates on the basis of their level of education rather than of their vocational qualifications" (Zdrojewski et al. 2008: 103).

Denmark, this reduces employment insecurity and facilitates the transition into an insider status for well-qualified entrants. In contrast, the nonstandardized training systems and relatively strict employment protection in Italy and Spain make the transition into the first employment quite long and difficult (Müller et al. 2002), leading to a generally high level of employment insecurity among first-time job-seekers.

The second argument regards the countries' efforts to promote young people's labor market integration via active labor market policies: While the southern European countries spend almost nothing on active labor market policies, some of the northern European countries spend a considerable amount of their GDP on education and training measures to upgrade the qualifications of the unemployed and to motivate them to seek work actively—both reducing their employment insecurity.

Before introducing the results of the country comparison, I shall outline some of the challenges of this cross-national type of comparison and give an overview on the country-specific analyses used in the comparisons.

Methodological considerations and overview on the country-specific analyses

Using a common conceptual framework, the *flexCAREER* project analyzed a range of processes and aspects in order to learn about the effects of increasing labor market flexibility on young people's objective insecurity experiences: Regarding the initial labor market entry, the project analyzed the duration of job search until first employment (as an indicator for individual employment insecurity) and the quality of the first job in most country studies. Regarding the further development of the employment career, the most interesting question was whether labor market entrants, especially those working in flexible forms of employment, were able to establish themselves in the labor market. Therefore considering the characteristics of the first job, the single country studies analyzed early-career employees' risk of unemployment (i.e., their job insecurity), risk of downward mobility, and chances of upward mobility.

One major challenge in cross-national endeavors such as the *flexCAREER* project is to gather appropriate and comparable data based on common methods, concepts, and indices while working in each individual country context. Furthermore, it is necessary to allow for country-specific research designs. For instance, consequences have to be drawn from the country-specific definition of the first 'real' job when a combination of education and work is comparatively frequent among young people, when jobs alongside education do not have the character of side jobs, or when it is common practice to switch between periods of studying and working. Additionally, the definition of a 'bad' and 'good' labor market entry depends to a large extent on the institutional features and the social and cultural norms of a given society. For some country analyses, this evaluation is based on the added job insecurity of fixed-term employment; for others, it is defined by the economic insecurities related to involuntary part-time employment, or the risk of being employed in a low-paid job.[28] Taking all this into account, the question of when someone has become established on the labor market is also dependent on the institutional context.

All things considered, the success of cross-national life-course studies depends crucially on finding a reasonable compromise between the consistency and comparability of the country studies while simultaneously allowing for country-specific idiosyncrasies. However, the possibility of allowing for country specifics is also an analytical advantage that reduces the bias occurring "because we, as life course researchers, often wear cultural blinders of some sort that are connected to the society in which we are socialized" (Blossfeld 2009: 281).

In this regard, a further enormous advantage of this kind of research is that the country case studies are produced by an international network of researchers who serve as national experts on their home countries, are familiar with the data sets available within each country, and are able to analyze them to the fullest advantage (Blossfeld 2009). Given the specific country contexts and the different microdata sets used for the single country contributions within the *flexCAREER* project, the definition of labor market entries (first 'real' jobs), 'bad' and 'good' entry positions, as well as upward and downward mobility criteria was left to the authors of each country study.[29]

The longitudinal individual-level analyses covered the period from the 1980s until the first years of the new millennium. The empirical analyses focused on cohorts of young people who left general education, formal vocational training (e.g., in the dual system), and college or university education in specific years.[30] When the data permitted, the first step when analyzing *labor market entry* examined the initial school-to-work transition in terms of the duration of job search and the quality of the first job.

---

28 Yet another aspect, analyzed in some of the country studies, was 'over-qualification,' that is, the skill requirements of the job are lower than the qualification attained by the individual (for the results on this issue, see Kurz et al. 2008).
29 Furthermore, it was decided not to use a common rule for closing 'gaps' between two educational spells that occur when first-time education system leavers re-enter education or enter military service within a fixed timeframe (in countries with compulsory military service, the respective spells were treated like educational spells, because these individuals are not able to enter employment before finishing their service).
30 For details, see the single country chapters in Blossfeld et al. (2008).

The definition of 'bad,' that is, flexible or precarious entry positions differs between countries in terms of the specific way in which employment flexibility has been implemented in the respective institutional contexts. Countries with strong employment protection have tried to introduce employment flexibility mainly through the introduction of fixed-term contracts or agency work (OECD 2004a). Consequently, the country studies on France, Germany, the Netherlands, Sweden, Italy, and Spain used fixed-term employment as an indicator for low-quality jobs. Entries into fixed-term jobs were also included in the study on the United Kingdom, although for employers in countries with weak employment protection (i.e., Denmark, the United Kingdom, and the United States), fixed-term contracts do not offer the advantage of additional flexibility. Furthermore, in the United Kingdom, fixed-term jobs may well be stepping-stones to permanent jobs (Booth et al. 2000). However, if we compare fixed-term jobs in the United Kingdom to those in Denmark, we find different degrees of social protection attached to them. In Denmark, all employees (including those on fixed-term jobs) enjoy generous social protection coverage, whereas social entitlements in the United Kingdom are generally limited, and fixed-term employees are even less protected (Barbier 2008).

Nevertheless, in countries with weak employment protection, other forms of a bad start into employment are more important: bad pay and poor career prospects. Therefore, the analyses for Denmark, the United Kingdom, and the United States focused on one or more of these indicators. The study on Denmark in the previous section used low-wage jobs as a type of bad entry position. The country study on the United States focused on *stopgap jobs*. These are highly flexible part-time jobs with low skill requirements, no social protection (e.g., no health insurance), low pay, and few prospects for career advancement. They are typically used by young people as a way to gain an initial foothold on the labor market (Oppenheimer and Kalmijn 1995). The situation is similar in the United Kingdom, where part-time jobs and seasonal and casual work are the most important forms of precarious work (Schmelzer 2008). In addition, the studies on France, the Netherlands, and Sweden included indicators for part-time jobs, which are also relevant in these countries.

The second step concentrated on *processes in the early career*, mainly, on the risk of unemployment and upward or downward mobility. Again, the exact processes under study varied between the countries, mainly based on considerations of what was appropriate in the country-specific institutional setting and what was possible in terms of the microdata available. The following subsections summarize and compare the findings of the country studies in terms of the labor market entry- and early-career analyses.

A cross-national comparison of changes at labor market entry

Changes in the initial labor market entry process

First of all, the results of the single country studies in the *flexCAREER* project confirmed that the labor market entry process is clearly structured by the institutional context of the respective country, in particular, by the degree of employment protection and by the organization of general and vocational education. Overall, in countries in which education is relatively standardized and stratified or in which vocational education has a clear, occupation-specific character, the labor market entry process has remained quite smooth even in recent years; that is, the job search after leaving school has been relatively short. Apart from Denmark, this is the case in Germany, the Netherlands, and Sweden. Entry is also smooth in countries where employment protection is low and, thus, the labor market is relatively open. This is true for the United Kingdom and the United States. However, since on-the-job training is the dominant mode of vocational education in the liberal countries, skill-job mismatches in the early career are common. This means, the entry process might occur quickly in these labor markets, but the first job might not match the qualification and might be of only short duration. In contrast, entry processes in the remaining insider-outsider labor markets (i.e., in France, Italy, and Spain) were expected to be characterized by long searching or waiting times. This was indeed observed for Italy. However, in France, employment entry occurred relatively quickly in the period under study (1992–2001), probably because flexible work forms reduced the costs of hiring young workers for employers (Kurz et al. 2008).

How did the duration of job search change over cohorts? Given the increased global competition and the related economic restructuring in the countries under study, the basic prediction was that the labor market entry process would have become more difficult for young people since the 1980s. In line with this expectation, the search phase became longer for young people in the United States, Germany, Italy, and Spain. However, as in Denmark, the duration of job search became shorter over cohorts in the United Kingdom, France, and the Netherlands. In Sweden, the duration of job search became longer for cohorts leaving the education system between 1990 and 1996, but shortened thereafter. These patterns can be attributed clearly to macroeconomic developments. Denmark, France, the Netherlands, and Sweden experienced economic upswings during the 1990s and the United Kingdom already since the mid-1980s. In Denmark, the youngest cohort entering the labor market during an economic upswing displayed a significantly lower transition rate into first employment than the cohort entering the labor market during an earlier upswing in the 1980s (see Section 2.2.5). An exception was the United States, where a slight prolongation of the job search phase could be observed, although there was an economic upswing in the 1990s.

Changes in the quality of the first job

As argued above, the typical way of relaxing national employment protection legislation to fight high levels of unemployment in insider-protection countries has been to weaken the protection for temporary forms of employment (OECD 2004). Indeed, in most of the respective countries under study (Germany, Sweden, Italy, and Spain), the individual risk of receiving a fixed-term job ran parallel to trends in aggregate unemployment figures. However, there were two exceptions: First, France exhibited no increase in the risk of fixed-term employment; in contrast to the other countries with strong employment protection, France even slightly strengthened the protection legislation for both temporary and permanent forms of employment (see Section 1.3). However, the country experienced an economic boom in the 1990s. The second exception was the Netherlands, which also experienced an economic upswing. However, despite decreasing unemployment, young people faced increasing risks of starting in bad entry jobs. The improved opportunities for school-leavers in the Netherlands in the mid-1990s were not accompanied by a falling, but by a rising risk of entering the labor market with a fixed-term contract or with a skill-job mismatch.[31]

Results for liberal countries were mixed. The analyses for the United Kingdom revealed increasing risks of starting in a precarious type of job for the educational cohorts from 1985 to 2004. In particular, the number of part-time and seasonal/casual jobs increased tremendously. In contrast, the risk of starting the employment career in a stopgap job in the United States actually decreased for the youngest cohort leaving the education system between 1993 and 2002 (Relikowski et al. 2008). The latter development ran parallel to the trend in aggregate unemployment figures.

As described in Section 1.3, Denmark experienced an economic boom in the 1990s accompanied by a strong decrease in aggregate unemployment rates. However, similar to the results for the Netherlands, the relevant educational cohort faced the highest risk of a bad entry job, defined as work with low pay. There are two possible explanations for this: First, the activation policy for unemployed people introduced in Denmark in this period probably motivated some people to take up even a low paid job in order to avoid participation in activation programs. Second, wage setting had been decentralized in the mid-1990s, which led to a reduction of wage levels (see Section 2.2.5). The results for the Danish and the Dutch country studies indicate that the increasing demand for flexible forms of work was more than

---

31 The risk peaked off, however, from the late 1990s onward.

a temporary phenomenon in times of economic stagnation: it seems to have remained attractive for employers in times of an economic upswing as well.

In summary, the findings from the previous country studies on labor market entry do not support the view that there is a general linear trend toward a longer job searching phase and toward ever more flexible or precarious jobs in all countries under study. However, as Kurz et al. (2008: 345) have pointed out, taking the globalization argument seriously this is not what was to be expected.

> Economic globalization is characterized by an increasing volatility of markets to which companies try to adjust as quickly and flexibly as possible. [...] In times of economic upswings employers will hire young people more readily than in times of economic downswings. In fact, this is generally what we found: The searching phase has become longer, except in those countries that experienced an economic boom. The interesting question is, however, whether employers tend to reduce the extent of flexible or bad paid jobs in times of economic upswings. First of all, in countries that undergo economic stagnation and display high unemployment rates, labor market entrants are more and more likely to face precarious forms of work. [...] In countries that experienced economic upswings, there is in most cases no clear reduction of flexible or precarious jobs for labor market entrants. Quite in contrast, such jobs appear to be used as instruments to combat unemployment and are thus part of the 'success story' in these countries (Kurz et al. 2008: 345).

In my view, this is one of the most important results of Blossfeld et al.'s (2008) study.

A cross-national comparison of developments in the early employment career

If we want to know whether the flexibilization of young peoples' employment entry is only a temporary phenomenon at labor market entry, or whether it has become a general feature of the working life of the young cohorts under study, it does not suffice to focus solely on changes in the duration of job search and the quality of the first job. Therefore, we (the *flexCAREER* project team) also analyzed how the labor market entrants' employment career in the single countries developed further, concentrating on the 5 years after the individual had started the first job. Most analyses examined the transition rate to unemployment out of the first job, as well as upward and downward mobility processes.

Trends in the risk of unemployment and in career mobility

For the transition to unemployment out of the first job, we found increasing risks across cohorts in the United Kingdom, Germany, and Italy; declining risks in Denmark and France; and no time trend in the Netherlands. Except for the United Kingdom and the Netherlands, results corresponded to the development of the general unemployment rate in these countries.

Turning to upward and downward status mobility, findings from the single country studies were mixed. In some countries, mobility rates were found to have increased across cohorts. This was the case in Denmark and the United Kingdom for both upward and downward mobility, and in Italy for downward mobility. The development in downward mobility rates ran parallel to the development of unemployment risks, indicating more instability in the working lives of young cohorts. There were also countries for which no clear time trend was observable, namely, the Netherlands and Sweden. A decrease in both forms of mobility across cohorts was detected in the United States.

In summary, as with the results on the duration of job search at labor market entry, there is a relatively clear relationship between the macroeconomic developments in the respective countries and the trends in unemployment and downward mobility risks.

A bad entry job: Stepping-stone or trap?

How does a bad start into working life affect the further career? Does a difficult employment entry in terms of a 'bad' first job (defined in the respective country contexts as fixed-term, low-wage, stopgap, casual, or part-time job) increase the risk of unemployment and downward mobility? Or is it connected to upward mobility, indicating that a difficult employment entry is only a temporary phase in the employment career?[32] As outlined in the introductory part of this book (Section 1.2), these questions refer to two opposing scenarios anticipated in either the stepping-stone or the entrapment hypothesis.

As discussed in the hypotheses section, in countries with a relatively open employment system and a weak institutional link between the education and the employment system (such as the United Kingdom and the United States), the early career might consist of a series of stopgap jobs and short unemployment episodes as part of a matching process characterized by job hopping. It therefore seems unlikely that individuals will become entrapped in a bad employment position or that such a position will act as a scar for their further careers. In contrast, in countries with a close link between education and the employment system (such as Denmark, Germany, the Netherlands, and Sweden), it is likely that the first job has a stronger effect on further career perspectives. However, in the case of Denmark, this effect might be

---

32 Besides the influence of bad entry jobs, some of the flexCAREER country studies also examined the effect of the duration of the job search on early-career trajectories. These results are summarized in Kurz et al. (2008).

buffered by the high labor market flexibility.[33] Furthermore, in Denmark and the Netherlands, possible scar effects might be counteracted by the high supply of active labor market policies that should help young people with employment difficulties. Finally, in the countries with a relatively lose linkage between education and the employment system and an insider protection strategy (France, Italy, and Spain), a bad entry job might act as an obstacle for the further career.

However, these expectations were not confirmed by analyses on the effects of the quality of the first job on the risk of unemployment. Instead, results were basically similar for all countries under study: Having a bad first job increased the risk of unemployment.

With respect to upward and downward mobility, the effects of the quality of entry jobs were relatively homogeneous: An increase of both upward and downward mobility was observed in France, Sweden, and Italy for entrants who started in a fixed-term job, in the United Kingdom for young people who began their working life in a part-time or casual/seasonal jobs, and in the United States for those who started in a stopgap job. Thus, it seems that, in these countries, low-quality entry jobs generally induce more turbulence in the employment careers of young people. In contrast, we did not find that having had a fixed-term contract in the first job had any effect on upward and downward mobility in the Netherlands. Employees in Denmark who started their career in low-wage jobs had relatively good upward mobility prospects and a relatively low downward mobility risk. However, this result was probably related to bottom effects.[34]

Development of social inequalities

Given the rising flexibilization of young people's labor market entry, the different country studies also investigated whether there was a persistence of social inequalities related to educational qualification and occupational class. As sketched in the introductory chapter (see Section 1.2), this prediction is based on stratification research (Breen 1997; Erikson and Goldthorpe 1992; Shavit and Blossfeld 1993). It presents a sharp contrast to theses by

---

33   Indeed, as already mentioned, empirical studies have shown that the risk of starting in a low-wage job has always been relatively high in Denmark. Young people tend to be hired at the bottom of the wage distribution within a firm and then move upwards as they gain experience and establish careers (Bingley and Westergaard-Nielsen 1997; Eriksson and Westergaard-Nielsen 2004; OECD 1996a).

34   In the Danish country study, I analyzed wage mobility taking the wage level of origin into account (see Section 2.2.4), and found that the wage level of origin had a significant effect on both mobility directions (see Section 2.2.5, Table 2.5): the higher the wage level, the lower the chances of making an upward move and the higher the risk of making a downward move. This finding is related to bottom and ceiling effects.

individualization and globalization theorists like Beck (1992) and Castells (2000).

First of all, the results of the single *flexCAREER* country studies indicated that social inequalities are persistent: We could still observe a rather clearly stratified distribution of risks at labor market entry and in the early career. With regard to labor market entry, the duration of the job search was clearly structured by educational level in most countries. Results were similar for the quality of the first job: Part-time work (United Kingdom, France), stopgap jobs (United States), and low pay (Denmark) were more common at the bottom of the educational hierarchy. In most countries, this was also true for fixed-term contracts (in France, the Netherlands, Sweden, and Spain). In Germany and Italy, however, fixed-term contracts were also particularly widespread at the top of the educational hierarchy. However, for more highly educated employees, fixed-term contracts do not generally have to be considered as precarious. As Mertens and McGinnity (2005) have shown for the German case, fixed-term contracts in highly qualified positions are well compensated in monetary terms. With regard to the early career, education and occupational position clearly stratified the risks of unemployment and downward mobility in all the countries under study.

A further question addressed how these inequalities have developed across cohorts of labor market entrants. The basic prediction was that, during the course of increasing global competition, the inequality gap between employees with more and less market power would increase. For Denmark, this prediction could not be confirmed (see Section 2.2.5); however, I found social inequalities among labor market entrants with different educational levels to be persistent. Nonetheless, a rise in inequalities between educational levels could be observed in the other countries under study (Kurz et al. 2008). This increase in risks followed a specific pattern: For insider-protection strategy countries (France, Germany, Sweden, Italy, and Spain), the main issue for labor market entrants was to gain a foothold in the labor market. In most of these countries—except for the Netherlands and Sweden where active labor market policies seem to play an important role in integrating poorly qualified young people into the labor market—a widening gap between well and poorly qualified entrants could be observed with respect to the duration of job search. In countries with weak employment protection, the main risk for labor market entrants was identified as starting and being stuck in bad job positions, moving downward, or being restricted when trying to move upward. According to the analyses, the relative risk of starting in part-time work (United Kingdom) or stopgap jobs (United States) increased between educational groups in these countries. The poorly qualified also faced an increasingly higher risk of downward mobility (United Kingdom) and lower chances for upward mobility (United States). In sum, for all the countries compared with Denmark here, one could observe an increase in country-specific flexible forms of work and a destabilization of subsequent employment careers for entrants with lower education and/or lower occupational class.[35]

2.4. Preliminary conclusion on the development of objective economic insecurity in Denmark and the other countries

This chapter commenced with two questions:
1. *How have the immediate school-to-work transition and the early career changed in different labor market entry regimes since the early 1980s?*
2. *Do changes in this life-course transition in Denmark reveal a distinctive pattern compared to other OECD countries?*

These global questions were decomposed into four more detailed research questions: (1) What can be regarded as a 'bad,' that is, precarious employment position for youth in different national contexts? (2) Has the risk of a bad start to the employment career increased across cohorts? (3) Is a bad career entry typically a trap, or can it serve as a stepping-stone toward more rewarding jobs? (4) Do changes in youth employment trajectories lead to a persistence or even reinforcement of social inequalities related to educational qualification and occupational class?

At the end of Section 2.2, I have already answered these questions for the Danish case. Now, I am able to answer them from a cross-national comparative perspective before returning to the two global research questions addressing young people's risk of being exposed to the two insecurity dimensions studied here within the dynamics of labor market entry and establishment processes at the beginning of their working lives: employment insecurity (i.e., insecurity over being able to find a new job) and job insecurity (i.e., insecurity over keeping the current job).

Table 2.6 summarizes the most relevant results of the country comparison in section 2.3.

---

[35] Except for the Netherlands, where the development of inequality was not studied (see Wolbers 2008).

Table 2.6: Summary: Labor market entry regimes and changes in school-to-work transitions and early career trajectories since the 1980s

Labor market entry regime:	Danish flexicurity	Liberal	N. European insider protection	S. European insider protection
Countries under study:	Denmark	United Kingdom, United States	France, Germany, Netherlands, Sweden	Italy, Spain
Increasing duration of job search?[a]	No linear trend[b]	UK: no (decreasing), USA: yes	NL: no (decr.), S: no linear trend,[c] F: no (decr.), D: yes	Yes
(Main) indicators for 'bad' entry jobs:	Low-wage job	Part-time work, seasonal/casual job (UK), stopgap job (USA)	Fixed-term employment	Fixed-term employment
Increasing risk of a 'bad' start?	Yes	UK: yes, USA: no (decr.)	Yes, except for F (decr.)	Yes
Bad entry: Trap or stepping-stone?	Trap	Trap	Trap	Trap
Reinforcement of social inequalities?	No, but persistence	Yes	Yes	Yes

Source: Own illustration, based on Kurz et al. 2008.
Notes: a Denmark, France, the Netherlands, and Sweden experienced economic upswings during the 1990s and the United Kingdom already since the mid-1980s.
b In Denmark, the youngest cohort entering the labor market during the economic upswing in the 1990s displayed a lower transition rate into first employment than the cohort entering during an earlier upswing in the 1980s. However, two earlier cohorts who finished education in times of rising unemployment showed lower chances of making a transition into a first job.
c In Sweden, the duration of job search became longer for the cohorts leaving the education system between 1990 and 1996, but shortened thereafter.

The first detailed research question was: *What can be regarded as a 'bad,' that is, precarious employment position for youth in different national contexts?* As the table shows, the definition of 'bad' (i.e., flexible or precarious) entry positions differs between countries depending on the specific way in which employment flexibility is implemented in the respective institutional context. In the Danish labor market with its long tradition of weak dismissal protection, fixed-term jobs are as insecure as any other job. Furthermore, part-time work is mostly chosen voluntarily and regulated by the same collective agreements as full-time work. In the study on Denmark, I have therefore focused on *low-wage jobs* as a type of bad entry position. These are jobs with earnings within the lowest decile of the wage distribution. Countries of the liberal type are also characterized by a long history of employment flexibility. However, besides bad pay, a bad start into employment in these countries may also be characterized by low career prospects. The country study on the United States focuses on *stopgap jobs*: highly flexible part-time jobs with low skill requirements, no social protection (e.g., no health insurance), low pay, and few prospects for career advancement. The situation is similar in the United Kingdom, where part-time jobs and seasonal or casual work are the most important forms of precarious work. In contrast to Denmark and the liberal countries, countries belonging to one of the two insider-protection regime types have a rather short history of employment flexibility, and they have deregulated their labor markets since the 1980s mainly through an increased use of fixed-term contracts or agency work. Consequently, the country studies on France, Germany, the Netherlands, Sweden, Italy, and Spain use fixed-term employment as an indicator for low-quality jobs.

The second detailed research question asked: *Has the risk of a bad start to the employment career increased across cohorts?* With regard to the duration of job search after leaving school, there is no clear answer to this question, because the job-search duration proves to be dependent on both national institutional arrangements and the macroeconomic development in the specific country. In times of economic upswing, the job search phase after leaving school becomes shorter (see Table 2.6). However, when the above question addresses the quality of the first employment, the answer is yes for the majority of countries under study (including Denmark): Almost all the countries reveal an increasing risk of entering a precarious type of job. Moreover, once certain forms of flexible work have become established as a route into the labor market, there is a tendency to maintain them even when the macroeconomic situation improves.

The third detailed research question was: *Is a bad career entry typically a trap, or can it serve as a stepping-stone toward more rewarding jobs?* Regardless of which labor market entry regime we examine, entering a bad job increases the risk of unemployment in all the countries studied here; in some countries, it is also related to more downward mobility during the subsequent years of the early career.

Finally, the fourth detailed research question asked: *Do changes in youth employment trajectories lead to a persistence, or even reinforcement of social inequalities related to educational qualification and occupational class?* While Denmark reveals a persistence of social inequalities, all the other countries reveal increasing social inequalities with regard to educational levels or occupational positions during the course of globalization.

Moving up to the level of the two more global research questions, these findings can be summarized as follows:

How have the immediate school-to-work transition and the early career changed in different labor market entry regimes since the early 1980s?

Given increased global competition and the economic restructuring in the countries under study, the immediate school-to-work transition and the early career have changed tremendously since the early 1980s. In all labor market entry regimes, the school-to-work transition has become increasingly difficult, and flexible and precarious forms of work have become more typical in the first job after leaving the education system. With regard to the early employment career, unemployment risks have risen across successive cohorts depending on the specific macroeconomic cycles in the countries under study. Furthermore, irrespective of national context, labor market entry in a bad job has negative effects on the stability of the further career in terms of unemployment and status mobility. Both the immediate labor market entry phase and the subsequent early career are characterized by persistent and growing social inequalities among young people in the different countries.

Do changes in this life-course transition in Denmark reveal a distinctive pattern compared to other OECD countries?

Denmark does not differ significantly from the other countries included here. Two dimensions of economic insecurity are addressed in the present country comparison: employment and job insecurity. Employment insecurity is studied with regard to the chances of finding a first job by looking at the duration of job search in the single countries. The duration of job search is not only relatively low for the youngest school-leaver cohort in Denmark; this pattern can also be observed in the United Kingdom, France, and the Netherlands; that is, in countries that have also experienced economic upswings affecting the labor market entry phase of the youngest cohorts studied. Job insecurity is analyzed by looking at the risk of entering the first unemployment. Similar to the duration of job search, this risk is also influenced by the development of national unemployment rates. The declining job insecurity found for young employees in Denmark is not exceptional, because a declining job-loss risk is also found for early-career employees in France. Furthermore, as in the other employment regimes, independent from macroeconomic cycles, school leavers in Denmark face an increasing risk of starting their careers in a precarious job, this appears to increase their unemployment risks in the further career, and it is young people with a lower education who are more likely to being exposed to these risks.

However, in comparison to young people in other countries, the situation of labor market entrants and early-career employees in Denmark is probably not all that bad, because a 'long duration of job search,' a 'bad job,' and 'unemployment' have a specific meaning in this institutional context. First, in an international comparison, it can be assumed that the job-search duration of first-time education system leavers in Denmark is short, given the close link between the vocational system and the employment system, the high mobility on the flexible Danish labor market, and the high supply of active labor market policies. Second, with regard to 'bad' jobs, even if young people in Denmark work in low-wage jobs, they are covered by health insurance; besides, education and most public services are free of charge (Westergaard-Nielsen 2008). In the liberal countries, low-wage earners have to pay for some of these things and may have problems affording them. Third, in case of unemployment, labor market entrants in Denmark profit from the country's specific combination of flexibility and security, in particular, from the high mobility on the flexible labor market (reducing employment insecurity) combined with high public expenditure on labor market policies that is both active (further reducing employment insecurity) and passive in terms of generous unemployment benefits (reducing income insecurity). In case of unemployment, labor market entrants in Denmark can rely on a short duration of unemployment, because the hire-and-fire principle leads to a relatively high level of external vacancies thus promoting job mobility (Gangl 2003a; Mills and Blossfeld 2005). Furthermore, those who are unable to find their own way back into the labor market are supported by active labor market policies along with relatively generous unemployment and cash benefits providing them with sufficient and regular income to reduce their economic insecurity.

Overall, these (mainly unskilled) young people, who are at risk of ending up in the 'gray area' of the Danish labor market beyond the reach of labor market integration measures (Jacobsen 2006) and are hopping from one low-wage job to another, are probably still better integrated into the labor market than some of the young fixed-term employees and certainly most of the unemployed in the insider-outsider regimes. Moreover, the economic insecurity experienced by low-wage job-hoppers in Denmark is certainly less precarious than that of the 'working poor' in the liberal countries. And during an unemployment spell, they face a relatively low poverty risk: Using representative national surveys, the EPUSE study[36] found that in the mid-1990s, the proportion of the unemployed in poverty (taking the 50% mean equivalized household income line) was only 8 percent in Denmark—compared to between 25 (the Netherlands) and 49 percent (the United Kingdom) in the other countries studied (Gallie 2000).

The interesting question, however, is whether all this is reflected in the insecurity perception of young people in different national labor markets. This is the subject of Part 3 of this book.

---

36 'Employment Precarity, Unemployment and Social Exclusion (EPUSE)' was conducted within the EU's Framework Programme Research. Using large-scale samples drawn from both national data sets and the European Community Household Panel, the study compared the situation of the unemployed in eight countries: Denmark, France, Germany, Ireland, Italy, the Netherlands, Sweden, and the United Kingdom (Gallie 2000).

3. Insecurity perception: The translation of unemployment risks into job-loss worry in times of flexible employment

3.1. Preliminary note

In this empirical part, economic insecurity is conceptualized as a multidimensional, subjective phenomenon. Due to the nature of the available data, the focus is on the insecurity perception of early-career employees, that is, those young people who have managed to find a first job.

As outlined in Chapter 1, economic security is closely linked to having sufficient and regular work for young people, because earning one's own income also means economic independence. This central role of labor market earnings makes the risk of unemployment one of the core dimensions of a young worker's economic insecurity.

One of the results of the cross-national comparison of labor market entries presented in the previous chapter has showed that, depending on macroeconomic cycles in the countries under study, unemployment risks in the early career have increased across successive cohorts. However, countries differ significantly in how far they provide security with respect to potential job loss and unemployment (Anderson and Pontusson 2007; Bredgaard et al. 2005; Gallie 2007). Thus, 'unemployment' has a different meaning in different labor market entry regimes. As individuals take structural factors into account when thinking about the possibility of losing their job, it is feasible to assume that young people's job-loss worries will also differ in a cross-national comparison.

However, little is known about how these cross-national institutional differences are mapped into young workers' insecurity perception. After controlling for individual and macroeconomic factors, does an early-career employee in late-1990s Sweden worry more when thinking about possible job loss than an early-career employee in late-1990s Denmark?

Based on survey data from an international subsample of early-career employees, I shall address the following two research questions:

1. *How do institutional frameworks differ with regard to insecurity perception?*
2. *Does the specific Danish combination translate into less job-loss worry in young workers in Denmark compared to those in other OECD countries?*

In particular, I shall analyze the following dimensions of individual insecurity perception in early-career employees: (1) the risk of *job insecurity perception* (i.e., the individual's estimate of the probability of losing her or his job), (2) the risk of *employment insecurity perception* (i.e., the individual's estimate of the risk of not finding another—more or less equivalent—job), (3) the risk of *income insecurity perception* (i.e., the individual's estimated probability of an income loss due to unemployment), and (4) the overall risk of *job-loss worry* (i.e., the extent to which a person worries about losing her or his job), which is equated with the employees' overall extent of economic insecurity perception.

In contrast to the first empirical study presented in the previous chapter, this second study applies an integrated cross-national design. Drawing on one international data set, countries will be represented in the regression models by dummy variables while taking Denmark as the reference country; that is, the perceived job insecurities of respondents in the other countries will be compared to the insecurities of their counterparts in this classic flexicurity regime.

The data comes from a subsample of early-career employees extracted from pooled cross-sectional international survey data gathered in 1997 and 2005 as part of the *Work Orientations* studies by the *International Social Survey Program* (ISSP). This particular subsample has been created by selecting respondents in the first 6 years after leaving formal education, with this graduation time proxied by using country- and education-specific *typical graduation ages*.

Scientific contribution

Different institutional frameworks produce different labor market entry and early-career patterns (see Chapter 2, or, e.g., Blossfeld et al. 2005; Brzinsky-Fay 2007; Gangl 2003b). These institutional differences lead to variations in the labor market risks and economic insecurities confronting young people not only at initial labor market entry but also during the early employment career. However, up to now, there are hardly any empirical studies on how these institutional differences are reflected in young workers' individual perceptions of economic insecurity.

An exception is the project 'Families and Transitions in Europe' (FATE) (Biggart 2007), which studied some specific aspects of young people's lives in nine local regions throughout Europe with a survey of youth in their final year of education plus qualitative follow-up interviews with the young people and their parents one year later. The project's overall aim was to examine the role of the family in enabling transitions from education to work. The issue of economic insecurity was addressed indirectly by looking at young people's economic independence during the school-to-work transition in terms of their sources of income (financial support by their parents and/or income from employment, loans, or grants). The project's empirical findings have shown that in most countries, young people cannot live an autonomous life as long as they have not achieved a stable position in the labor market.[37] However, the project did not go beyond the first year of the employment career, and, because its focus was a different one, it did not use any particular model of economic insecurity.

Due to the lack of adequate data (Clark and Postel-Vinay 2009; Green 2009), there are hardly any international studies on job insecurity perception that account for the multidimensional character of job-loss worry. Exceptions are an OECD study on job insecurity across the EU (1997)[38] as well as studies by Green (2009) as well as Anderson and Pontusson (2007). All these contributions draw on cross-sectional data, because there is still no international longitudinal dataset addressing the multi-dimensional character of job insecurity perception. The study presented here is also based on cross-sectional data.

To summarize: This is the first cross-national quantitative study on young worker's perception of economic insecurity that accounts for more dimensions than job insecurity.

3.2. A cross-national comparison of young worker's job-loss worry

3.2.1. Introduction

In recent years, long-term, full-time work has declined in modern societies in favor of so-called 'nonstandard' employment forms such as part-time, fixed-term, and own-account self-employment (i.e., without employees). As recent research has shown, these trends are most pronounced at labor market entry, leading to a longer entry process and increasing difficulties for education system leavers to establish themselves in the labor market. This increases young people's difficulties in making choices and long-term binding life-course decisions that frequently may translate into decisions for their private

---

37 An exception is Denmark, the country with "[the] most abundant levels of state support [...], where the need to support young people's independence is recognised as an explicit goal of social policy" (Biggart 2005: 7).
38 However, this OECD study used objective indicators for employment and income insecurity.

lives, such as opting for cohabitation instead of marriage or forgoing parenthood until they have obtained a job with a longer term perspective (Blossfeld 1995; Kurz et al. 2005; Mills 2004; Mills and Blossfeld 2005; Oppenheimer 1988, 2003; Oppenheimer et al. 1997). These social consequences highlight the relevance of studying people's insecurity perception in their early employment career across countries in order to learn about its individual and institutional determinants. This empirical study investigates the link between rising employment flexibility and young people's job-loss worries. When analyzing this relationship, I shall focus on the role of different institutional settings and labor market regulation in industrial societies.

It seems reasonable to suppose that individuals take a number of objective factors into account when estimating the subjective probability of losing their job and when evaluating the consequences of a possible job loss (Anderson and Pontusson 2007). Besides the assumed effect of current labor market conditions and individual factors like education or gender, it is institutional frameworks that substantially determine such considerations and, hence, the overall levels of individual job-loss worry. Blossfeld et al. (2008) have described in detail how country-specific institutional settings channel insecurities generated by the global economy to labor market entrants. Central roles in this regard can be assigned to a country's employment protection and the related labor market policies. The objective of this empirical study is to explore how different national combinations of these institutional features translate into young people's insecurity perceptions. I shall compare the Danish flexicurity model, the liberal institutional frameworks, and the insider-protection models of Continental Europe and study whether the specific Danish framework generates less job-loss worry. In particular, my analyses will compare young workers from Denmark, Great Britain,[39] the United States of America, France, Germany, the Netherlands, Sweden, Italy, and Spain.

This chapter is structured as follows: In the next subsection, I shall study the meaning of 'unemployment' and illustrate the importance of job security for youth in different national contexts. Then, I shall introduce the research design of the country study and outline which relevant aspects need to be considered when studying regime-specific job-loss worry in the early career. This involves a decomposition of the different dimensions of job-loss worry and a discussion of its institutional, macroeconomic, and individual determinants that I subsequently use to derive hypotheses on how the

---

39 Whereas the flexCAREER country study I referred to in the cross-national comparison in Chapter 2 used data from the United Kingdom, the ISSP data was conducted only in Great Britain, that is, the United Kingdom without Northern Ireland. Unfortunately, all the OECD measures I am using in the present study were available for the United Kingdom alone.

different institutional backgrounds influence the distinct insecurity dimensions. After describing the data and methods used, I shall present the results of my empirical analyses. The chapter ends with a preliminary conclusion that summarizes and discusses the most important findings on subjective economic insecurity in Denmark and the other countries.

3.2.2. The meaning of 'unemployment' and the importance of job security for young people in different national contexts

The meaning of 'unemployment' for youth in different labor markets

As this empirical part focuses on the translation of unemployment risks into young workers' job-loss worry, I shall start with a more detailed look at the meaning of 'unemployment' for youth in the countries under study. When comparing the relation of young people's job loss risk and their insecurity perception across countries, it does not suffice to look at national unemployment rates. One person who has been unemployed for one year contributes as much to the national yearly average unemployment rate as a group of 12 persons who have been unemployed for one month. However, these 12 persons are probably much better off. Consequently, two countries with identical youth unemployment rates may provide young people with different structural contexts in terms of employment risks and chances. Thus, it makes sense to take a more detailed look at cross-national differences in the temporal structure of unemployment. With regard to young peoples' perception of economic insecurity or their job-loss worry, a key factor is whether unemployment represents "a state of short-term joblessness or one of long-term economic inactivity" (Hofäcker 2010: 179). Whereas in flexible labor markets, unemployment is usually considered to be of a short-term nature and thus assumed to be perceived as a 'normal' passage from one job to another, in less flexible labor markets, it is usually considered to have a more long-term character that may lead to an entrapment in unemployment even for young people at the beginning of their careers.

The OECD (2009a) splits total unemployment into different durations by reporting the number of persons registered as unemployed for less than 1 month, between 1 and 3 months, between 3 and 6 months, between 6 and 12 months, and for 12 months or more. Following Hofäcker (2010), who performed the same analysis for mid- and late-career workers, I used the two extreme durations to calculate percentages of short- and long-term unemployed youth. Figure 3.1 shows the yearly cross-sectional percentage shares of unemployed youth (i.e., persons between 15 and 24[40]) in each country who were short-term unemployed (defined as being unemployed for less than 1 month) and long-term unemployed (defined as being unemployed for 12 months or more) from 1985 to 2005. The following example for Denmark shows how the data points have to be interpreted: In 2005, almost 50 percent of all unemployed youth were unemployed for less than 1 month, while only 4 percent were unemployed for 1 year or more. Note that the unemployed youth we are looking at, and who are registered at their local employment agencies as "actively seeking work," consist of two groups: early-career employees who have lost their job as well as first-time job seekers who have recently left the education system.

Figure 3.1: Short- and long-term youth unemployment for both sexes, percentage shares: 1985–2005

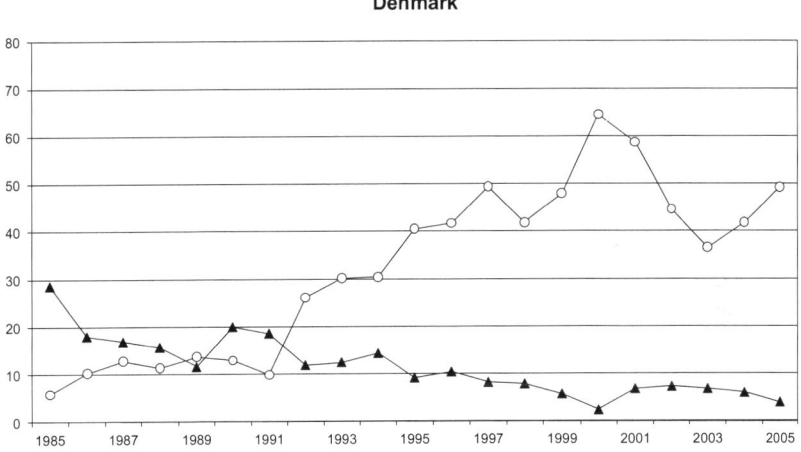

—O— 15-24 year olds' short-term unemployment (less than one month)
—▲— 15-24 year olds' long-term unemployment (more than one year)

---

40 This age-specific definition implies that only unemployed persons with a university degree from Great Britain and Spain had a slight chance to be selected here; in the remaining seven countries, the typical graduation ages for university graduates are over 24 (see Table A.2 in the appendix).

Figure 3.1: continued

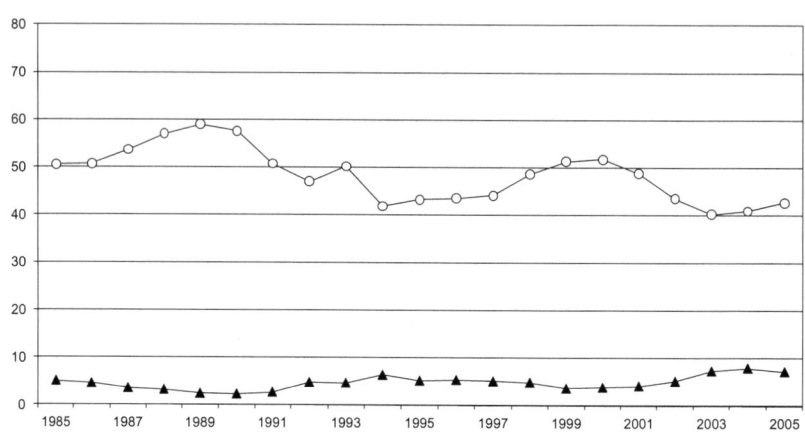

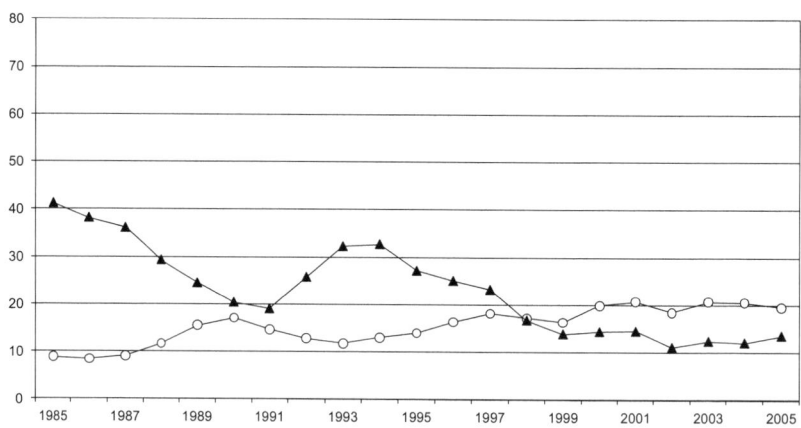

—○— 15-24 year olds' short-term unemployment (less than one month)
—▲— 15-24 year olds' long-term unemployment (more than one year)

Figure 3.1: continued

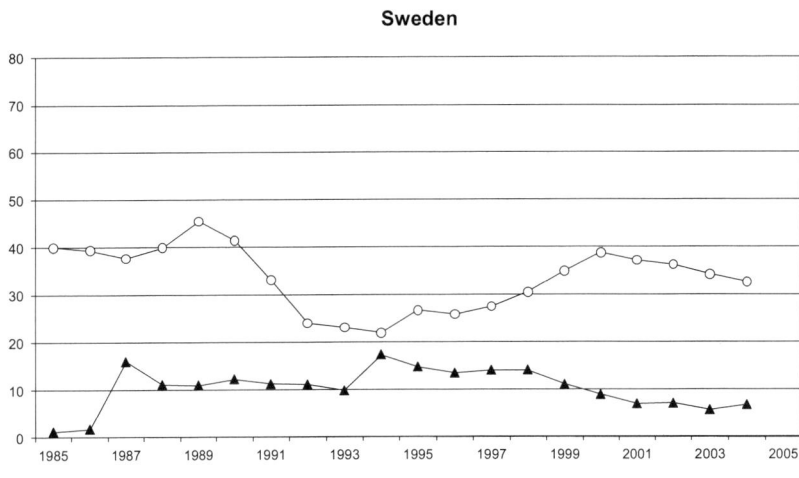

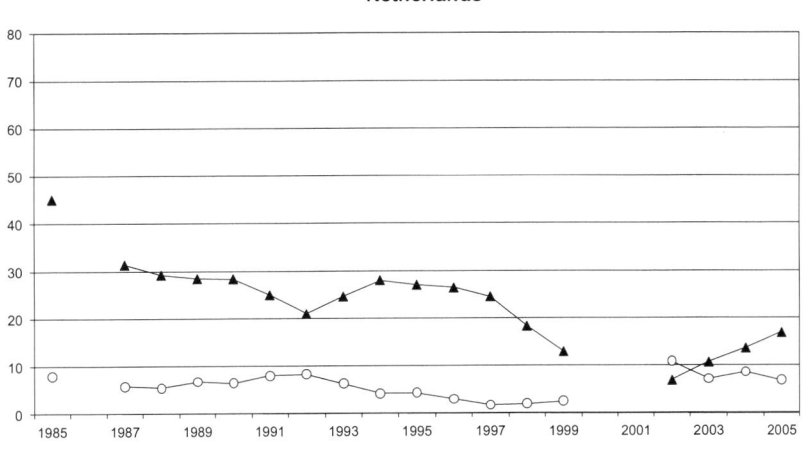

—O— 15-24 year olds' short-term unemployment (less than one month)
—▲— 15-24 year olds' long-term unemployment (more than one year)

Figure 3.1:continued

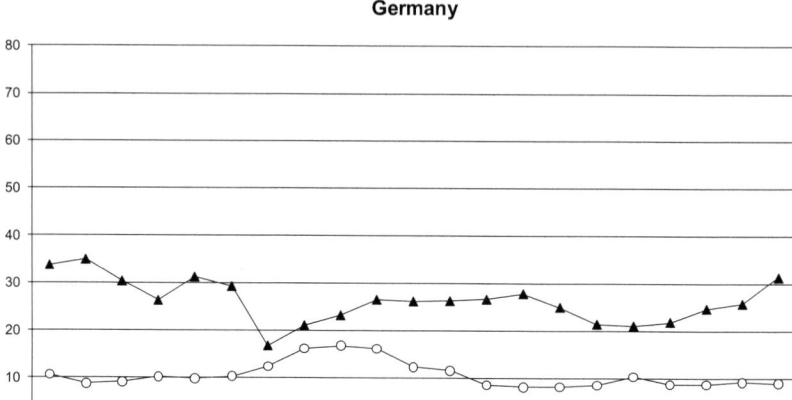

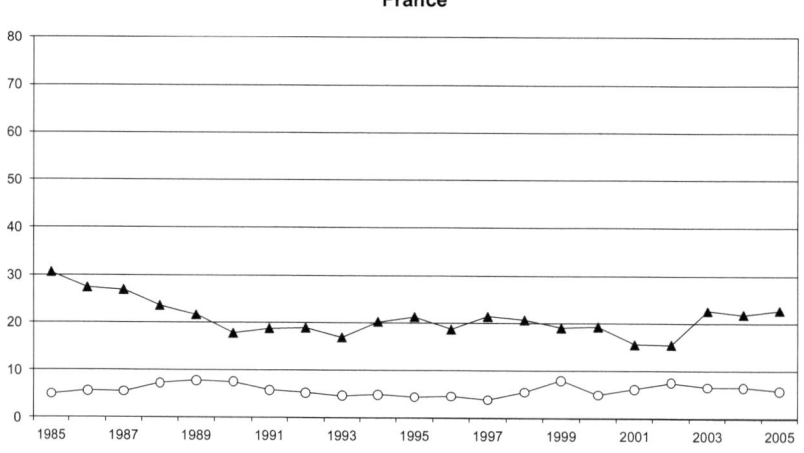

—○— 15-24 year olds' short-term unemployment (less than one month)
—▲— 15-24 year olds' long-term unemployment (more than one year)

112

Figure 3.1: continued

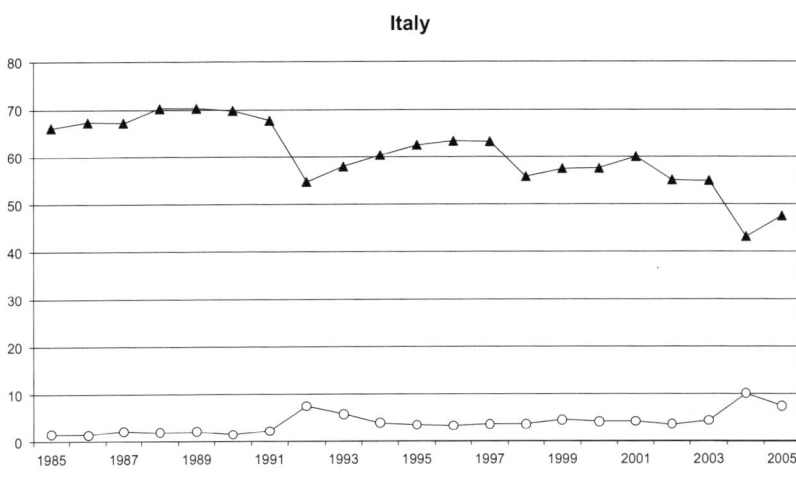

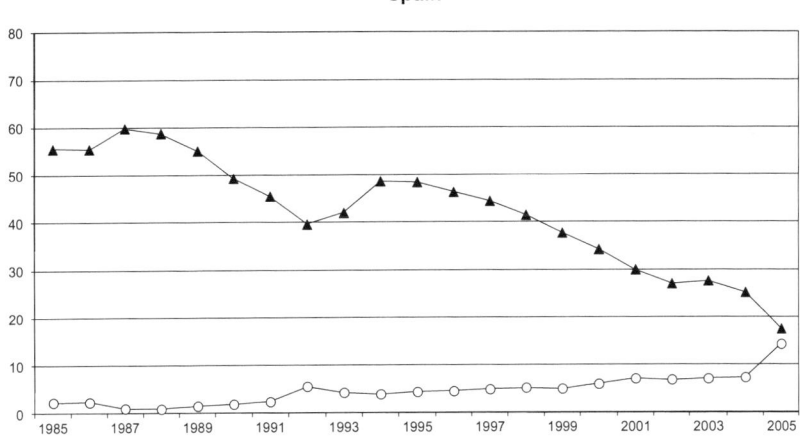

—○— 15-24 year olds' short-term unemployment (less than one month)
—▲— 15-24 year olds' long-term unemployment (more than one year)

Source: OECD 2009a.

Young people's unemployment duration varies with labor market entry regimes, but also reflects macroeconomic and legislative changes in the different countries. In *Denmark*, the extent of long-term youth unemployment exceeded the level of young people's short-term unemployment in the late 1980s. Then, in 1992, the Danes started to raise their public spending on labor market measures for youth (Drøpping et al. 1999; OECD 1994). As a result, since 1992, we find a reverse picture with long-term unemployment rates constantly below a rising share of short-term unemployment. Although this success story is related to further changes in labor legislation targeted at unemployed youth such as *Instant Activation* (Jacobsen 2006) and the *Youth Unemployment Program* (Jensen et al. 2003), both introduced in 1996,[41] the general 'activation reforms' of 1994 and the coinciding economic boom of the mid-1990s have also contributed to this success. With regard to the specific aims of the different measures, the considerable rise in short-term unemployment has been a result of rising transition rates from unemployment back into work, but also into activation measures and back into general schooling (Jensen et al. 2003).

In the *liberal countries* included in this study, unemployment patterns appear to be diverse. In the United States, long-term unemployment is clearly of low importance: Over the whole period between 1985 and 2005, it accounts for less than 10 percent of total youth unemployment, whereas short-term unemployment accounts for 40 to 60 percent. This result reflects the fact that in liberal labor markets, the hire-and-fire concept and on-the-job training systems generally promote mobility while the only limited duration of welfare benefits simultaneously obliges unemployed people to find a new job quickly. However, this argumentation obviously does not apply to the United Kingdom, because the respective figures initially show higher shares of long-term than short-term unemployment. However, in 1998, both graphs intersected and switched positions. This shift was a result of the New Deal program launched by Tony Blair's New Labor government, which has been elected in 1997. One target of the active welfare-to-work incentives was the labor market integration of youth by means of re-training (Schmelzer 2008). Since 1998, the share of short-term unemployment among unemployed youth in the United Kingdom has remained constantly above the share of long-term unemployment—although this difference has been much smaller compared to that in the United States and Denmark.

Among the countries classified as *Northern European insider-protection regimes* Sweden stands out as a remarkable exception with long-term unemployment rates constantly below short-term unemployment. Sweden is

---

41 For details on these measures, see section 1.4.

commonly described as ranking employment security higher than job security (Halldén and Hällsten 2008). Indeed, until 1999, Sweden's share of spending on active labor market policies (as a percentage of GDP) was higher than Denmark's, and since 1999, both shares have been very similar (OECD 2009b). Furthermore, the education system is as flexible as that in Denmark, allowing reentries at any time; students finishing vocational training are, in principle, eligible for studies at higher levels, and additional qualifications can be acquired in the comprehensive adult education system (Bygren et al. 2002). Consequently, a large share of the short-term unemployment spells probably end in transitions back into education or into active labor market programs. The graphs for the Netherlands, Germany, and France are generally in line with what can be expected in the northern European variant of the insider-protection regime type: For unemployed youths, short-term unemployment of less than one month is at low levels, mostly accounting for only around 10 percent of total youth unemployment, whereas, in contrast, unemployment of more than one year is much more widespread.[42] Obviously, the introduction of employment flexibility to these countries in the 1990s (mainly through the use of fixed-term contracts or agency work, see OECD 2004a) was not sufficient to improve young people's labor market integration in terms of any considerable reduction in the duration of unemployment.

The picture is even worse in both of the *Southern European insider-protection regimes* that combine highly rigid labor markets with marginal government spending on active labor market policies. Consequently, we find extremely low levels of short-term unemployment accompanied by extraordinarily high long-term unemployment rates for youth reaching values up to 70 percent in Italy and initially ranging up to 60 percent in Spain. In these labor markets, it is very difficult to leave unemployment; the 'outsider' status generally entails manifest labor market problems. However, prospects for unemployed youth in Spain have improved recently, reflecting the economic boom of the late 1990s (Hofäcker 2010).

Overall, the results from the previous analysis point to considerable differences in the meaning of 'unemployment' for youth in different institutional contexts. In post-1992 Denmark, in the United States, but also in Sweden, unemployment is unlikely to become a trap for youth, but represents a temporary state. In contrast, in most insider-protection countries, unemployment proves to be considerably more long-term than short-term—at

---

42 Here, the Netherlands represents an exception in 2002. Although the data for the two previous years is missing, it can be assumed that long-term unemployment already dropped below short-term unemployment shares in 2000 or 2001 as a result of the introduction of flexicurity in 1999 (Bredgaard et al. 2005; Wilthagen 1998). However, from 2003 to 2005, the pattern reversed again, converging to a 'normal' insider-protection pattern with higher long-term and lower short-term unemployment.

least when using the strict definition of short-term unemployment as less than one month. Despite the flexibilization processes in these countries, separation is still a distinctive feature of the insider-outsider labor markets: Entries or returns into the labor market are difficult, especially in the two southern European countries, because their relatively strict overall employment protection continues to reduce job turnover (Gangl 2003a). These differences are likely to be reflected in young people's individual perception of their reemployment chances and, hence, in their overall job-loss worry.

The above-mentioned differences in the temporal structure of youth unemployment could also lead to differences in the importance ascribed to job security. In countries in which unemployment has a short-term character, job security could rank subsequent to other job characteristics like 'being interesting' or a high income, although, as the next subsections will show, this is not generally the case. Furthermore, I shall use empirical data to show that job security is of comparably high importance for both early-career employees and mid- and late-career employees in each country, contradicting a common view of postmodern young people portraying them as embracing flexibility and mobility as something 'cool' and an aspect of their personal freedom.

On the importance of job security

According to Näswall and De Witte (2003b: 191), it is not the objectively given situation that determines how individuals react to it, but the way they interpret it. In other words, "job insecurity will only affect human behavior if people are aware of it" (Stejin 2005); and one has to add, "if job security is important to them." Hence, before studying job insecurity perception in more detail, I shall take a look at the importance of job insecurity across countries.

Table 3.1 shows the importance of different job attributes across the countries under study. The table reports the proportion of respondents in each country who rated the respective job characteristic as 'very important.' It shows that in most countries, job security was regarded as the most important job attribute. The exceptions are Denmark, France, and (in 2005) Great Britain, where having an interesting job was rated higher. Similar results are reported by other surveys such as a study based on the 2001 *Eurobarometer* (Muñoz de Bustillo and de Pedraza 2007).

Table 3.1: Employed and unemployed persons between 18 and 65: Very important job attributes in 1997 and 2005 (in parentheses)

	DK	GB	USA	D-W	D-E	F	NL*	S	I*	E
Job security	36.9 (31.0)	**61.6** (48.0)	**55.2** (**61.4**)	**65.9** (**62.7**)	**72.3** (**72.9**)	62.4 (58.7)	36.3 (–)	**54.4** (**56.4**)	66.0 (–)	**60.5** (**68.8**)
High income	9.5 (9.3)	14.6 (14.8)	22.1 (29.9)	12.6 (15.0)	16.9 (28.1)	17.1 (21.2)	8.6 (–)	12.4 (17.2)	28.1 (–)	31.4 (60.3)
Good advancement opportunities	8.3 (6.0)	22.9 (21.5)	34.8 (41.6)	15.1 (16.2)	11.5 (18.9)	17.1 (20.9)	19.1 (–)	10.0 (11.4)	27.1 (–)	31.4 (43.7)
Being interesting	**60.0** (**57.4**)	47.7 (**49.0**)	48.5 (56.9)	50.0 (45.4)	43.9 (48.9)	**65.5** (**65.1**)	35.6 (–)	49.3 (49.8)	50.4 (–)	34.4 (48.5)
Allowing one to work independently	47.6 (43.7)	18.0 (18.7)	27.3 (35.8)	39.0 (36.9)	32.0 (40.4)	22.7 (21.4)	28.4 (–)	30.0 (30.5)	29.3 (–)	26.9 (38.0)
Allowing one to help other people	34.7 (25.5)	20.4 (20.7)	28.2 (43.0)	15.1 (20.2)	19.0 (29.0)	16.2 (17.3)	22.4 (–)	18.8 (23.0)	23.5 (–)	27.6 (37.2)
Being useful to society	27.0 (20.6)	19.8 (19.9)	29.5 (45.9)	12.6 (18.6)	13.2 (27.8)	17.2 (19.8)	17.2 (–)	14.4 (14.5)	22.1 (–)	28.9 (39.7)
Allowing one to decide one's working times	16.2 (17.5)	9.9 (12.3)	16.0 (17.4)	11.0 (13.7)	9.8 (13.8)	19.8 (20.4)	16.6 (–)	17.3 (20.3)	29.2 (–)	17.8 (36.6)

Source: Own calculations based on the ISSP data sets *Work Orientations II* (1997) and *Work Orientations III* (2005).

Notes: The survey question was: "From the following list, please tick one box for each item to show how important you personally think it is in a job." The table shows the percentage of respondents in each country who chose 'very important' for the respective job attribute in 1997 and in 2005 (in parentheses).

*The Netherlands and Italy were not included in the 2005 ISSP's Work Orientations surveys.

The repeatedly high importance of job security reflects the considerable significance of this job attribute across countries, particularly in the period of increasing labor market flexibilization during the late 1990s and early 2000s.

Looking at employed respondents, does their particular career phase influence their evaluation? Figure 3.2 displays the distribution of the combined percentages of early-, mid-, and late-career employees who rated job security as 'very important' or 'important' for each country.[43] It shows that the importance of job security varies only marginally with people's career phase; that is, job security is just as important for people in their early career as it is for mid- or late-career employees.

Figure 3.2: Early-, mid-, and late-career employees: Importance of job security, 1997 and 2005

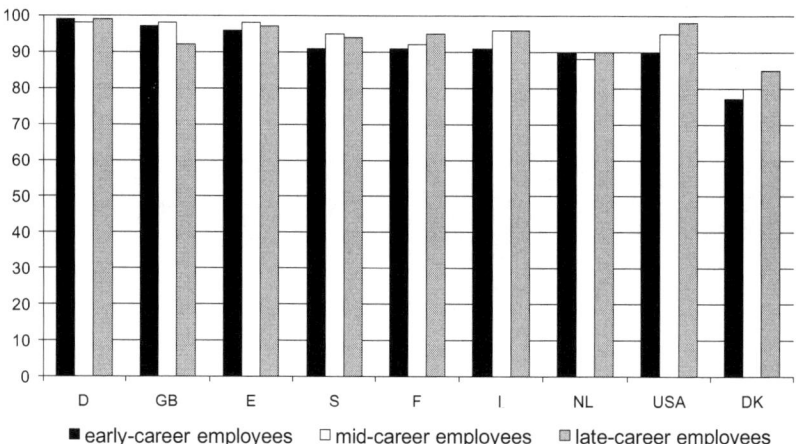

Source: Own analysis of pooled ISSP data from 1997 and 2005.

The importance of job security for early-career employees stands in stark contrast to a widespread public image of young people in modern societies that portrays them as being perfectly adjusted to the requirements of a postmodern world of rapid change—including its greater hazards and risks (Eckersley 1997)—and as having learned to tolerate or even appreciate chaos, uncertainty, and insecurity (Rushkoff 1996). Eckersley (1997: 243) describes this 'postmodern' perspective on young people as seeing them "riding on a wave of change [...] while adults flounder in its wake." This view implies that

---

43 'Early career' is defined as the first 6 years in the labor market after leaving the education system; 'late career' reflects the last 10 years before making the transition into retirement; and mid career is regarded as the period between these two career phases. For a schematic representation of the career phase definition, see Figure A.2 in the appendix.

nowadays, youth increasingly embrace flexibility and mobility as valuable assets of personal freedom, and that this should be reflected in a lower significance of job security.

Yet, my analysis demonstrates that job security still appears to be of critical importance for young people. The remaining part of this chapter will be devoted to a more thorough analysis of how young people perceive job insecurity and its expected consequences.

3.2.3. Research design

In the first chapter of this book, I defined *economic insecurity* in terms of the security of having stable access to sufficient and regular income (see Section 1.2). For early-career employees, I decomposed this into three dimensions that I also expect to find in young workers' insecurity perception. All the dimensions of subjective economic insecurity are related to the threat of unemployment. The overall category of perceived economic insecurity is therefore named *job-loss worry*.

What needs to be considered when studying regime-specific job-loss worry in the early career? The possibility of capturing this multidimensional phenomenon empirically depends initially on how researchers understand it conceptionally. Therefore, in the following subsections, I shall describe my model of job-loss worry, its dimensions, as well as its institutional and individual determinants. Furthermore, I shall explain the phenomenon of country-specific relative insecurity perception, which counteracts the negative relationship between national employment protection strictness and individual job insecurity and therefore has to be taken into account when postulating hypotheses on regime-specific job-loss worry.

Job-loss worry as a multidimensional phenomenon

Job insecurity perception is regarded as an important complement to standard objective labor market measures of job insecurity such as fixed-term employment rates or unemployment figures (e.g., Näswall and De Witte 2003a). Its analysis makes it possible to link macrolevel changes such as globalization and rising employment flexibility with microlevel individual perceptions of job-loss risk and economic insecurity along with the associated behavioral outcomes. But how can it be measured adequately in empirical terms?

Clark and Postel-Vinay (2009) have pointed out that survey questions on perceived job insecurity typically appear in two broad forms: The first asks individuals to report their degree of satisfaction with respect to their job security (*satisfaction questions*); the second asks them to estimate the probability of losing their job (*probability questions*). While probability questions measure one specific aspect of job insecurity (i.e., the estimated subjective probability of job loss), satisfaction questions include "information on the respondent's perception of at least two different components of job insecurity, namely the subjective probability of job loss and its costs" (Clark and Postel-Vinay 2008: 210).

For my analysis, I shall draw upon a model of job-loss worry by Anderson and Pontusson (2007) that includes both aspects of job insecurity perception.[44] It starts from the psychological two-variable function illustrated in Figure 3.3:

Figure 3.3: Basic model of job-loss worry

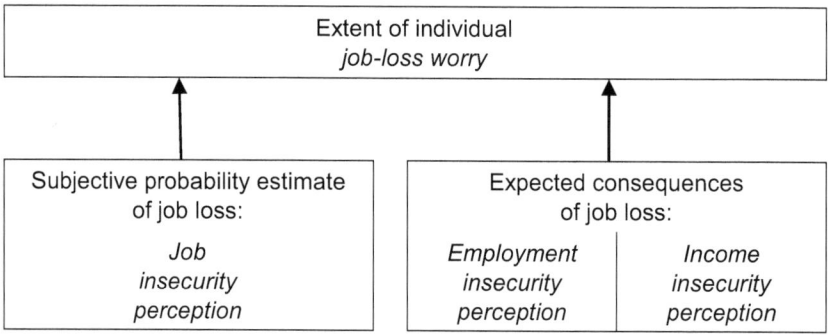

Source: Own illustration, based on Anderson and Pontusson 2007.

The extent to which a person worries about losing their job (*job-loss worry*) is a function of (1) the individual's estimate of the probability of losing her or his job (*job insecurity perception*); (2) the individual's perception of the consequences of losing that job, namely, (2a) the estimated probability of not finding another (more or less equivalent) job (*employment insecurity perception*); and (2b) the estimated probability of an income loss while being unemployed (*income insecurity perception*).

Among the dimensions of job-loss worry, employment insecurity perception plays an important role: People who perceive high job insecurity, but have good prospects of finding a new job in case of unemployment, probably do not worry so much about the consequences of possibly losing their current job. Furthermore, low employment insecurity reduces the expected duration of possible unemployment, and thus should also mediate the detrimental effect of income insecurity on job-loss worry.

---

44 Anderson and Pontusson's (2007) model, in turn, builds on OECD (1997). Note that the authors use different notions for some of the insecurity dimensions.

It seems reasonable to suppose that individuals take a number of objective factors into account when estimating the probabilities that they might lose their job, have difficulties in finding a new job, and experience an income loss while being unemployed (Anderson and Pontusson 2007). Besides labor market conditions and individual factors like age, education, and gender, it is institutional frameworks that substantially determine such considerations and, hence, the overall degrees of individual job-loss worry.

The objective of this empirical study is to explore how national combinations of certain institutional features translate into young people's insecurity perceptions, and whether the specific Danish framework generates less job-loss worry. The country comparisons are based on the regime typology developed in Chapter 1 (Section 1.5) that distinguishes between four labor market entry regimes: (1) the *Danish flexicurity regime* combining relatively weak employment protection (i.e., high labor market flexibility via generally low dismissal protection) and high government spending on active labor market policies; (2) the *liberal regime* (represented by the United Kingdom and the United States) combining weak employment protection and low government spending on active labor market policies; (3) the *Northern European insider-protection regime* (represented by France, Germany, the Netherlands, and Sweden) combining relatively strict employment protection (i.e., low labor market flexibility for labor market 'insiders' and high flexibility for 'outsiders' mainly via fixed-term employment) and relatively high supply of active labor market policies; and (4) the *Southern European insider-protection regime* (represented by Italy and Spain) combining strict employment protection and low government spending on active labor market policies.

In the following subsection, I shall discuss the institutional, macroeconomic, and individual determinants of early-career employees' job-loss worry in general terms.

The determinants of young workers' job-loss worry

The objective factors that individuals take into account when estimating the probabilities on which their job, employment, and income insecurity perceptions are based can be grouped under three headings: labor market conditions, individual aspects, and institutional frameworks. This study's main focus is on institutional factors and, in particular, on the role of employment protection legislation and labor market policies.

I consider three main types of institutional regulations: first, the level of employment protection that safeguards established workers against potential job loss and also influences the chances of making the transition from unemployment back into the labor market; second, the level of public spending on active labor market policies supposed to prevent long-term unemployment; and third, the level of public spending on passive labor market policies to secure against severe income losses in case of unemployment. In this subsection, I shall outline how these regulations influence the single dimensions of job-loss worry and how the countries included in this study differ with regard to these institutional factors. Furthermore, I shall outline the effects of labor market conditions and individual factors.

Institutional determinants and country-specific relative insecurity perception

If we were to suppose that subjectively perceived insecurities would completely correspond to objectively given ones, the effects of employment protection legislation and active and passive labor market policies on the single dimensions of job-loss worry would be as follows: A high level of national employment protection would reduce job insecurity perception, but might increase employment insecurity perception (due to the concomitant insider-outsider gap on the labor market); high public spending on active labor market policies would reduce employment insecurity perception; and generous unemployment and cash benefits would reduce income insecurity perception.

However, it is rather unlikely that perceived insecurities will correspond completely to objectively given ones. Some of the initially mentioned institutional effects might be counteracted by the phenomenon of *country-specific relative insecurity perception* that I assume to have a moderating effect, especially on the relationship between national employment protection and individual job insecurity perception. The idea is that people frame their situation not so much by using objective data, but instead perceive their position within the context of what is considered to be 'normal' in a particular social environment. *Significant others* such as family members, peers, or colleagues have a strong impact on this perception. In the European insider-outsider labor markets, the typical form of employment has long been a safe, permanent job. Because young fixed-term employees in these countries probably tend to compare themselves with the still safely employed parent generation, they may well perceive relatively high levels of job insecurity.[45] Therefore, in the insider-protection regimes, country-specific relative

---

[45] However, comparisons do not just take the one direction. For the German insider-outsider labor market, Dörre et al. (2006) have been able to show that job insecurity perceptions of core and flexible employees in the same firm were interrelated. It was not just the flexible employees who were constantly confronted with the precariousness of their situation when comparing themselves to the established core workers. Conversely, the presence of the flexible employees undermined the job security perception of those working in objectively nonprecarious jobs.

insecurity perception can be expected to increase a young worker's level of perceived job insecurity. Conversely, in the flexible labor markets of Denmark, Great Britain, and the United States, it probably *de*creases young people's job insecurity perception because all employees face a similarly high risk of dismissal.

Taken together, the hypothesized effects of employment protection, active labor market policies, and passive labor market policies on the single dimensions of young workers' job-loss worry can be summarized as follows: (1) Strict employment protection legislation increases job and employment insecurity perception, whereas (2) high public spending on active labor market policies reduces employment insecurity perception and (3) high public expenditure on passive labor market policies (generous unemployment and cash benefits) reduce income insecurity perception. These relationships are included in Figure 3.4, which illustrates my model of job-loss worry.

Figure 3.4: The determinants of young workers' job-loss worry

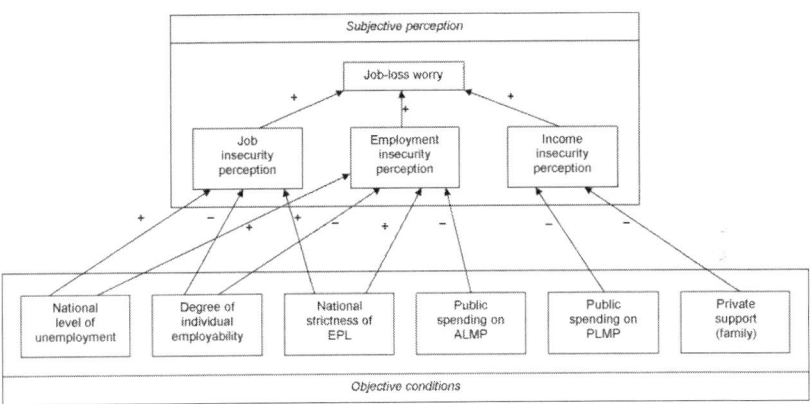

Source: Own illustration, modified version of Anderson and Pontusson's (2007) model.
Notes: EPL: employment protection legislation; ALMP: active labor market policies; PLMP: passive labor market policies.

Labor market conditions and individual factors

In addition to the institutional determinants discussed above, a few other objective factors have to be taken into account when analyzing the various dimensions of job-loss worry (see Figure 3.4): (1) on the macrolevel, the national unemployment rate, which I assume to increase job and employment insecurity perception; (2) on the microlevel, the degree of individual employability—the key issue here is *human capital*—which I assume to decrease job and employment insecurity perception; and, finally, (3) also on the microlevel and in contrast to public nonmarket support via passive labor market policies, private nonmarket support (by the family) in case of unemployment, which I assume to decrease income insecurity perception. In the following empirical analyses, these factors will be considered as control variables.

3.2.4. Hypotheses

Against this theoretical background, I am now able to formulate regime-specific expectations regarding the prevailing patterns of insecurity perception (see Table 3.2).

For early-career employees in *Denmark*, I expect a medium level of job insecurity perception, because the *significant others* with whom they compare themselves are likely to be exposed to an equally high dismissal risk (country-specific relative insecurity perception). I also expect that the low Danish employment protection (via more external vacancies and high labor market mobility) raises people's prospects of finding a new job. In addition, the very high supply of active labor market policies should further reduce perceived employment insecurity in this regime type. Taken together, the weak employment protection and the high supply of active labor market policies should lead to a very low share of young workers who report employment insecurity in the Danish flexicurity cluster. Furthermore, I assume low income insecurity perception in this labor market regulation regime[46] because of generous unemployment compensation. Hence, despite their low dismissal protection, I expect early-career employees in Denmark to worry very little about possible job loss.

---

46 Even though I cannot test this influence directly, see the data and methods section.

Table 3.2: Expected labor market entry regime-specific insecurity perception patterns

Labor market entry regime:	Danish flexicurity	Liberal	N. European insider protection	S. European insider protection
Countries included:	Denmark	Great Britain, United States	France, Germany, Netherlands, Sweden	Italy, Spain
Strictness of employment protection: [a]	Low	Very low	High	Very high
Strategies of numerical flexibility:	Low dismissal protection	Low dismissal protection	Fixed-term employment	Fixed-term employment
Expenditures on active labor market policies:[b]	Very high	Low	High (very high in Sweden)	Low
Expenditures on passive labor market policies:[c]	High	Low	High	Low
Effect of country-specific rel. insecurity perception:	Decreases job insecurity perception	Decreases job insecurity perception	Increases job insecurity perception	Increases job insecurity perception
Expected insecurity perception patterns for early-career employees:				
Job insecurity:	Medium	Medium	High (because of 'outsider' status)	High (because of 'outsider' status)
Employment insecurity:	Very low	Low	High	Very high
(Income insecurity:[d])	(Low)	(High)	(Low)	(High)
Job-loss worry:	Very low	Low	High	Very high

Notes: a Based on the OECD's summary indicators of EPL strictness for the late 1990s and for 2003 (OECD 2004).
b Based on the countries' expenditures for active labor market policies as a percentage of their GDP (OECD 2009b) in the years of the analyzed ISSP interviews (1997 and 2003).
c Based on the countries' expenditures for unemployment compensation as a percentage of GDP (OECD 2009b) in the years of the analyzed ISSP interviews.
d Income insecurity cannot be analyzed separately; it will be proxied within the models on job-loss worry (for more information, see the data and methods section 3.2.5).

Among early-career employees in the *liberal cluster*, here represented by Great Britain and the United States, I expect to find a medium level of job insecurity perception, as in Denmark, due to the country-specific relative insecurity perception. The supply of active labor market policies in the liberal countries is low, that is, there are only few active labor market programs helping the unemployed to find their way back into employment. However, due to the very weak employment protection, people's chances of finding a new job are relatively good. This should significantly reduce their employment insecurity perception; however, due to the low level of active labor market policies, this will probably not be lower than that in Denmark. Furthermore, due to the poor level of unemployment compensation, income insecurity perception in this labor market regulation regime may loom large.

Yet, despite high income insecurity perception, I expect to find relatively few respondents in this cluster who report substantial worries about losing their job, because mobility chances were high and unemployment rates were comparatively low in liberal labor countries (especially in the United States) at the times of the interviews[47]; both factors are expected to increase people's reemployment chances.

The *Northern European insider-protection cluster* in my sample includes France, Germany, the Netherlands, and Sweden. In this regime type, I expect an important insider-outsider cleavage, with the majority of early-career employees having an outsider status. Due to the high overall employment protection, established employees in permanent jobs (the 'insiders') should perceive low job insecurity, whereas employees in the early stages of their career are likely to assess their job-loss risk as comparatively high. Based on earlier research (e.g., Buchholz 2008), it seems plausible to suppose that a high proportion of early-career employees in this cluster actually does have fixed-term contracts.[48] Hence, I expect to find a high share of early-career employees in this regime who report job insecurity. In addition, country-specific relative insecurity perception can be expected to further increase the level of young worker's perceived job insecurity, because younger workers in flexible work contracts will tend to compare themselves with the more securely established "insider" generation. The high supply of active labor market policies should reduce employment insecurity perception among early-career employees, even though, except for Sweden, the countries in this cluster spend somewhat less on active labor market policies than the Danish

---

47 See Table A.4 in the appendix.
48 Unfortunately, I am not able to control for fixed-term employment in all models. The 2005 surveys do not provide information on fixed-term employment; however, in the 1997 survey wave, one third (34%) of the early-career respondents in the Northern European insider-protection regime were employed on fixed-term basis.

state[49]. Given, however, that this effect may be mediated by high employment protection, I expect a somewhat higher share of respondents who report perceived employment insecurity in the Northern European insider-protection cluster than in Denmark. Furthermore, I assume low income insecurity perception in this cluster, because of relatively generous unemployment compensation. However, not all early-career employees have the possibility of falling back on benefits in case of job loss, because of entitlements requiring long, continuous employment histories. Furthermore, benefit reception is restricted to a short duration. Finally, living on unemployment compensation is probably generally not a satisfying perspective for young people wishing to build up a career. All in all, I therefore expect to find more job-loss worry in the Northern European insider-protection cluster than in Denmark and in the liberal cluster, but less than in the Southern European insider-protection cluster.

The *Southern European insider-protection cluster* in my sample is represented by Italy and Spain. Both countries have very strict employment protection; consequently my expectations with regard to the perception of job insecurity among early-career employees in this country cluster are the same as those for the northern European variant of this regime type: I expect to find high job insecurity perception, because of both the young people's outsider status (many of them work on the basis of fixed-term contracts[50]) and the reinforcement effect of country-specific relative insecurity perception. In contrast to northern Europe, however, the interaction between strict employment protection and the low supply of active labor market policies should lead to significantly higher levels of perceived employment insecurity among early-career employees than in the other three labor market regulation regimes above. This hypothesis is also based on the very high shares of long-term unemployment among unemployed youth in these countries displayed in Figure 3.1. Furthermore, due to the very low levels of unemployment compensation and the fact that young people under 24 are not even eligible for unemployment benefits in Italy and Spain (Howell 2004; OECD 2002a)—which means that they have to rely on private income support (e.g., from their families)—I assume high income insecurity perception in the southern European cluster. All this should lead to very high job-loss worry among young workers in the Southern European insider-protection cluster.

Taken together, my *central hypothesis* is that the lowest level of job-loss worry should be found among early-career employees in Denmark followed—in descending order—by the liberal countries and the countries of the Northern European insider-protection regime. Highest levels of insecurity

---

49 See Figure A.1 in the appendix.
50 In the 1997 survey wave, almost one half (45%) of the interviewed early-career employees in the Southern European insider-protection regime were fixed-term employees.

perception are expected to be found in the Southern European insider-protection regime. The following empirical analyses will study how closely the insecurity perceptions of young workers in my sample match my expectations summarized in Table 3.2.

3.2.5. Data and methods

My empirical test of the hypotheses formulated in the previous section was based on cross-sectional data, because, so far, no international longitudinal dataset is available that could be used to address the multidimensional character of job insecurity perception.

This study draws on pooled survey data for Denmark, France, Germany, Great Britain, Italy, the Netherlands, Spain, Sweden, and the United States conducted in 1997 and 2005 as part of the *Work Orientations* study by the *International Social Survey Program* (ISSP).[51] To restrict the analysis to early-career employees, I extracted a subsample from the ISSP data consisting of employees in their first 6 years in the labor market. Since the data is cross-sectional and gives no information on when the respondents finished their education, I used education-specific *typical graduation ages* for each country when selecting the individuals for the sample. These typical graduation ages were taken from OECD publications (1997b; 2002b) and from the UNESCO Statistics Data Center (UNESCO 2009).[52] The resulting subsamples of people aged between 18 and 33 had the following sizes: 262 for Denmark, 310 for France, 176 for Germany, 109 for Great Britain, 54 for Italy, 87 for the Netherlands, 100 for Spain, 87 for Sweden, and 235 for the United States.[53]

The resulting data set provides information on each of the different dimensions of job-loss worry. I constructed the same indicators as those used by Anderson and Pontusson (2007) and Green (2009): To measure job insecurity perception, respondents were asked how much they agreed or disagreed with the statement 'my job is secure' (on a scale from 1 to 5). The dummy variable 'high job insecurity perception' indicated whether or not

---

51 The Netherlands and Italy were included only in the 1997 survey wave.
52 See Table A.2 in the appendix for details.
53 For the descriptive comparison of early-, mid-, and late-career employees in Figure 3.2, the late-career workers were identified on the basis of sex-specific median retirement ages for each country taken from EUROSTAT (2007) and the U.S. Department of Labor (Gendell 2001) respectively. As actual retirement ages tend to vary significantly within countries and early retirement is still a widespread phenomenon (Blossfeld et al. 2006), the age span defined for late career employees included the 10 years before as well as the 5 years after reaching the respective median retirement age. Mid-career employees were identified by taking the ages between the early- and the late-career group.

respondents disagreed or strongly disagreed with the statement. This item, "though admittedly a little imprecise" (Green 2009: 6), was assumed to correspond to the respondents' subjective probability of losing her or his job.

To gauge individuals' employment insecurity perception, I used responses to the questions: "How easy or difficult do you think it would be for you to find an acceptable job?" (1997) and "How difficult or easy do you think it would be for you to find a job at least as good as your current one?" (2005), respectively (answers for both questions on a 5-point scale ranging from 'very easy' to 'very difficult'). The dummy variable 'high employment insecurity perception' indicated whether or not respondents answered this with 'fairly difficult' or 'very difficult.' This indicator captured part of the expected consequences (or costs) of job loss; however, it did not pick up worries of income loss during an extended unemployment spell (income insecurity perception).

Finally, the overall extent of individual job-loss worry was measured with a question asking: "To what extent, if at all, do you worry about the possibility of losing your job?" (answers were coded on a 4-point scale ranging from 'I don't worry at all' to 'I worry a great deal'). The dummy variable 'high job-loss worry' indicated whether or not respondents reported that they worried 'a great deal' or 'to some extent.' Like Anderson and Pontusson (2007) as well as Green (2009), I used this indicator as a measure of the overall psychological impact of job insecurity perception because "it captures both the combined impact of risk and the cost of job loss (including the uncertainty over these), and how the respondent is affected" (Green: 2009: 6).[54]

Unfortunately, the ISSP data do not contain items that could be used as an indicator for the respondent's perception of income insecurity. Following Anderson and Pontusson (2007), I used two indicators for nonmarket income support as proxies for income insecurity instead: public spending on unemployment compensation as a percentage of GDP (from the OECD's Social Expenditure Database, see OECD 2009b) to measure public income support and a dummy variable for respondents who have an employed spouse to proxy private support (Lim 1996).

In addition, I included a number of control variables that have been shown to be related to some of the job-loss worry dimensions under study.[55] With regard to the microlevel, these were dummies for the respondent's gender (Anderson and Pontusson 2007; Green 2003, 2009; Gallie 2003), age

---

54 In principle, one should also be aware of effects due to the respondent's personality (e.g., differences in risk perception and in strategies for dealing with risk: optimistic vs. defensive-pessimistic risk dealing). However, due to the lack of adequate indicators, I had to ignore these in my job-loss worry models.
55 See Table A.5 in the appendix.

(Anderson and Pontusson 2007; Clark and Postel-Vinay 2009; Erlinghagen 2008; Green 2009; Green et al. 2000; OECD 1997a), and education (Anderson and Pontusson 2007; Clark and Postel-Vinay 2009; Erlinghagen 2008; Green 2009; OECD 1997a) measured in years. Further dummies were for union membership (Anderson and Pontusson 2007) and fixed-term employment (Anderson and Pontusson 2007; Clark and Postel-Vinay 2009; Erlinghagen 2008; Green 2003, 2009). In some of the models on job-loss worry, I also used a dummy variable indicating whether children were living in the respondent's household, which I assumed to be associated positively with more worry about job loss. For this dummy as well as for the dummy variable 'employed spouse,' I included gender-specific interaction effects in the respective models, because women whose spouses are employed (and/or who have children) are likely to worry less about job loss than men with the same private background (Blossfeld and Drobnič 2001).[56]

With regard to the level of firms, I used a dummy variable for sector (Anderson and Pontusson 2007; Clark and Postel-Vinay 2009); and with regard to the macrolevel, I included the national average rate of unemployment (Anderson and Pontusson 2007; Clark and Postel-Vinay 2009; Erlinghagen 2008; Green 2009) for the 6 years prior to the respective ISSP surveys (from the OECD's Employment Statistics Database, see OECD 2009a) as well as country dummies or, alternatively, some of the following three variables representing the institutional environment: the OECD's (2004) summary measure of employment protection legislation strictness (Anderson and Pontusson 2007; Clark and Postel-Vinay 2009; Erlinghagen 2008) and— as indicators for labor market policies—data from the OECD's Social Expenditure Database (OECD 2009b) on government spending on active labor market policies (Anderson and Pontusson 2007) and on unemployment compensation (Anderson and Pontusson 2007) both as a percentage of GDP.[57]

In the following sections, I shall examine the cross-country differences in perceived job insecurity, employment insecurity, and job-loss worry by showing their distributions by country and presenting results of logit models to explain their variation both within as well as between countries.

---

56 A number of other variables could influence at least one of the insecurity dimensions, but these could not be included in the models because they were either not surveyed at all or missing for single countries or interview waves. These were: firm size (Green et al. 2000), industry (Erlinghagen 2008; Gallie 2003; Green et al. 2000; OECD 1997a), tenure (Erlinghagen 2008; Green et al. 2000), and occupational class (Erlinghagen 2008; Gallie 2003; Green et al. 2000; OECD 1997a).
57 For an overview of all OECD indices used, see Table A.4 in the appendix.

3.2.6. Empirical findings

Job insecurity perception

Figure 3.2 shows that job security was highly important for early-career employees in all the countries under study. Nonetheless, Denmark stands out as having the lowest percentage of respondents who were worried about losing their job: only 78 percent—compared to 90–99 percent of respondents in other countries. This exceptional result for Denmark may be traced back to the respondents' awareness of the objective conditions providing them with high levels of employment and income security. The consequences of possible job loss are not as negative as in the other employment regimes; the chances of quickly finding a new job are high; and in the meantime, generous unemployment compensation guarantees a relatively low income loss. Notably, however, despite this institutional safety net, there was still a strong majority of 78 percent who considered security to be an important or very important job feature.

However, the Danish employment system does not meet this high job security demand: The OECD's aggregate measure of employment protection legislation places Denmark in the group of countries with the overall lowest level of employment protection (OECD 2004). Considering this discrepancy, it is necessary to ask how early-career employees in Denmark actually evaluate their own job insecurity.

To answer this question, Figure 3.5 shows the combined percentages of early-career employees across the nine countries under study who 'disagree' and 'strongly disagree' when asked about the statement 'my current job is secure.'

As the graph shows, there was considerable cross-national variation in job insecurity perception among early-career employees, ranging from 43 percent in Spain to only 9 percent in the United States. Denmark displayed the second lowest share of early-career employees who perceived job insecurity, a percentage that was only marginally lower than Great Britain. Considering the almost nonexistent dismissal protection in Denmark and the two liberal countries, these relatively low rates of job insecurity perception may seem surprising at first sight; but they can be explained by the moderating effect of country-specific relative insecurity perception.

Figure 3.5: Percentage shares of early-career employees who perceived job insecurity, 1997 and 2005

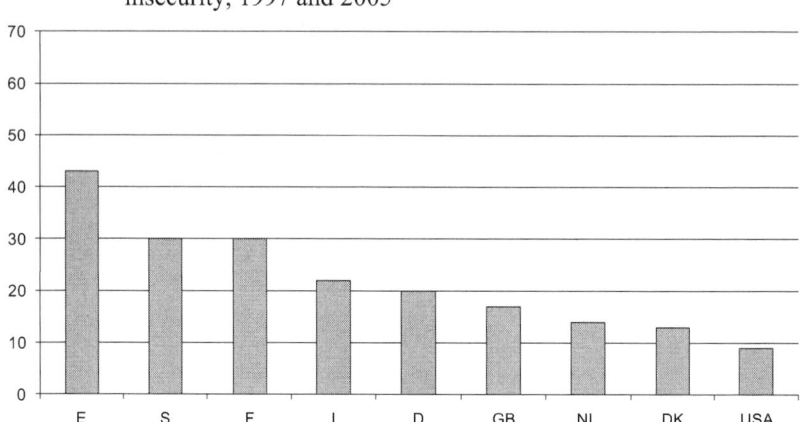

Source: Own analysis of pooled ISSP data from 1997 and 2005.

However, at this point, I am still unable to say whether this result is related to such effects. The finding could also be accounted for by differences in national unemployment rates or by the composition of the workforce, for example, in terms of education. To test for these effects, I estimated logit models for job insecurity perception (Table 3.3).

Regarding individual characteristics, the logit models showed that education certainly was negatively associated with the job insecurity perception in early-career employees. Respondents who had only up to 9 years of education reported job insecurity significantly more frequently than those who had 10 or more years of education. In contrast, gender and age turned out to be of no significant importance for job insecurity perception in early-career employees.

Models 4 and 5 additionally controlled for union membership, private sector employment, and fixed-term contracts.[58] Results indicated that being a fixed-term employee was a strong predictor of perceiving job insecurity—whereas the other two variables had no significant influence on early-career employees' job insecurity perception.

---

58 Note that no information was available on union membership and the sector of employment in the United States, and these were excluded from both models. Furthermore, information on fixed-term employment was recorded only in 1997; consequently, Model 5 is based on data from that year alone.

Table 3.3: High job insecurity perception of early-career employees (logit models)

	1	2	3	4[a]	5[a]
Constant	-3.06**	-2.05**	-2.56**	-1.94**	-3.44**
Labor market conditions:					
Average unempl. rate, past 6 years	0.11**		0.08+		
Labor market policies:[b]					
EPL score (high = more protection)	0.32*				
Individual characteristics:					
Female	0.27	0.25	0.25	0.28	0.29
Aged 18–24 years (ref.: 25–33 years)	-0.16	-0.08	-0.10	-0.05	-0.31
≤ 9 years of educ. (ref.: ≥ 10 years)	0.61+	0.69+	0.69+	0.76+	0.94+
Union member				-0.12	0.22
Job characteristics:					
Fixed-term contract					1.98**
Priv. sector empl. (ref.: publ. sect. empl.)				-0.14	0.27
Country dummies:					
Flexicurity regime:					
Denmark (ref.)		–	–	–	–
Liberal regime:					
Great Britain		0.37	0.32	0.37	1.38*
United States		-0.31	-0.24	–	–
N. European insider-protection regime:					
France		1.02**	0.71*	0.97**	1.77**
Germany		0.51	0.32	0.48	0.90
Netherlands		0.24	0.26	0.33	-0.06
Sweden		1.16**	0.94*	1.23**	1.66**
S. European insider-protection regime:					
Italy		0.62	0.22	0.61	1.00
Spain		1.62**	0.83	1.54**	1.88**
No. of cases	1,374	1,374	1,374	1,134	622
–2*diff (LogL)	81.77	85.80	91.56	61.22	124.86

Source: Own calculations based on a subsample of the pooled ISSP data sets *Work Orientations II* (1997) and *Work Orientations III* (2005).

Notes: a Model 4 did not include the United States; model 5 was based solely on the 1997 data and did not include the United States.
b EPL: employment protection legislation.
** significant at $p < 0.01$; * significant at $p < 0.05$; + significant at $p < 0.10$.

Turning to macrostructural conditions, I found that respondents in countries with higher levels of unemployment were significantly more likely to state that their current job was insecure (see Models 1 and 3). Model 1 also showed that stricter employment protection was associated significantly with higher job insecurity perception in early-career employees. This confirmed my expectation that in countries with high levels of employment protection, an insider-outsider cleavage would make it harder for young people to establish an employment career. Among the respondents from the 1997 survey wave, 34 percent in the Northern European and 45 percent in the Southern European insider-protection regime had fixed-term contracts.

Models 2 to 5 included country dummies instead of the above institutional variable, using Denmark as the reference category. Notably, young workers in France, Great Britain, Spain, and Sweden (in Model 5) displayed significantly higher levels of reported job insecurity than their counterparts in Denmark. However, the coefficient for Spain was only significant when the unemployment rate was not accounted for (see Models 2, 4, 5 vs. Model 3). Hence, higher insecurity perceptions in Spain were probably due to the very high unemployment rates around the times of the interviews[59] rather than a consequence of a generally higher level of insecurity perception. After controlling for the unemployment rate, the interviewed employees from Spain, the country with the strictest employment protection legislation among the countries under study, perceived themselves as relatively well-protected labor market insiders.

Respondents in Germany did not differ significantly from those in Denmark. One possible explanation is that many of them had completed an apprenticeship in the so-called *dual system* of education. Supervised by national institutions, this system provides highly standardized qualification and curriculum standards that are partly set in accordance with companies' requirements (e.g., Allmendinger 1989; Blossfeld 1992). This design is known to reduce the risk of youth unemployment to a large extent, and thus is likely to further decrease job insecurity perception of early-career employees in Germany despite its relatively high employment protection. Germany and Denmark were joined by the Netherlands in which a concerted action involving the state, employers, and employees effectively reduced unemployment and established a climate of relative economic security (Delsen 2000; Werner 1997) even before the official turn to flexicurity in 1999.

What is remarkable is that, even after controlling for individual characteristics, early-career employees from Denmark, Great Britain, and the United States were still among those reporting low job insecurity perception, despite their low levels of overall employment protection. Compared to these countries, the insider-outsider gap in Sweden and France seemed to lead to higher levels of job insecurity perception—most likely because early-career employees in these countries compared themselves to established core workers.

---

59 See Table A.4 in the appendix.

Employment insecurity perception

Figure 3.6 displays young workers' perceived rate of employment insecurity; it shows the percentage of early career employees who consider it 'difficult' or 'very difficult' that they would find 'an acceptable job.' A crucial point to note is the remarkable degree of variation in employment insecurity perception across the countries under study.

Figure 3.6: Percentage shares of early-career employees who perceive employment insecurity, 1997 and 2005

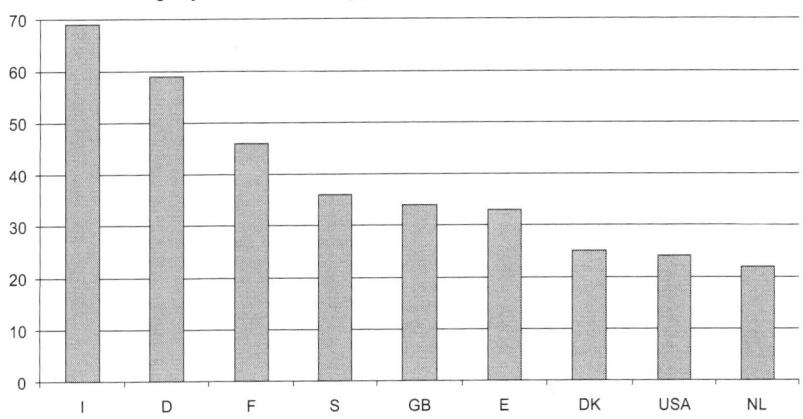

Source: Own analysis of pooled ISSP data from 1997 and 2005.

Especially in two countries, a clear majority of respondents found it difficult or very difficult to find an acceptable job: These were Italy and Germany. Almost one half of the interviewed early-career employees shared this assessment in France, and over one third in Great Britain, Spain, and Sweden. Only one quarter of respondents shared this view in Denmark, and even fewer in the United States and the Netherlands. Again, these differences may well have depended on national unemployment rates and compositional effects with regard to individual employability attributes. Therefore, logit models calculating the risk of employment insecurity perception were calculated to investigate how far these effects accounted for country-level differences (Table 3.4).

With regard to individual characteristics, education was once again the key factor in respondents' assessments of reemployment prospects. Those with less years of education significantly more often reported employment insecurity. Other individual controls were not significant.

Table 3.4: High employment insecurity perception of early-career employees (logit models)

	1	2	3	4[a]
Constant	-1.35**	-1.20**	-1.63**	-1.19**
Labor market conditions:				
Average unempl. rate, past 6 years	-0.01		0.07+	
Labor market policies: [b]				
EPL score (high = more protection)		0.55**		
Publ. spend. on ALMP, % GDP		-0.39*		
Individual characteristics:				
Female	0.20	0.20	0.21	0.19
Aged 18–24 years (ref.: 25–33 years)	-0.11	-0.14	-0.16	0.03
≤ 9 years of educ. (ref.: ≥ 10 years)	0.60+	0.61+	0.61+	0.38+
Union member				0.21
Job characteristics:				
Priv. sector empl. (ref.: publ. sect. empl.)				-0.37+
Country dummies:				
Flexicurity regime:				
Denmark (ref.)	–	–	–	
Liberal regime:				
Great Britain		0.48	0.44	0.63
United States		0.04	0.10	–
N. European insider-protection regime:				
France		0.92**	0.67**	1.09**
Germany		1.51**	1.35**	1.70**
Netherlands		-0.10	-0.08	-0.09
Sweden		0.57+	0.39	0.60+
S. European insider-protection regime:				
Italy		1.89**	1.57**	2.07**
Spain		0.41+	-0.25	0.59+
No. of cases	1,368	1,368	1,368	1,123
-2*diff (LogL)	64.61	115.35	119.43	104.35

Source: Own calculations based on a subsample of the pooled ISSP data sets *Work Orientations II* (1997) and *Work Orientations III* (2005).
Notes: a Model 4 did not include the United States.
b EPL: employment protection legislation; ALMP: active labor market policies.
** significant at p < 0.01; * significant at p < 0.05; + significant at p < 0.10.

Considering statistical discrimination against women (Sattinger 1998), which is likely to affect women's estimates of their replacement job prospects, it was surprising to find no significance for the gender dummy, especially when it is considered that the respondents in the sample were aged between 18 and 33 at the interview date, that is, in an age span when women are likely to have their first child—a fact that employers take into account when assessing their potential productivity. Model 4 additionally controlled for private sector employment, which significantly decreased the level of reported employment insecurity for early-career employees.

As regards macrostructural context conditions, respondents in countries with higher levels of unemployment over the past 6 years prior to the interview were significantly more likely to perceive employment insecurity (see Model 3). However, the unemployment covariate proved to be nonsignificant after controlling for labor market policies (see Model 1). The effect of these policies was in line with my expectation that higher employment protection would be associated with higher employment insecurity perception in early-career employees. Since high employment protection results in low external vacancy levels (Gangl 2003), it is relatively difficult to make the transition from unemployment back into the labor market in the European insider-outsider employment systems. Hence, employees in these countries generally perceive higher levels of employment insecurity, in particular, when they are labor market entrants who lack previous labor force experience. However, public spending on active labor market policies appears to generate more positive assessments of alternative employment prospects, and this is possibly able to mediate the detrimental effects of insider-outsider markets for early-career employees.

Models 2 to 4 again replaced the institutional variables by country dummies, with Denmark as the reference category. Results of Models 2 and 4 showed that young workers in the two liberal countries and in the Netherlands did not differ significantly from their Danish counterparts, whereas early-career employees reported a significantly higher degree of employment insecurity perception in all other countries. This contradicted my expectation that young employees in the liberal country cluster would report slightly more employment insecurity than those in Denmark, given that the Danish flexicurity model provides a remarkably higher level of active labor market policies[60]. Nevertheless, my results suggest that the combination of lower employment protection levels with higher mobility chances in Great Britain and the United States compensates for the low public spending on active labor market policies, and thus leads to a comparably low level of perceived employment insecurity.

The equally low level of employment insecurity perception in the Netherlands, initially placed in the Northern European insider-outsider protection regime, appears to be somewhat surprising. However, employees in the Netherlands were only interviewed in 1997 when unemployment over the previous 6 years had been lower than in Denmark, and the share of public

---

60 See Figure 4 and Table A.4 in the appendix.

spending on active labor market policies had been relatively high.[61] I believe that this combination may explain the low employment insecurity perception of early-career employees in the Netherlands.

Notably, the country dummies for Sweden and Spain were only significant when the unemployment rate was not controlled (see Models 1, 2). Once it was included in the analysis (see Model 3), respondents seemed to be more confident in their self-perception as labor market insiders, and did not anticipate difficulties in finding a new job if they wanted to. Hence, higher levels of employment insecurity perception in these two countries can be traced back mainly to the unfavorable economic situation at the time of the interview, when both countries were suffering from comparatively high unemployment rates.[62]

Job-loss worry

Following the above discussion of job and employment insecurity perception, I shall now turn to an empirical investigation of job-loss worry and its determinants among young employees. Figure 3.7 shows the combined percentages of respondents who said that they worried 'a great deal' or 'to some extent' about losing their job across the nine countries.

Figure 3.7: Percentage shares of early-career employees who worry about job-loss, 1997 and 2005

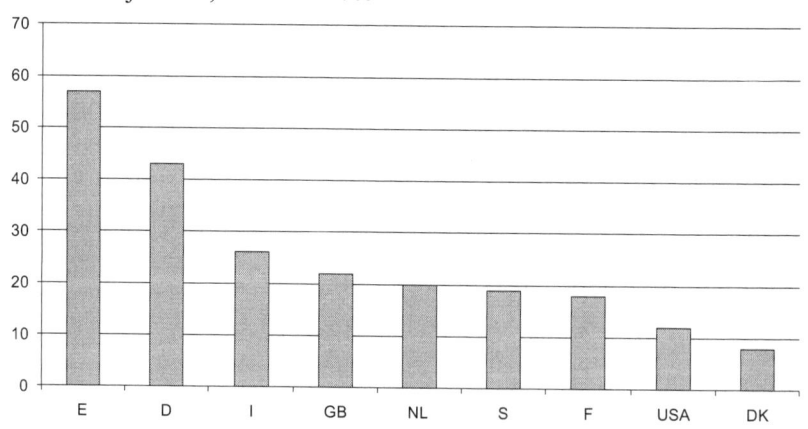

Source: Own analysis of pooled ISSP data from 1997 and 2005.

---

61   Only Denmark's and Sweden's relative investments in active labor market policies were higher (see Table A.4, appendix).
62   See Table A.4 in the appendix.

When comparing the extent of job-loss worry of early-career employees in different countries, I found a notable degree of cross-national variation: Worries about potential job loss ranged from 57 percent in Spain to only 8 percent in Denmark.

Table 3.5 includes the same covariates used in the models on job and employment insecurity perception plus the following proxy variables for nonmarket income support that I assumed would affect income insecurity perception: 'public spending on unemployment compensation, as a percentage of GDP' to measure public income support and a dummy variable for 'employed spouse' to proxy private support. In addition, I controlled for children living in the respondent's household, which I expected to be associated with more worry about job loss.[63] For both dummies, 'employed spouse' and 'child(ren) in the household,' I included gender interaction variables in the respective models to control for gender-specific effects.

On the individual level, age was a highly significant determinant of job-loss worry. Apparently, younger respondents (i.e., those aged 18–24 years) worried significantly more about possible job loss than those aged 25–33 years. This might be explained by a lower degree of experience and seniority (the older age group contains more people approaching mid-career), and, related to that, more fixed-term employment in the younger age group.[64] Indeed, after controlling for fixed-term contracts, the age dummy was no longer significant (Model 5).

Although education proved to be a key determinant of job and employment insecurity perception, it lost its explanatory power for job-loss worry after controlling for the country of employment (Models 2 to 6). Apparently, when controlling for country-level differences, possible job loss was a cause of worry for all early-career employees, regardless of their educational level. Furthermore, neither having an employed spouse nor having children had any statistically significant effect on young employees' job-loss worry.

---

63 Note that full information on the spouse's employment and on children was not available for France, Great Britain, and the Netherlands. Therefore, the data from these countries were excluded from Model 6.

64 Indeed, 39 percent of the respondents aged between 18 and 24 were fixed-term employed compared to only about half as many (19%) of those between 25 and 33.

Table 3.5: High job-loss worry of early-career employees (logit models)

	1	2	3	4[a]	5[a]	6[a]
Constant	-2.97 **	-2.71 **	-3.06 **	-2.71**	-3.12 **	-2.73**
Labor market conditions:						
Average unempl. rate, past 6 yrs.	0.07 +		0.06			
Labor market policies:[b]						
EPL score (high = more protection)	0.35 *					
Publ. spend. on ALMP, % GDP	-0.44 +					
Publ. spend. on UE comp., % GDP	0.18					
Individual characteristics:						
Female	0.06	0.13	0.13	0.19	0.05	-0.03
Aged 18–24 years (ref.: 25–33 years)	0.69 **	0.50 *	0.48 *	0.56**	0.40	0.59 *
≤ 9 years of educ. (ref.: ≥ 10 years)	0.59 +	0.52	0.52	0.43	0.20	0.40
Union member				0.08	0.11	
Empl. spouse						0.19
Empl. spouse * female						-0.13
Child(ren) in the household (hh.)						0.18
Child(ren) in the hh. * female						-0.13
Job characteristics:						
Fixed-term contract					1.31 **	
Priv. sector empl. (ref.: publ. sect. empl.)				-0.16	-0.28	
Country dummies:						
Flexicurity regime:						
Denmark (ref.)		–	–	–	–	–
Liberal regime:						
Great Britain		1.11 **	1.08 *	1.16 **	1.18 +	–
United States		0.35	0.40	–	–	0.37
N. European insider-protection regime:						
France		0.97 **	0.76 +	0.99 *	1.50 **	–
Germany		1.95 **	1.82 **	1.99 **	1.96 **	1.96 **
Netherlands		0.90 +	0.92	0.91 +	0.69	–
Sweden		0.95 *	0.81 +	0.97 *	1.12 +	0.95 *
S. European insider-protection regime:						
Italy		1.17 *	0.90 +	1.28 *	1.40 *	1.25 *
Spain		2.51 **	1.99 **	2.57 **	2.60 **	2.51 **
No. of cases	1,380	1,380	1,380	1,138	626	886
–2*diff (LogL)	115.94	162.75	165.26	142.48	115.15	157.43

Source: Own calculations based on a subsample of the pooled ISSP data sets *Work Orientations II* (1997) and *Work Orientations III* (2005).

Notes: a Model 4 did not include the United States; model 5 was based solely on the 1997 data and did not include the United States; model 6 did not include F, GB, and NL.

b EPL: employment protection legislation; ALMP: active labor market policies; UE comp.: unemployment compensation.

** significant at $p < 0.01$; * significant at $p < 0.05$; + significant at $p < 0.10$.

Turning to the macrolevel, Model 1 indicated that respondents from countries with higher unemployment rates over the past years tended to worry more often about possible job loss. However, institutional characteristics of the countries under study appeared to mediate the effects of national unemployment rates: For early-career employees, the level of employment protection was associated positively with more job-loss worry (see Model 1). This was in line with my earlier findings that high employment protection significantly increased young peoples' job and employment insecurity perception by creating an insider-outsider gap in the labor market. On the other hand, public spending on active labor market policies reduced individual job-loss worry, although public spending on unemployment compensation had no significant effect on young workers' job-loss worry.

Either this variable was not a sufficiently good proxy for income security (e.g., because not all labor market entrants were entitled or eligible to receive unemployment benefits), or low income insecurity perception did not reduce job-loss worry in early-career employees, because being dependent on public or private nonmarket support was not a satisfying perspective for young people at the beginning of their careers.

Model 5 additionally controlled for fixed-term employment. Not surprisingly, early-career employees with a fixed-term contract worried more about job loss, because this was more than just an abstract possibility for them.

When I replaced institutional-level determinants with country dummies (see Models 2 to 6), I found that compared to early-career employees in the Danish flexicurity regime, young workers in both European insider-protection regimes worried more about possible job loss and its consequences, whereas only those in the United States did not differ significantly from those in Denmark. However, when controlling for the national level of unemployment (see Model 3) or for fixed-term employment (see Model 5), the coefficient for the Netherlands also did not differ significantly from the one for Denmark, suggesting that the Dutch institutional context with its high spending on labor market policies[65] appeared to generate similar feelings of security once the economic cycle had been controlled.

In contrast to earlier regressions, young respondents from Great Britain differed from those in Denmark by reporting that they more often worried about the possibilities of losing their job, probably because, compared to Denmark, the country offers few active labor market policies while its unemployment level prior to the first interview wave (1997) was higher than not only Denmark but also the United States.

---

65 See Table A.4 in the appendix.

Overall, together with the United States, Denmark stands out as a country with a notably low level of job-loss worry among early-career employees.

3.2.7. Preliminary conclusion on subjective economic insecurity in Denmark and the other countries

At the beginning of the present chapter, I illustrated how job security is just as important for young workers as it is for older, more experienced ones. However, as the empirical findings of the study presented in Chapter 2 have shown, flexible and precarious forms of employment and employment instability have gained in importance in all the countries covered by this study—especially at labor market entry. Furthermore, one of the main results of the study in Chapter 2 is that, irrespective of national context, labor market entry in a 'bad' job has negative effects on the stability of the further career in terms of unemployment. In this respect, Denmark does not differ significantly from the other countries included in the cross-national comparison. However, I concluded Chapter 2 with the assumption that in comparison to young people in other countries, the situation of labor market entrants and early-career employees in Denmark is probably nowhere near as bad, because 'unemployment' is an experience involving less economic insecurity due to the high mobility on the flexible Danish labor market (that reduces employment insecurity) combined with the country's high expenditure on active labor market policies (that further reduces employment insecurity) and generous unemployment benefits (that reduce income insecurity). In case of unemployment, labor market entrants in Denmark can rely on a short duration of unemployment, because the hire-and-fire principle leads to a relatively high level of external vacancies (Mills and Blossfeld 2005; Gangl 2003a).[66] Furthermore, those who are unable to find their own way back into the labor market will be supported by active labor market policies, while relatively generous unemployment and cash benefits will continue to provide them with sufficient income and reduce their economic insecurity.

The interesting question, however, is whether this is reflected in the insecurity perception of young people in different national labor markets. This is the subject of the study presented in this chapter. Drawing on survey data from the *International Social Survey Program* (ISSP), the study has explored the following two research questions:

1. How do institutional frameworks differ with regard to insecurity perception?

---

66 This assumption is confirmed by the high share of short-term youth unemployment in Denmark (see Figure 3.1).

2. Does the specific Danish combination translate into less job-loss worry in young workers in Denmark compared to those in other OECD countries?

In line with Anderson and Pontusson (2007), I distinguish the following dimensions of job-loss worry: (1) the individual's estimate of the probability of losing her or his job (*job insecurity perception*), (2) the individual's estimate of the probability of not finding another (more or less equivalent) job (*employment insecurity perception*), and (3) the individual's estimate of the probability of experiencing an income loss when becoming unemployed (*income insecurity perception*)—each one of them leading to (4) the overall extent to which a person worries about losing her or his job (*job-loss worry*). To explain cross-national differences in early-career employees' job-loss worries, I have used the regime typology developed in Chapter 1 (Section 1.5) that distinguishes between four labor market entry regimes: the Danish flexicurity, the liberal regime (represented by Great Britain and the United States), the Northern European insider-protection regime (represented by France, Germany, the Netherlands, and Sweden), and the Southern European insider-protection regime (represented by Italy and Spain).

Considering the countries' institutional frameworks against the background of the effects of employment protection legislation and active and passive labor market policies as well as the phenomenon of country-specific relative insecurity perception, I formulated the following regime-specific expectations regarding the prevailing patterns of insecurity perception (see Section 3.2.4, Table 3.2): (1) For early-career employees in Denmark, I anticipated a medium level of job insecurity perception, a very low level of employment insecurity perception, and a low level of income insecurity perception that, taken together, should lead to a very low level of job-loss worry. (2) For young workers in the liberal cluster, I expected a medium level of job insecurity perception, a low level of employment insecurity perception, and a high level of income insecurity perception that I expected to cumulate in a low level of job-loss worry. (3) For early-career employees in the Northern European insider-protection cluster, I anticipated a high level of job insecurity perception, a high level of employment insecurity perception, and a low level of income insecurity perception, a combination that should cause a high level of job-loss worry. (4) For young employees in the Southern European insider-protection cluster, I expected a high level of job insecurity perception, a very high level of employment insecurity perception, and a high level of income insecurity perception that, taken together, should culminate in a very high level of job-loss worry.

In summary, my central hypothesis is that the lowest level of job-loss worry should be found among early-career employees in Denmark followed—in descending order—by the liberal countries and the countries of the Northern European insider-protection regime. Highest levels of insecurity perception are expected in the Southern European insider-protection regime.

I have tested my hypotheses by estimating logit models on each of the insecurity dimensions (except for income insecurity[67]) using data from the ISSP studies 1997 and 2005 to control for other variables that might have an influence.

With regard to the two research questions, the empirical findings can be summarized as follows:

How do institutional frameworks differ with regard to insecurity perception?

The results regarding *job insecurity* suggest that young workers in Denmark, Great Britain, and the United States perceive lower levels of job insecurity than those in France and Sweden, despite the higher levels of overall employment protection in the latter regimes. This finding was expected, and may be explained by the insider-outsider gap in the latter countries that probably lead early-career employees to compare themselves with established core workers. Country-specific relative insecurity perception may also explain why early-career employees in Denmark and in the liberal regimes do not report much job insecurity: Almost every worker in these countries, irrespective of their age or tenure, can be easily dismissed—why should young respondents then rate their jobs as particularly insecure?

The findings on *employment insecurity perception* indicate that young workers in both liberal countries are as optimistic about finding new employment in case of job loss as those in Denmark. Hence, it seems that the higher mobility chances in Great Britain and the United States counterbalance the very low public spending on active labor market policies in these countries.

The main result regarding *job-loss worry* is that the United States does not differ significantly from Denmark in any of the models, despite the United States' low public spending on active labor market policies and on unemployment compensation—which leads us to the second research question:

Does the specific Danish combination translate into less job-loss worry in young workers in Denmark compared to those in other OECD countries?

---

67 As explained in the data and methods section (see section 3.2.5), the ISSP data do not contain items that can be used as an indicator for the respondent's perception of income insecurity; instead I have used two indicators for nonmarket income support as proxies for income insecurity within the models on job-loss worry.

Most job-loss worries of young people are generated by the insider-outsider labor market regimes of Continental Europe, where young people have the greatest difficulties in establishing themselves securely in the labor market. In comparison to these regimes, early-career employees in Denmark clearly do worry less. Also in comparison to Great Britain, Denmark seems to provide young workers with more perception of economic security. However, the institutional framework of the United States obviously produces a similarly low degree of job-loss worry.

The fact that in the United States, low public expenditure rates on labor market policies are accompanied by low levels of young workers' job-loss worry shows that extensive active labor market policies and generous unemployment benefits are not the only necessary conditions for reducing young people's perception of economic insecurity. The high mobility on the flexible United States labor market seems to act as 'functional equivalent' for extensive labor market policies. In the United States, it is not active state involvement that accounts for low job-loss worry among early-career employees but the combination of flexible labor market structures with a perception of a marginal safety net as something 'normal.' Hence, for young people at the beginning of their employment careers, both the Danish flexicurity approach, as well as the liberal 'flexibility approach,' may represent alternative routes toward a low perception of economic insecurity—at least in times of low unemployment.

To conclude, the most important findings of this study can be summarized as follows: (1) Even under globalization, young employees obviously still frame their situation with reference to their national context rather than to global standards (country-specific relative insecurity perception). (2) The flexicurity system of Denmark offers a context of high security and low job-loss worry. (3) Despite all differences, the institutional framework of the United States obviously produces the same securities at the individual level as the Danish system: When comparing the analyses on job insecurity perception, employment insecurity perception, and job-loss worry, the United States is the only country that does not differ from Denmark on the three dimensions of insecurity perception in any of the models used here. Nonetheless, whether this continues to be true since the financial crises beginning in 2008 remains an open question. (4) Finally, though most of the institutional patterns appear to be robust, macroeconomic developments also seem to influence individual insecurity perception, especially in countries with insider-outsider labor markets. This complex relationship between institutional and macroeconomic framework conditions may provide both a challenge as well as a fertile ground for further studies.

4. Summary and discussion

The present study traces how globalization and the related rise in employment flexibility are linked to young people's labor market risks and economic insecurity. It takes a cross-national perspective with a focus on Denmark, the "darling of flexicurity literature" (Madsen 2006: 14), famous for its successful combination of flexibility and individual security. However, the empirical analyses go beyond the usual conceptualization of economic insecurity as an 'objective' phenomenon linked to specific labor market risks and also include an investigation of young people's perception of economic insecurity.

I shall start this final chapter by reconstructing the arguments on the importance of studying economic insecurity of labor market entrants in Denmark from a cross-national perspective that I presented in the introductory chapter. In particular, I shall recapitulate why it is important to study young people's economic insecurity from two perspectives—as both objective experiences and subjective perceptions—and why Denmark makes such an interesting case as a reference country. After this recapitulation of my arguments, I shall outline the structure of the empirical part of the study and summarize my findings on young people's economic insecurity. I shall conclude with a discussion of what policymakers might learn from the Danish case and outline an agenda for further research.

Line of argumentation and structure of the study

At the beginning, I defined *economic insecurity* in terms of the security of having stable access to sufficient and regular income. The starting point of the present study is that for today's young labor market entrants, this security is threatened by the volatility of global markets, the diffusion of precarious forms of work, and the rising risk of unemployment.

I started Chapter 1 by sketching the mechanisms behind the flexibilization of young people's employment relationships. I explained how increased global competition and the related employment flexibilization have changed young people's school-to-work transitions and early careers. Employers in modern societies respond to the volatility of global markets by transferring market risks to their workers. Because first-time jobseekers usually lack work experience and relevant networks, they are a particularly vulnerable outsider group on the labor market. Therefore, it can be assumed that flexible and precarious entry jobs have become more frequent, and that unemployment risks in the early career have risen across successive cohorts. Thus, the primary thesis of this study is that more recent cohorts of school-leavers face increasing economic insecurity and uncertainty at labor market entry.

Young people develop context-specific strategies to respond to rising economic insecurity (Mills and Blossfeld 2005). I have sketched two of these strategies, namely, the postponement or forgoing of parenthood and the trend to remain in education. However, the consequences of economic insecurity for young people at the beginning of their careers cannot be understood fully without analyzing individual insecurity perception. The subjective conceptualization of insecurity is an important complement to objective measures because it is not their objectively given situation, but rather "the way individuals interpret their environment [that] affects how they react to it." (Näswall and De Witte 2003b: 191). Consequently, the analysis of insecurity perception delivers a useful analytical strategy for linking macrolevel changes such as globalization and rising employment flexibility to microlevel individual perceptions of job-loss risk and economic uncertainty—and the behavior to which this perception leads.

However, I have also argued that both kinds of analyses need to consider that employers do not spread their risks evenly across their employees, but that it is young people with low investments in education who face a higher risk of starting their employment careers in more precarious, flexible forms of employment. But it is not only the distribution of risk that reshapes along already established social inequalities but also the consequences. Some individuals will be able to use bad entry positions as stepping-stones, whereas especially unskilled labor market entrants may well become entrapped in the labor market periphery of bad entry jobs.

Whether early-career employees are generally able to use nonoptimal entry positions as stepping-stones or are more likely to be trapped in them largely depends on historically grown and country-specific institutional settings that filter the impact of globalization. Institutional characteristics pertinent to young people's labor market entry process include the national level of employment protection, the focus of labor market policies, and the organization of general and vocational education.

I have explained why Denmark is a special case for applying the *flexibilization hypothesis*, namely, because of its long tradition of combining a high level of labor market flexibility with high levels of social security. Compared to most of the other countries regarded in the present study, the central changes in the Danish labor market have not been associated with increasing employment flexibility, but with the turn toward activation in the 1994 labor market reforms and the coinciding economic boom that both led to a tremendous decrease in unemployment—especially for youth. However, the mid-1990s also saw the decentralization of wage setting down to the level of firms in Denmark, widening the scope for employers to adjust to changing labor market conditions. Furthermore, compulsory activation is suspected of having a negative side effect, in that some people who are pushed by job-search requirements to seek work will end up in jobs with lower wages than might otherwise be the case. Taking all this into account, one of the main research questions in this book has been whether changes in the immediate school-to-work transition and the early career in Denmark reveal a distinctive pattern compared to other OECD countries when looking at labor market entry cohorts from the early 1980s to the beginning of this millennium.

To provide a basis for cross-national comparisons, four labor market entry regimes were distinguished in terms of the main national attributes of labor market regulations and employment sustaining policies. These were (1) the *Danish flexicurity regime* combining relatively weak employment protection (i.e., high labor market flexibility via generally low dismissal protection) and high government spending on active labor market policies; (2) the *liberal regime* containing countries with weak employment protection and low government spending on active labor market policies, namely, the United Kingdom and the United States of America; (3) the *Northern European insider-protection regime* containing countries with relatively strict employment protection (i.e., low labor market flexibility for labor market 'insiders' and high flexibility for 'outsiders' mainly via fixed-term employment) and relatively high supply of active labor market policies, that is, France, Germany, the Netherlands, and Sweden; and (4) the *Southern European insider-protection regime* composed of countries with strict employment protection accompanied by low government spending on active labor market policies, namely, Italy and Spain.

This regime typology serves as a tool to study the objective and the subjective economic insecurity of young people at labor market entry. Due to missing longitudinal data including information on both objective insecurity experiences and insecurity perception, I have had to study both topics separately and link them theoretically. Therefore, the empirical part of this book is split in two chapters with different conceptualizations of insecurity.

The first empirical part (Chapter 2) studies 'The development of employment risks at labor market entry since the 1980s.' The focus is on 'objective insecurities,' that is, risky events and experiences that are linked to young people's economic insecurity. I have applied a comparative cross-national study design: first, a case study on Denmark and, second, a comparison with other country studies conducted for the same research project, the *flexCAREER* project (Blossfeld et al. 2008). All these studies have used a longitudinal, school-leaver cohort design; that is, different cohorts were followed from leaving the education system until the end of their early career. This design makes it possible to capture the dynamics of the labor market entry process and to see how young people's labor market risks develop over time.

The second empirical study (Chapter 3) focuses on 'Insecurity perception: The translation of unemployment risks into job-loss worry in times of flexible employment.' Here, economic insecurity is conceptualized as a multidimensional, subjective phenomenon. Due to the nature of the available data, the focus is on insecurity perception in early-career employees; that is, those young people who have completed the school-to-work transition. The study has an integrated cross-national design: Using data from one international data set, the countries are represented by dummy variables in the models and Denmark is taken as the reference country. In other words, perceived job insecurities of respondents from the other countries are compared to those of respondents in Denmark. The data come from a subsample of early-career employees, extracted from pooled, cross-sectional international survey data conducted in 1997 and 2005 as part of the *Work Orientations* studies by the *International Social Survey Program* (ISSP). The subsample has been created by selecting respondents in the first 6 years after leaving education, with the graduation time proxied by using country- and education-specific *typical graduation ages*. The cross-sectional design makes it possible to study insecurity perception of early-career employees during a time when all the countries under study have already undergone major flexibilization processes.

The following subsections summarize the main findings from both empirical studies.

Insecurity experiences: Key findings from the empirical study on objective economic insecurity

Two main research questions stand at the beginning of Chapter 2:

1. *How have the immediate school-to-work transition and the early career changed in different labor market entry regimes since the early 1980s?*
2. *Do changes in this life course transition in Denmark reveal a distinctive pattern compared to other OECD countries?*

These global research questions are decomposed into a set of more detailed research questions that are then applied to Denmark and the other countries under study: What can be regarded as a 'bad,' that is, precarious, employment position for youth in different national contexts? Has the risk of a bad start to the employment career increased across cohorts? Is a bad career entry typically a trap, or can it serve as a stepping-stone toward more rewarding jobs? Do changes in youth employment trajectories lead to a persistence or even reinforcement of social inequalities related to educational qualification and occupational class?

These questions are answered by studying the following processes and aspects: For the initial labor market entry, I have considered the duration of job search until first employment and the quality of the first job. For the further development of the employment career, the most interesting question is whether labor market entrants, especially those working in flexible forms of employment, are able to establish themselves in the labor market. Therefore, the models on early-career employees' risk of unemployment, on the risk of downward mobility, and on the chances of upward mobility in the different countries controlled for the characteristics of the first job.

Evidence from Denmark

The country study on Denmark found the following answers to the questions raised above:

For the highly flexible Danish labor market—in which fixed-term jobs are as insecure as any other job and part-time work is mostly chosen voluntarily and regulated by the same collective agreements as full-time work—I identified 'bad' jobs as *low-wage jobs*, that is, jobs with earnings within the lowest decile of the wage distribution.

I found an increasing risk of a bad start of the employment career across cohorts entering the Danish labor market. Even though the 1994 labor market reforms were accompanied by an economic upswing and a strong decrease in unemployment rates, members of the relevant educational cohort had a lower transition rate into first employment than those who left education during the earlier economic upswing between 1984 and 1987. Furthermore, individuals who entered the labor market after 1994 faced a high risk of starting their career in a low-wage job. I offered two possible explanations for this last result: First, the activation policy for unemployed people that had been introduced in Denmark in this period probably motivated some people to take up even a low paid job in order to avoid participation in activation programs. Second, wage setting had been decentralized in the mid-1990s, which led to a reduction of wage levels.

With regard to the question whether a bad career entry is typically a trap, or whether it can serve as a stepping-stone toward more rewarding jobs, the findings for Denmark favor the entrapment hypothesis. Low-wage employees had a significantly higher risk of making a transition into unemployment than employees in more highly paid jobs.

Finally, I found a persistence of social inequalities among labor market entrants with different educational levels on the Danish labor market. The empirical results showed that unskilled people were still clearly disadvantaged. The activation reforms improved their chances only in terms of a reduced transition rate into registered unemployment—a development fitting the policy changes and the general economic trend. At the same time, earlier cohorts of unskilled employees were found to have had higher transition rates into a first employment. Furthermore, unskilled persons in the youngest cohort still showed the highest risk of starting in a low-paid job as well as low upward and high downward mobility rates.

However, in order to find out whether labor market entry processes in Denmark follow a distinctive pattern, the changes in labor market entry processes in Denmark need to be put into perspective by comparing them to developments in other countries.

Evidence from the country comparison

Within the framework of the four detailed research questions, the results from the cross-national comparison can be summarized as follows:

The definition of 'bad,' that is, flexible or precarious, entry positions differs among the countries according to the specific way in which employment flexibility has been implemented in the respective institutional contexts. As mentioned already, in the study on Denmark, I focused on low-wage jobs as a type of bad entry position. Like Denmark, countries of the liberal type are also characterized by a long history of employment flexibility. However, besides bad pay, a bad start into employment in these countries might also be characterized by low career prospects. The country study on the United States focused on *stopgap jobs*,—highly flexible part-time jobs with low skill requirements, no social protection (e.g., no health insurance), low pay, and few prospects for career advancement; the study on the United Kingdom focused on part-time jobs and seasonal or casual work as the most important forms of precarious work. In contrast to Denmark and the liberal countries, countries belonging to an insider-protection regime type have a rather short history of employment flexibility, and they have mainly deregulated their labor markets since the 1980s through the increased use of fixed-term contracts or agency work. Consequently, the country studies on France, Germany, the Netherlands, Sweden, Italy, and Spain use fixed-term employment as an indicator for low-quality jobs.

The second detailed research question asked: Has the risk of a bad start to the employment career increased across cohorts? There is no clear answer to this question in terms of the duration of job search after leaving school, because this proves to depend on the macroeconomic development in the specific country. In times of economic upswing, the job search phase after leaving school becomes shorter. However, in terms of the quality of the first employment, the majority of countries under study (including Denmark) reveal an increasing risk of entering a precarious type of job. Moreover, once certain forms of flexible work become established as a route into the labor market, there seems to be a tendency to maintain them even when the macroeconomic situation improves.

With regard to the *trap or stepping-stone* question, the general finding is clear: In all the countries studied, entering a 'bad' job increases the risk of unemployment. In some countries, it is also related to more downward mobility during the subsequent years of the early career.

Regarding the development of social inequalities, I have found that these have persisted in Denmark, whereas in all the other countries, inequalities with regard to educational levels or occupational positions are increasing during the course of globalization.

Summarizing all these findings delivers answers to the two more global research questions posed at the beginning of Chapter 2:

How have the immediate school-to-work transition and the early career changed in different labor market entry regimes since the early 1980s?

Given increased global competition and the economic restructuring in the countries under study, the immediate school-to-work transition and the early career have changed tremendously since the early 1980s. In all the labor market entry regimes, the school-to-work transition has become increasingly difficult, and flexible and precarious forms of work are more typical in the first job after leaving the education system. With regard to the early employment career, unemployment risks have risen across successive cohorts while depending on macroeconomic cycles in the countries under study. Furthermore, irrespective of national context, labor market entry in a 'bad' job has negative effects on the stability of the further career in terms of unemployment and status mobility. Both the immediate labor market entry phase and the subsequent early career are characterized by persistent and growing social inequalities among young people in the different countries.

Do changes in this life course transition in Denmark reveal a distinctive pattern compared to other OECD countries?

I have found that Denmark does not differ significantly from the other countries. This comparison is based on two dimensions of economic insecurity: employment insecurity and job insecurity. Employment insecurity is studied in terms of the chances of finding a first job, by looking at the duration of job search in the single countries. It is not just in Denmark that the duration of job search is relatively low for the youngest school-leaver cohort. This pattern can also be observed in France, the Netherlands, and the United Kingdom, that is, in countries that have also experienced economic upswings affecting the labor market entry phase of the youngest cohorts studied. Job insecurity is studied by looking at the risk of entering a first unemployment. Similar to the duration of job search, and as expected, this risk also turns out to be influenced by macroeconomic changes and the development of national unemployment rates. The declining job insecurity found for young employees in Denmark is not exceptional, because a declining job-loss risk is also found for early-career employees in France. Furthermore, as in the other employment regimes, independent from macroeconomic cycles, school leavers in Denmark reveal an increasing risk of starting their careers in a precarious job, and this significantly increases unemployment risks in the further career, with young people who are less well-educated being more likely to be exposed to these risks.

I then considered the general increase of situations related to higher economic insecurity for young people in different labor markets against the background of the singular strategies countries have applied to implement employment flexibility. This raises the question whether different country-specific institutional settings lead to differences in insecurity perception. Given the institutional framework combining high labor market mobility with high social protection, I assumed that the economic insecurity experienced by young people in Denmark would be less precarious and they would generally worry less about having stable access to sufficient and regular income.

Insecurity perception: Key findings from the empirical study on subjective economic insecurity

Chapter 3 delivers the insight that job insecurity is important to young people, but—as the study presented in Chapter 2 illustrates—it has deteriorated in recent years. In all the countries compared, flexible and precarious forms of employment and employment instability have gained in importance at labor market entry, and labor market entry in a bad job raises the risk of unemployment in the further career.

Hence, the key objective of this empirical part of the study is to explore how the Danish flexicurity model, the liberal institutional framework, and the two insider-protection regime types of continental Europe translate into insecurity perceptions among early-career employees and to see whether the specific Danish framework generates less job-loss worry.

I have studied the following dimensions of job-loss worry: (1) the individual's estimate of the probability of losing her or his job (*job insecurity perception*), (2) the individual's estimate of the probability of not finding another (more or less equivalent) job (*employment insecurity perception*), and (3) the individual's estimate of the probability of experiencing an income loss when becoming unemployed (*income insecurity perception*); all three contributing to (4) the overall extent to which a person worries about losing their job (*job-loss worry*). As no subjective indicator for the respondents' income insecurity perception is available, this dimension cannot be analyzed separately, but has to be proxied within the models on job-loss worry.[68]

Results of the models on the single insecurity perception dimensions provide answers to the two research questions:

How do institutional frameworks differ with regard to insecurity perception?

The models on job insecurity perception suggest that young workers in Denmark and the United States perceive lower levels of job insecurity than those in France and Sweden, despite the higher levels of overall employment protection in the Northern insider-protection regime. This finding is explained by the phenomenon of country-specific relative insecurity perception: In the insider-outsider regimes, early-career employees probably compare themselves with established core workers, whereas in Denmark and in the liberal regimes, there are no *significant others* with lower unemployment risk to compare themselves with due to the generally low employment protection applying to all workers irrespective of age or tenure.

The results on employment insecurity perception suggest that young workers in both liberal countries do not perceive higher employment insecurity than those in Denmark, despite the very low public spending on active labor market policies. This finding is explained by the higher mobility chances in Great Britain and the United States that seem to counterbalance the lack of activation programs that help to reintegrate unemployed people into the labor market in Denmark.

With regard to job-loss worry, the central finding is that respondents in the United States do not differ significantly from those in Denmark—despite the United States' marginal public spending on both active labor market policies and unemployment compensation. In all the other countries under study, early-career employees worry significantly more.

Does the specific Danish combination translate into less job-loss worry in young workers in Denmark compared to those in other OECD countries?

With regard to the previously summarized findings, this question has to be answered with no. Evidently, the completely different institutional framework of the United States produces a similarly low degree of job-loss worry among young people in their early career. The high mobility on the highly flexible labor market in the United States seems to act as 'functional equivalent' for extensive active labor market policies and generous unemployment benefits. Probably the common perception of a marginal safety net as something 'normal' also has to be taken into account when trying to explain this result.

---

68   For details, see the data and methods section 3.2.5.

In addition to the results outlined above, two additional important findings of this study have to be mentioned: (1) Even under globalization, young employees obviously still frame their situation with reference to their national context rather than to global standards (country-specific relative insecurity perception). (2) Though most of the institutional patterns appear to be robust, macroeconomic developments also seem to influence individual insecurity perception, especially in countries belonging to one of the insider-protection regime types.

Providing young people with economic security: What can policymakers from countries with insider-outsider labor markets learn from Denmark?

Young people's perception of economic insecurity depends to a high degree on their relative situation compared to others (country-specific relative insecurity perception). The empirical analyses in Chapter 3 have shown that the labor markets of continental Europe with generally high employment protection produce relatively high job-loss worry in young people. This is probably because only insiders are covered by the employment protection in these labor markets, whereas outsiders (such as persons with less labor force experience) are employed in flexible, precarious jobs and carry the whole burden of increasing labor market flexibility demands. Conversely, in Denmark and the United States, two countries with generally low employment protection, job-loss worry among early-career employees is significantly lower despite the high risk of dismissal. This is because all employees face the same risk in these labor markets irrespective of tenure or age. A second reason for low levels of young workers' job-loss worries on the labor markets with low employment protection is the good reemployment prospects in highly mobile labor markets in which more vacancies open up that are potentially available to all.

One possible strategy to reduce young people's perception of economic insecurity would thus be to transform insider-outsider labor markets into more flexible employment systems by reducing overall employment protection. But which country should policymakers take as a role model? Both the Danish flexicurity approach and the United States' liberal 'flexibility approach' seem to produce similarly low degrees of job-loss worry among young workers. Hence, both approaches could represent alternative routes toward a lower perception of economic insecurity. However, the Danish one with its huge welfare system is much more costly.

Yet, if economic security is the target, a change toward the Danish model would be recommendable, because it is an open question whether job-loss worry rates of young people in the United States have remained comparable to those in Denmark since the financial crises beginning in 2008. In times of economic downshifts and increasing unemployment, the Danish flexicurity model provides more income security due to its relatively generous unemployment and cash benefit systems. Additionally, in times of economic crises, the high supply of active labor market policies can be assumed to be advantageous, especially for labor market entrants and early-career employees.

What should policymakers take into account when trying to learn from the Danish case? First of all, that Danish flexicurity is not an export model (Madsen 2006), and it cannot simply be copied by other countries. As both Bredgaard et al. (2005) and Madsen (2006; 2005) have pointed out, it is the product of a long evolutionary process supported by stable institutions and social compromises in different policy areas. This process has resulted in a specific labor market model that is now labeled as *flexicurity*. It would be wrong to describe the specific Danish institutional mix as the product of some elaborate master plan. However, it may serve as a best-practice model.

It is only in such a sense that a general message from the cross-national comparison in Chapter 3 could be that the central European countries should aspire to reduce their general employment protection. However, this should be accompanied by institutional changes increasing all workers' income and employment security to initiate the necessary level of (voluntary) labor market mobility. It would be naïve to expect that if the central European countries were to reduce their employment protection in general, higher mobility would simply emerge by itself. In these countries, a safe, permanent job has been the normal form of employment for a long time, and it would take considerable time (more than one generation, I suppose) before the workforce would adapt to a new 'openness.' An increase in both employment and income security could accelerate this process, and this again would require institutions providing this kind of *mobility protection*[69] in terms of active and passive labor market policies.

For the European insider-protection regimes, this implies a need for massive institutional restructuring at the end of which they would no longer be insider-protection regimes. Whereas the northern European insider-protection countries already spend relatively high shares of their GDP on labor market policies, the southern countries would have to catch up in this respect. In other words, such system change would be easier to reconcile with the institutional path dependencies of the northern European insider-protection countries than with those of the southern European countries.

For both the northern and the southern European insider-protection countries, a reduction in general employment protection would certainly be a

---

69   Auer (2006) speaks of 'protected mobility.'

painful transformation incorporating a longer temporal increase in perceived economic insecurity for the whole workforce. However, policymakers in countries with insider-outsider labor markets would be shortsighted if they were to believe that young people can gain useful work experience and build up relevant labor market networks while working in fixed-term jobs, and then move up into permanent jobs and form a family. By the time these employees perceive themselves as being established on the labor market, it might be too late. In all the countries covered by this study, the main childbearing ages are between 24 and 30 (Mishra and Smyth 2010), and this age span overlaps with the country-specific age ranges of the early career[70]. It is particularly highly educated people who are affected by this overlap. Even at the end of their early career, many young employees still feel like 'outsiders.' They worry about possible job loss and thus even forgo parenthood—and declining birth rates are a major concern in most modern societies.

Insecurity perception: An agenda for further research

The findings in this study indicate that the economic security of young people at labor market entry has deteriorated in recent years, that economic security is something that is important to them, and that it is determined by national institutional settings. However, I have to agree with Lars Osberg, who concluded his essay on economic insecurity 12 years ago with the words: "Much remains to be done in improving the measurement of economic insecurity [...]" (Osberg 1998: 32).

One improvement would be to study the different dimensions of young people's objective and subjective economic insecurities at labor market entry and in the early career together—longitudinally, with a comparative cross-national design.

The empirical analyses in Chapter 3 have shown that there is more to young people's perception of economic insecurity than job insecurity, and that it makes sense to treat it as a multidimensional phenomenon. For example, it reveals the role of low employment insecurity perception in reducing young employees' job-loss worry.

However, worry—as a subjective response to perceived economic insecurity—is influenced by the prevalence of risky events, such as leaving the safe resort of the education system, entering a precarious job, or having a spouse who is laid off. Hence, objective and subjective economic insecurities need to be studied together.

Furthermore, the phenomenon needs to be examined longitudinally. This is the only way that would enable us to answer relevant questions like: How

---

70 See Table A.2 in the appendix.

do the different dimensions of economic insecurity develop over the life course? Which insecurities do first-time job-seekers perceive? How do these change when they enter the labor market? How is insecurity perception in young men and women linked to family formation? Are there differences between early- and mid-career employees? Many of these questions were studied in the GLOBALIFE project (Blossfeld et al. 2005); however, with only an 'objective' conceptualization of economic insecurity.

Moreover, a cross-national design similar to the GLOBALIFE (Blossfeld et al. 2005) or *flexCAREER* project (Blossfeld et al. 2008) would enable us to learn more about the role of institutional settings in translating insecurity experiences into insecurity perception. A joint project involving a network of researchers from different countries serving as national experts on their home countries who produce country case studies would certainly deepen our understanding of cross-national differences in young people's economic insecurity. Such researchers are familiar with the data sets available within each country, and would be able to analyze them to the fullest advantage; they can provide explanations for the impact of institutional and sociostructural conditions on economic insecurity in different phases of the life course in their country.

Ideally, quantitative analyses should be accompanied by qualitative ones. The best option would be a longitudinal cross-national event-oriented qualitative study design in which young people are interviewed before, during, and after their labor market entry. There are probably more dimensions of young people's economic insecurity than those covered by the present study, and it would be worthwhile to find out about them.

Mills and Blossfeld (2005) have defined the transition to adulthood as a stepwise process in which young people adopt specific roles and participate in certain activities. In this regard, labor market entry is only one of the steps young people take on their way to adulthood. The GLOBALIFE project has shown that economic insecurity has consequences for family formation, with those in more precarious positions more likely to postpone or forgo partnership and parenthood (Mills et al. 2005). This applies especially to men in the so-called *male-breadwinner nations*. As suggested a few times in the course of this book, it would be interesting to conduct a combined study on objective insecurity experiences, subjective insecurity perception, and the transition to parenthood—with a design considering the suggestions I have made above. It is outside the scope (and beyond the means) of this work to study the association between economic insecurity perception and the transition to parenthood on the individual level. However, I shall conclude this book with a cross-country comparison of the distribution of job-loss worry among early-career employees and fertility levels that could motivate further research on the topic. Figure 4.1 compares the country-specific percentages of respondents in the 1997 ISSP's surveys who said that they worry 'a great deal' or 'to some extent' about losing their job with the same year's national *total fertility rates* (TFR).[71]

Figure 4.1: Percentage shares of early-career employees worrying about job loss and national total fertility rates, 1997

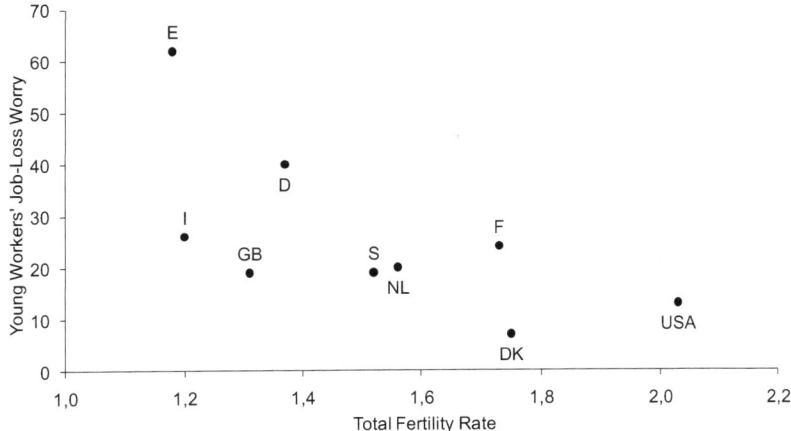

Source: Job-loss worry: Own analysis of ISSP subsample; TFR: *Internationale ifb-Datenbank Familie und Demografie* 2009.

It can be seen that those countries with lower shares of young people worrying about the possibilities of job loss in 1997 display higher numbers of children per woman in 1997 and vice versa.

One could object that the TFR also refers to women who are either in their mid career or not employed, whereas the measure of the extent of job-loss worry refers to early-career employees.[72] Furthermore, this is not the only factor influencing a country's fertility level (e.g., the level of female employment, the availability of part-time jobs, the scope and generosity of family allowances and public childcare services, etc.). Nonetheless, a look at the figure does suggest that it would make sense to assume that the relationship is negative, and this could certainly serve as a starting point for further research.

---

71 The TFR in a specific year is defined as "the number of children that would be born to each woman if she were to live to the end of her childbearing years and if the likelihood of her giving birth to children at each age was the currently prevailing age-specific fertility rates" (OECD 2009c).

72 However, in all the countries under study, the main childbearing ages are between 24 and 30 (Mishra and Smyth 2010). This age span is covered by the country-specific age ranges of the subsamples of early-career employees used in the present study (see Table A.2 in the appendix).

References

Allison, P. D. (1982) 'Discrete-time Methods for the Analysis of Event Histories.' in S. Leinhardt (ed.) *Sociological Methodology*, San Francisco: Jossey-Bass.
Allmendinger, J. (1989) 'Educational systems and labour market outcomes.' *European Sociological Review* 5: 231-50.
Altvater, E. (2003) 'Öffentliche Güter für menschliche Sicherheit und soziale Demokratie.' *WISO* 3: 36-61.
Anderson, C. J and Pontusson, J. (2007) 'Workers, worries and welfare states: Social protection and job insecurity in 15 OECD countries.' *European Journal of Political Research* 46: 211-235.
Atkinson, J. (1984) 'Manpower Strategies for Flexible Organizations.' *Personnel Management* 15: 28–31.
Auer, P. (2006) 'Protected mobility for employment and decent work: labour market security in a globalized world.' *Journal of Industrial Relations* 48: 21-40.
Auer, P. and Cazes, S. (2003) 'The resilence of the long-term employment relationship.' in P. Auer and S. Cazes (eds.) *Employment stability in an age of flexibility. Evidence from industrialized countries*, Geneva: International Labour Office.
Barbier, J.-C. (2008) 'There is more to Job Quality than 'Precariousness': a Comparative, Epistemological Analysis of the 'Flexibility and Security' Debate in Europe.' in R. Muffels (ed.) *Flexibility and Employment Security in Europe: labor markets in transition*, Cheltenham, UK/Northampton, MA, USA: Edward Elgar.
Baumann, Z. (1999) *In Search of Politics*. Palo Alto, CA: Stanford University Press.
Beck, U. (1986) *Risikogesellschaft: Auf dem Weg in eine andere Moderne*. Frankfurt/M.: Suhrkamp.
Beck, U. (2000) *What is Globalization?* Cambridge: Polity Press.
Bernardi, F. (2006) 'Globalization and Men's Employment Careers in Italy.' in H.-P. Blossfeld, M. Mills and F. Bernardi (eds.) *Globalization, Uncertainty and Men's Careers. An International Comparison*, Cheltenham, UK/Northampton, MA, USA: Edward Elgar.
Bernardi, F. and Nazio, T. (2005) 'Globalization and the Transition to Adulthood in Italy.' in H.-P. Blossfeld, E. Klijzing, M. Mills and K. Kurz (eds.) *Globalization, Uncertainty and Youth in Society*, London/New York: Routledge.
Biggart, A. (2005) 'Families and Transitions in Europe.' *Final report of the Research project FATE*. Coleraine: University of Ulster.

Bingley, P. and Westergaard-Nielsen, N. (1997) *Individual Wage Mobility – the Case of Denmark 1980–1990*. University of Aarhus: Aarhus School of Business, Centre for Labour Market and Social Research.
Blossfeld, H.-P. (1992) 'Is the German Dual System a Model for a Modern Vocational Training System? A Cross-National Comparison of How Different Systems of Vocational Training Deal With the Changing Occupational Structure.' *International Journal of Comparative Sociology* 18: 168–81.
Blossfeld, H.-P. (1995) *The New Role of Women: Family Formation in Modern Societies*. Boulder: Westview Press.
Blossfeld, H.-P. (2009) 'Comparative Life Course Research. A Cross-National and Longitudinal Perspective.' in G. H. Jr. Elder and J. Z. Giele (eds.) *The Craft of Life Course Research*, New York/London: The Guildford Press.
Blossfeld, H.-P., Buchholz, S., Bukodi, E. and Kurz, K. (2008) *Young Workers, Globalization and the Labor Market. Comparing Early Working Life in Eleven Countries*. Cheltenham, UK/Northampton, MA, USA: Edward Elgar.
Blossfeld, H.-P. and Drobnič, S. (2001) *Careers of Couples in Contemporary Societies: From Male Breadwinner to Dual Earner Families*. Oxford: Oxford University Press.
Blossfeld, H.-P., Klijzing, E., Mills, M. and Kurz, K. (2005) *Globalization, Uncertainty and Youth in Society*. New York: Routledge Advances in Sociology.
Blossfeld, H.-P. and Stockmann, R. (1998/99) *Globalization and Chances in Vocational Training Systems in Developing and Advanced Industrialized Societies*. Armonk, NY: Sharpe.
Booth, A. L., Francesconi, M. and Frank, J. (2002) 'Temporary Jobs: Stepping Stones or Dead Ends?' *Economic Journal* 112: 189–213.
Bowers, N., Sonnet, A. and Bardone, L. (1998) *Background Report. Giving Young People a Good Start: the Experience of OECD Countries*. Paris: OECD.
Braun, T. (2003) 'Ein neues Modell für Flexicurity – der dänische Arbeitsmarkt.' *WSI Mitteilungen* 2: 92–99.
Brauns, H., Gangl, M. and Scherer, S. (1999) 'Education and Unemployment: Patterns of Labour Market Entry in France, the United Kingdom and West Germany.' *Arbeitspapier 6*, Mannheimer Zentrum für Europäische Sozialforschung.
Brauns, H. and Steinmann, S. (1999) 'Educational Reform in France, West-Germany, the United Kingdom: Updating the CASMIN Educational Classification.' *ZUMA-Nachrichten* 44: 7–45.

Bredgaard, T., Larsen, F. and Madsen, P. K. (2005) 'The Flexible Danish Labour Market – a Review.' *CARMA Research Paper 1*, Centre for Labour Market Research (CARMA), University of Aalborg.
Bredgaard, T., Larsen, F., Madsen, P. K. and Rasmussen, S. (2009) 'Flexicurity and atypical employment in Denmark.' *CARMA Research Paper 1*, Centre for Labour Market Research (CARMA), University of Aalborg.
Breen, R. (1997) 'Risk, Recommodification and Stratification.' *Sociology* 31: 473-89.
Breen, R. (2004) *Social Mobility in Europe*. Oxford: Oxford University Press.
Breen, R. (2005) 'Explaining Cross-national Variation in Youth Unemployment.' *European Sociological Review* 21: 125–34.
Bruhnes, B. (1989) 'Labor Market Flexibility in Enterprises: A Comparison of Firms in Four European Countries.' *OECD Labor Market Flexibility: Trends in Enterprises*, Paris: OECD.
Brzinsky-Fay, J. (2007) 'Lost in Transition? Labour Market Entry Sequences of School Leavers in Europe.' *European Sociological Review* 23: 409–22.
Buchholz, S. (2008) *Die Flexibilisierung des Erwerbsverlaufs: Eine Analyse von Einstiegs- und Aufstiegsprozessen in Ost- und Westdeutschland*. Wiesbaden: VS Verlag für Sozialwissenschaften.
Buchholz, S. and Kurz, K. (2008) 'A new mobility regime in Germany? Young people's labor market entry and phase of establishment since the mid-1980s.' in H.-P. Blossfeld, S. Buchholz, E. Bukodi and K. Kurz (eds.) *Young Workers, Globalization and the Labor Market. Comparing Early Working Life in Eleven Countries*, Cheltenham, UK/Northampton, MA, USA: Edward Elgar.
Bukodi, E., Ebralidze, E, Schmelzer, P. and Relikowski I. (2006) 'Increasing flexibility at labor market entry and in the early career. A new conceptual framework for the *flexCAREER* project.' *flexCAREER Working Paper 6*, University of Bamberg.
Bukodi, E., Ebralidze, E., Schmelzer, P. and Blossfeld, H.-P. (2008) 'Struggling to become an insider: does increasing flexibility at labor market entry affect early careers?' in H.-P. Blossfeld, S. Buchholz, E. Bukodi and K. Kurz (eds.) *Young Workers, Globalization and the Labor Market. Comparing Early Working Life in Eleven Countries*, Cheltenham, UK/Northampton, MA, USA: Edward Elgar.
Burchell, B. J. (2005) 'The welfare costs of job insecurity: psychological well-being and family life' in *Trends in social cohesion No. 15: Reconciling labour flexibility with social cohesion – Facing the challenge*, Strasbourg Cedex: Council of Europe Publishing.

Bygren, M., Duvander, A.-Z. and Hultin, M. (2002) 'Elements of uncertainty in life courses. Transitions to adulthood in Sweden.' in H.-P. Blossfeld, E. Klijzing, M. Mills and K. Kurz (eds.) *Globalization, Uncertainty and Youth in Society*, London/New York: Routledge.

Campbell, I. and Burgess, J. (2001) 'Casual Employment in Australia and Temporary Employment in Europe: Developing a Cross-National Comparison.' *Work, Employment and Society* 15: 171–84.

Capelli, P. and Neumark, D. (2004) 'External Churning and Internal Flexibility: Evidence on the Functional Flexibility and Core-periphery Hypotheses.' *Industrial Relations* 43: 148–82.

Castells, M. (2000) *The Rise of the Network Society. The Information Age.* Oxford: Blackwell Publishers.

CEDEFOP (1993) *The Determinants of Transitions in Youth*. Berlin: European Centre for the Development of Vocational Training.

Clark, A. and Postel-Vinay, F. (2008) 'Job security and job protection.' *Oxford Economic Papers* 61: 207–39.

Conley, H. (2008) 'The nightmare of temporary work: a comment on Fevre.' *Work, Employment and Society* 22: 731–36.

Cort, P. (2002) 'Vocational education and training in Denmark: Brief description.' *Cedefop Panorama Series*. Luxembourg: Office for Official Publications of the European Communities.

Delsen, L. (2000) 'Das niederländische Bündnis für Arbeit und seine Wirkungen.' *Arbeit: Zeitschrift für Arbeitsforschung, Arbeitsgestaltung und Arbeitspolitik* 9: 119-32.

Dicken, P. (2003) *Global Shift: Reshaping the global economic map in the 21st century*. New York: The Guilford Press.

DiPrete, T. A. and McManus, P. A. (1996) 'Institutions, technical Change and Diverging Life Chances: Earnings Mobility in the United States and Germany.' *American Journal of Sociology* 102: 34–79.

DiPrete, T. A., deGraaf, P. M., Luijkx, R., Tahlin, M. and Blossfeld, H. P. (1997) 'Collectivist versus Individualist Mobility Regimes? Structural Change and Job Mobility in Four Countries.' *American Journal of Sociology* 103: 318–58.

Doeringer, P.B. and Piore, M.J. (1971) *Internal Labor Markets and Manpower Analysis*. Lexington: D.C. Heath and Company.

Döhrn, R., Heilemann, U. and Schäfer, G. (1998) 'Ein dänisches Beschäftigungs-wunder?' *Mitteilungen aus der Arbeitsmarkt- und Berufsforschung* 2: 312–23.

Doogan, K. (2001) 'Insecurity and Long-Term Employment.' *Work, Employment and Society* 15: 419–41.

Doogan, K. (2005) 'Long-Term Employment and the Restructuring of the Labour Market in Europe.' *Time and Society* 14: 65–87.

Dörre, K., Kraemer, K. and Speidel, F. (2006) *The increasing precariousness of the employment society – driving force for a new rightwing populism?* Paper prepared for presentation at the 15th Conference of Europeanists, Chicago, available online at: <http://www.columbia.edu/cu/ces/pub/papers/Dorre.pdf> (accessed 5 February 2010).

Drøpping, J. A., Hvinden, B. and Vik, K. (1999) 'Activation policies in the Nordic countries.' in M. Kautto, M. Heikkilä, B. Hvinden, S. Marklund and N. Ploug (eds.) *Nordic Social Policy. Changing welfare states*, London/New York: Routledge.

Eckersley, R. (1997) 'Portraits of youth: Understanding young people's relationship with the future.' *Futures* 29: 243-49.

Elster, J. (1979) *Ulysses and the sirens*. Cambridge: Cambridge University Press.

Emmerich, K., Hoffman, E. and Walwei, U. (2000) 'Beschäftigung von Geringqualifizierten in Dänemark.' *IAB-Werkstattbericht* 3: 1–17.

Erikson, R. and Goldthorpe, J.H. (1992) *The Constant Flux. A Study of Class Mobility in Industrial Societies*. Oxford: Clarendon Press.

Eriksson, T. and Westergaard-Nielsen, N. (2004) 'Wage and Labor Mobility in Denmark, 1980–2000.' in E. P. Lazear and K. L. Shaw (eds.) *The Structure of Wages. An International Comparison*, Chicago: The University of Chicago Press.

Erlinghagen, M. (2008) 'Self-Perceived Job Insecurity and Social Context. A Multi-Level Analysis of 17 European Countries.' *European Sociological Review* 24: 183–97.

Esping-Andersen, G. (1990) *The three worlds of welfare capitalism*. Cambridge: Polity Press.

Esser, H. (1991) *Alltagshandeln und Verstehen*. Tübingen: Mohr.

Fevre, R. (2007) 'Employment Insecurity and Social Theory: The Power of Nightmares.' *Work, Employment and Society* 21: 517–35.

Gallie, D. (2000) *Unemployment, Work and Welfare. A Preliminary Assessment of the Implications of the EU's Framework Programme Research*. Paper presented to the seminar 'Towards a Learning Society: Innovation and Competence Building with Social Cohesion for Europe.' Quinta de Marinha, Guincho, Lisbon, available online at: <http://hicks.nuff.ox.ac.uk/projects/UWWCLUS/Papers/restrict/lisbon.pdf> (accessed 15 December 2009).

Gallie, D. (2003) 'The Quality of Working Life: Is Scandinavia Different?' *European Sociological Review* 19: 61-79.

Gallie, D. (2007) 'Welfare Regimes, Employment Systems and Job Preference Orientations.' *European Sociological Review* 23: 279–93.

Gallie, D., White, M., Cheng, Y. and Tomlison, M. (1998) *Restructuring the Employment Relationship*. Oxford: Clarendon Press.

Gangl, M. (2003a) 'The Only Way is Up? Employment Protection and Job Mobility among Recent Entrants to European Labour Markets.' *European Sociological Review* 19: 429-49.

Gangl, M. (2003b) 'The structure of labour market entry in Europe: a typological analysis.' in W. Müller and M. Gangl (eds.) *Transitions from Education to Work in Europe: The Integration of Youth into EU Labour Markets*, Oxford: Oxford University Press.

Gangl, M. (2003c) 'Returns to Education in Context: Individual Education and Transition Outcomes in European Labour Markets.' in W. Müller and M. Gangl (eds.) *Transitions from Education to Work in Europe: The Integration of Youth into EU Labour Markets*, Oxford: Oxford University Press.

Gangl, M. (2004) 'Institutions and the Structure of Labour Market Matching in the United States and West Germany.' *European Sociological Review* 20: 171-87.

Gangl, M. (2006) 'Scar Effects of Unemployment: An Assessment of Institutional Complementarities.' American Sociological Review 71: 986-1013.

Ganßmann, H. and Haas, M. (2001) *Arbeitsmärkte im Vergleich II. Flexibilität und Rigidität der Arbeitsmärkte in den Niederlanden, Dänemark und Schweden*. Marburg: Schüren.

Gendell, M. (2001): 'Retirement age declines again in 1990s.' *Monthly Labor Review*, U.S. Department of Labor, Bureau of Labor Statistics: Washington.

Goldthorpe, J.H. and McKnight, A. (2006) 'The Economic Basis of Social Class.' in S. Morgan, D.B. Grusky and G.S. Fields (eds.) *Mobility and Inequality: Frontiers of Research from Sociology and Economics*, Stanford: Stanford University Press.

Goudswaard, A. and Andries, F. (2002) '*Employment Status and Working Conditions. European Foundation for the Improvement of Living and Working Conditions.*' Luxembourg: Office for Official Publications of the European Communities.

Green, F. (2003) 'The Rise and Decline of Job Insecurity.' *Department of Economics Discussion Paper* 05/03, Canterbury: University of Kent.

Green, F. (2009, forthcoming) 'Subjective employment insecurity around the world.' *Cambridge Journal of Regions, Economy and Society* 3: 1-21.

Green, F., Felstead, A. and Burchell, B. (2000) 'Job insecurity and the difficulty of regaining employment: an empirical study of unemployment expectations.' *Oxford Bulletin of Economics and Statistics* 62 (Special Issue), 855–83.

Grimshaw, D. and Rubery, J. (1997) 'Workforce Heterogeneity and Unemployment Benefits: the Need for Policy Reassessment in the European Union.' *Journal of European Social Policy* 7: 291-318.

Grunow, D. (2006) *Convergence, Persistence and Diversity in Male and Female Careers. Does Context Matter in an Era of Globalization? A Comparison of Gendered Employment Mobility Patterns in West Germany and Denmark.* Opladen: Barbara Budrich Publishers.

Grunow, D. and Leth-Sørensen, S. (2006a) 'Danish women's unemployment, job-mobility and non-employment, 1980s and 1990s: Marked by globalization?' in H.-P. Blossfeld and H. Hofmeister (eds.) *Globalization, Uncertainty and Women's Careers: An International Comparison*, Cheltenham, UK/Northhampton, MA, USA: Edward Elgar.

Grunow, D. and Leth-Sørensen, S. (2006b) 'Mobility of Men in the Danish Labor Market.' in H.-P. Blossfeld, M. Mills and F. Bernardi (eds.) *Globalization, Uncertainty, and Men's Careers: An International Comparison*, Cheltenham, UK/Northhampton, MA, USA: Edward Elgar.

Guerrero, T.J. (1995) 'Legitimation durch Sozialpolitik? Die spanische Beschäftigungskrise und die Theorie des Wohlfahrtsstaates.' *KZfSS* 47: 727-52.

Hall, P. A. and Soskice, D. (2001) 'An Introduction to Varieties of Capitalism.' in P. A. Hall and D. Soskice (eds.) *Varieties of Capitalism: The Institutional Foundations of Comparative Advantage*, New York: Oxford University Press.

Halldén, K. and Hällsten, M. (2008) 'Increasing Employment Instability Among Young People? Labor Market Entries and Early Careers in Sweden 1980–2000.' in H.-P. Blossfeld, S. Buchholz, E. Bukodi and K. Kurz (eds.) *Young Workers, Globalization and the Labor Market. Comparing Early Working Life in Eleven Countries*, Cheltenham, UK/Northampton, MA, USA: Edward Elgar.

Hjarnø J. and Jensen, T. (1997) 'Diskriminering af unge med indvandrerbaggrund ved jobsøgning. Dansk national rapport efter oplæg fra ILO.' *Papers, Migration No. 21. Dansk Center for Migration og Etniske Studier (DAMES)*, Esbjerg: Sydjysk Universitetsforlag.

Hofäcker, D. (2010, forthcoming) *Older Workers in a Globalizing World. An International Comparison of Retirement and Late-Career Patterns in Western Industrialized Countries.* Cheltenham, UK/Northampton, MA, USA: Edward Elgar.

Howell, D. R. (2004) 'Labor Market Institutions and Unemployment: An Assessment.' in D. R. Howell (ed.) *Fighting Unemployment. The Limits of Free Market Orthodoxy*, New York: Oxford University Press.

Internationale ifb-Datenbank Familie und Demografie (2009), International Database on Family and Demography, State Institute for Family Research at the University of Bamberg (ifb).

Jacobsen, A. (2005) 'Renewed vigour for working life.' *Nordic Labour Journal* 10: 18-19.

Jensen, P., Svarer, M. and Rosholm, M. (2003) 'The Response of Youth Unemployment to Benefits, Incentives, and Sanctions.' *European Journal of Political Economy* 19: 301–16.

Jochem, S. (2009) 'Skandinavische Beschäftigungspolitik – Stärken und Schwächen im internationalen Vergleich.' *WSI Mitteilungen* 1: 3-9.

Kim, A. and Kurz, K. (2003) 'Prekäre Beschäftigung im Vereinigten Königreich und Deutschland. Welche Rolle spielen unterschiedliche institutionelle Kontexte?' in W. Müller and S. Scherer (eds.) *Mehr Risiken – Mehr Ungleichheit? Abbau von Wohlfahrtsstaat, Flexibilisierung von Arbeit und die Folgen*, Frankfurt/New York: Campus Verlag.

Klijzing, E. (2005.) 'Globalization and the early life course. A description of selected economic and demographic trends.' in H.-P. Blossfeld, E. Klijzing, M. Mills and K. Kurz (eds.) *Globalization, Uncertainty and Youth in Society*, London/New York: Routledge.

Kohn, M. L. (1987) 'Cross-national research as an analytic strategy.' *American Sociological Review,* 52: 713-31.

Kronauer, M. and Linne, G. (2005) 'Flexicurity: Leitbild, Rhetorik oder halbherziger Kompromiss?' in M. Kronauer and G. Linne (eds.) *Flexicurity. Die Suche nach der Sicherheit in der Flexibilität*, Berlin: Edition sigma.

Kurz, K. (2005) *Beschäftigungsunsicherheiten und langfristige Bindungen. Analysen zu Partnerschaftsverhalten, Familiengründung und zum Erwerb von Wohneigentum.* Wiesbaden: VS Verlag für Sozialwissenschaften.

Kurz, K., Buchholz, S., Schmelzer, P. and Blossfeld, H.-P. (2008) 'Young People's Employment Chances on Flexible Labor Markets. A Comparison of Changes in Eleven Modern Societies.' in H.-P. Blossfeld, S. Buchholz, E. Bukodi and K. Kurz (eds.) *Young Workers, Globalization and the Labor Market. Comparing Early Working Life in Eleven Countries*, Cheltenham, UK/Northampton, MA, USA: Edward Elgar.

Kurz, K., Hillmert, S. and Grunow, D. (2006) 'Increasing Instability in Employment Careers? Men's Job Mobility and Unemployment in West Germany: Comparison of the Birth Cohorts 1940, 1955 and 1964.' in H.-P. Blossfeld, M. Mills and F. Bernardi (eds.) *Globalization, Uncertainty and Men's Careers. An International Comparison*, Cheltenham, UK/Northampton, MA, USA: Edward Elgar.

Kurz, K. and Steinhage, N. (2001) 'Global Competition and Labor Market Restructuring: The Transition into the Labor Market in Germany.' *GLOBALIFE Working Paper 15*, University of Bielefeld.

Kurz, K., Steinhage, N. and Golsch, K. (2005) 'Case study Germany. Global competition, uncertainty and the transition to adulthood.' in H.-P.

Blossfeld, E. Klijzing, M. Mills and K. Kurz (eds.) *Globalization, Uncertainty and Youth in Society*, London/New York: Routledge.
Layte, R., O'Connell, P. J., Fahey, T. and McCoy, S. (2005) 'Ireland and Economic Globalization. The Experiences of a Small Open Economy.' in H.-P. Blossfeld, E. Klijzing, M. Mills and K. Kurz (eds.) *Globalization, Uncertainty and Youth in Society*, London/New York: Routledge.
Leth-Sørensen, S. (1997) 'The IDA Database: a Longitudinal Database of Establishments and Their Employees.' *Statistics Denmark Working Paper 95*, Copenhagen: Statistics Denmark, the IDA Project.
Leung, K. (1989) 'Cross-cultural differences: Individual-level vs. culture-level analysis.' *International Journal of Psychology* 24: 703-19.
Liebig, T. (2007) 'The Labour Market Integration of Immigrants in Denmark.' *OECD Social, Employment and Migration Working Papers 50*, Paris: OECD.
Lim, V. K. G. (1996) 'Job insecurity and its outcomes: Moderating effects of work-based and non work-based social support.' *Human Relations* 49: 171–94.
Lindenberg, S. (1983) 'Utility and morality.' *Kyklos* 36: 450-68.
Luijkx, R., Kalmijn, M. and Muffels, R.J.A. (2006) 'The Impact of Globalization on Job and Career Mobility of Dutch Men: Life-history Data from the mid-1950s to the Year 2000.' in H.-P. Blossfeld, M. Mills and F. Bernardi (eds.) *Globalization, Uncertainty and Men's Careers. An International Comparison*, Cheltenham, UK/Northampton, MA, USA: Edward Elgar.
Madsen, P. K. (1999) 'Denmark: Flexibility, security and labour market success.' *ILO Employment and Training Papers* 53, University of Copenhagen.
Madsen, P. K. (2006) 'Flexicurity – kein Exportmodell.' *Kennzeichen DK* 78: 14-15.
Marsden, D. (1999) *A theory of employment systems: micro-foundations of societal diversity*. Oxford: Oxford University Press.
Martínez-Pastor, J. I., Bernardi, F.and Garrido L. (2008) 'Increasing Employment Instability Among Young People? Labor Market Entries and Early Careers in Spain since the Mid-1970s.' in H.-P. Blossfeld, S. Buchholz, E. Bukodi and K. Kurz (eds.) *Young Workers, Globalization and the Labor Market. Comparing Early Working Life in Eleven Countries*, Cheltenham, UK/Northampton, MA, USA: Edward Elgar.
McDonald, P. (2006) 'Low Fertility and the State: The Efficacy of Policy.' *Population and Development Review* 32: 485-510.
Mertens, A. and McGinnity, F. (2005) 'A 'Two-Tier' Labour Market for Fixed-Term Jobs? Evaluating Evidence from West Germany Using Quantile Regression.' *Schmollers Jahrbuch* 125: 75–85.

Meulders, D., Plasman, O. and Plasman, R. (1994) *Atypical Employment in the EC*. Aldershot: Dartmouth.

Mills, M. (2004) 'Stability and Change: The structuration of partnership histories in Canada, the Netherlands, and the Russian Federation.' *European Journal of Population* 20: 141-175.

Mills, M. and Blossfeld, H.-P. (2003) 'Globalization, Uncertainty and Changes in Early Life Courses.' *Zeitschrift für Erziehungswissenschaften* 6: 188–218.

Mills, M. and Blossfeld, H.-P. (2005) 'Globalization, Uncertainty and the Early Life Course. A Theoretical Framework.' in H.-P. Blossfeld, E. Klijzing, M. Mills and K. Kurz (eds.) *Globalization, Uncertainty and Youth in Society*, London/New York: Routledge.

Mills, M., Blossfeld, H.-P. and Klijzing, E. (2005) 'Becoming an adult in uncertain times: a 14-country comparison of the losers of globalization.' in H.-P. Blossfeld, E. Klijzing, M. Mills, and K. Kurz (eds.) *Globalization, Uncertainty and Youth in Society*, London/New York: Routledge.

Mishra, V. and Smyth R. (2010) 'Female labor force participation and total fertility rates in the OECD: New evidence from panel cointegration and Granger causality testing.' *Journal of Economics and Business* 62: 48–64.

Muffels, R. (2008) 'Flexibility and Employment Security in Europe: Setting the Scene.' in R. Muffels (ed.) *Flexibility and Employment Security in Europe: labor markets in transition*, Cheltenham, UK/Northampton, MA, USA: Edward Elgar.

Müller, W. and Gangl, M. (2003) *Transitions from Education to Work in Europe*. Oxford: Oxford University Press.

Müller, W., Gangl, M. and Scherer, S. (2002) 'Übergangsstrukturen zwischen Bildung und Beschäftigung.' in M. Wingens and R. Sackmann (eds.) *Bildung und Beruf. Ausbildung und berufsstruktureller Wandel in der Wissensgesellschaft*, Weinheim/München: Juventa Verlag.

Münch, R. (2001) *Offene Räume. Soziale Integration diesseits und jenseits des Nationalstaats*. Frankfurt/M: Suhrkamp.

Muñoz de Bustillo, R. and de Pedraza, P. (2007) 'Determinants of subjective job insecurity in 5 European countries.' *AIAS Working Paper* 58, University of Amsterdam.

Näswall, K. and De Witte, H. (2003a) ''Objective' vs. 'Subjective' Job Insecurity: Consequences of Temporary Work for Job Satisfaction and Organizational Commitment in Four European Countries.' *Economic and Industrial Democracy* 24: 149-88.

Näswall, K. and De Witte, H. (2003b) 'Who Feels Insecure in Europe? Predicting Job Insecurity from Background Variables.' *Economic and Industrial Democracy* 24: 189-215.

Nielsen, H. (2003) *Opgørelse af kønsforskelle i ledigheden hos nyuddannede.* Århus: Handelshøjskolen i Århus, Nationaløkonomisk Institut.
Nielsen, H., Rosholm, M., Smith, N. and Husted, L. (2001) 'Intergenerational Transmissions and the School-to-Work Transition of 2nd Generation Immigrants.' *IZA Discussion Paper 296*, Bonn: Institute for the Study of Labor.
OECD (1994) 'Recent Labor Market Developments and Prospects.' *Employment Outlook*. Paris: OECD.
OECD (1996) 'Earnings Inequality, Low-Paid Employment and Earnings Mobility.' *Employment Outlook*. Paris: OECD.
OECD (1997a) 'Is job insecurity on the increase in OECD countries?' *Employment Outlook*. Paris: OECD.
OECD (1997b): *Education at a Glance*. OECD: Paris.
OECD (1998a) 'Getting started, settling in: the transition from education to the labour market.' *Employment Outlook*. Paris: OECD.
OECD (1998b) 'Thematic Review of the Transition from Initial Education to Working Life. Denmark.' *Background Report*. Paris: OECD.
OECD (2001) 'Labour Market Policies that Work.' *Policy Brief*. Paris: OECD.
OECD (2002a) 'The Ins and Outs of Long-Term Unemployment.' *Employment Outlook*. Paris: OECD.
OECD (2002b): *Education at a Glance*. OECD: Paris.
OECD (2004a) 'Employment Protection Regulation and Labour Market Performance.' *Employment Outlook*. Paris: OECD.
OECD (2004b) 'Wage-setting institutions and outcomes.' *Employment Outlook*. Paris: OECD.
OECD (2009a) *Employment Statistics Database*, available online at: <stats.oecd.org> (accessed 1 January 2009).
OECD (2009b) *Social Expenditures Database*, available online at: <www.oecd.org/els/social/expenditure> (accessed 1 January 2009).
Offe, C. (1977) *Opfer des Arbeitsmarktes. Zur Theorie der strukturierten Arbeitslosigkeit.* Neuwied/Darmstadt: Luchterhand.
Oppenheimer, V. K. (1988) 'A theory of marriage timing.' *American Journal of Sociology* 94: 563-91.
Oppenheimer, V. K. and Kalmijn, M. (1995) 'Life-Cycle Jobs.' *Research in Social Stratification and Mobility* 14: 1–38.
Oppenheimer, V. K., Kalmijn, M. and Lim, N. (1997) 'Men's career development and marriage timing during a period of rising inequality.' *Demography* 34: 311-30.
Oppenheimer, V. K. (2003) 'Cohabiting and Marriage During Young Men's Career-Development Process.' *Demography* 40: 127-49.
Osberg, L. (1998) 'Economic Insecurity.' *SPRC Discussion Paper 88*, Sydney: Social Policy Research Centre, University of New South Wales.

Pedersen, P. J. (2005) 'Unemployment Traps - Marginal Groups in the Danish labour market.' *European Economy* 2: 83-95.
Regini, M. (2000a) 'Between deregulation and social pacts: The responses of European economies to globalization.' *Politics and Society* 28: 5-33.
Regini, M. (2000b) 'The Dilemmas of Labour Market Regulation.' in G. Esping-Andersen and M. Regini (eds.) *Why deregulate labour markets,* Oxford: Oxford University Press.
Relikowski, I., Zielonka, M. and Hofmeister, H. (2008) 'Labor Market Entries and Early Careers in the United States of America, 1984–2002. Increasing Employment Instability Among Young People?' in H.-P. Blossfeld, S. Buchholz, E. Bukodi and K. Kurz (eds.) *Young Workers, Globalization and the Labor Market. Comparing Early Working Life in Eleven Countries,* Cheltenham, UK/Northampton, MA, USA: Edward Elgar.
Roseveare, D. and Jorgensen, M. (2004) 'Migration and Integration of Immigrants in Denmark.' *OECD Economics Department Working Papers* No. 386, Paris: OECD.
Rushkoff, D. (1996) *Playing the Future: How Kids' Culture Can Teach Us to Thrive in an Age of Chaos.* New York: Harper Collins.
Sattinger, M. (1998) 'Statistical discrimination with employment criteria.' *International Economic Review* 39: 205–237.
Scherer, S. (2004) 'Stepping-stones or traps? The consequences of labour market entry positions on future careers in West Germany, Great Britain and Italy.' *Work, Employment and Society* 18: 369-94.
Scherer, S. (2005) 'Patterns of Labour Market Entry – Long Wait or Career Instability? An Empirical Comparison of Italy, Great Britain and West Germany.' *European Sociological Review* 22: 1–14.
Schizzerotto, A. (2001) 'The Transition to Adulthood in Three European Countries as an Empirical Test of Various Theories on the Condition of Today's Youth.' in L. Chisholm, A. de Lillo, C. Leccardi and R. Richter *Family Forms and the Young Generation in Europe. Report on the Annual Seminar 2001,* Vienna: Austrian Institute for Family Studies.
Schmelzer, P. (2008) 'Increasing Employment Instability Among Young People? Labor Market Entries and Early Careers in Great Britain since the 1980s.' in H.-P. Blossfeld, S. Buchholz, E. Bukodi and K. Kurz (eds.) *Young Workers, Globalization and the Labor Market. Comparing Early Working Life in Eleven Countries,* Cheltenham, UK/Northampton, MA, USA: Edward Elgar.
Schömann, K., Rogowski, R. and Kruppe, T. (1998) *Labour market efficiency in the European union. Employment protection and fixed-term contracts.* London/New York: Routledge.
Shavit, Y. and Blossfeld, H.-P. (1993) *Persistent Inequality: Changing Educational Attainment in Thirteen Countries.* Boulder: Westview Press.

Shavit, Y. and Müller, W. (1998) *From School to Work. A Comparative Study of Educational Qualifications and Occupational Destinations*. Oxford: Clarendon Press.

Singelmann, J. (1978) *The Transformation of Industry: from Agriculture to Service Employment*. Beverly Hills, CA: Sage Publications.

Soskice, D. (1999) 'Divergent Production Regimes: Coordinated and Uncoordinated Market Economies in the 1980s and 1990s.' in H. Kitschelt, P. Lange, G. Marks and J. D. Stephens (eds.) *Continuity and Change in Contemporary Capitalism*, Cambridge: Cambridge University Press.

Statistics Denmark (2004) *Statistical Yearbook 2004*. Copenhagen: Statistics Denmark.

Statistics Denmark (2005) *Statistical Yearbook 2005*. Copenhagen: Statistics Denmark.

Steffensen, L. L. (2005) 'Pure Luck.' *Nordic Labour Journal* 10: 10.

Stejin, B. (2005) 'The Insecure Middle Class and Unionsation: An Empirical Investigation of Class, Job Insecurity, and Union Membership.' in H. De Witte (ed.) *Job insecurity, union involvement and union activism*, Hampshire, UK/Burlington, VT, USA: Ashgate Publishing.

Taylor, R. (2002) *Britain's World of Work. Myths and Realities*. London: Economic and Social Research Council.

Tuma, N. B. (1985) 'Effects of Labor Market Structure on Job Shift Patterns.' in J.J. Heckman and B. Singer (eds.) *Longitudinal Analysis of Labor Market Data*, Cambridge: Cambridge University Press.

UNESCO (2009) *UNESCO Statistics Data Center*, available online at: <http://stats.uis.unesco.org> (accessed 17 May 2009).

van der Velden, R. K. W. and Wolbers, M. H. J. (2003) 'The Integration of Young People into the Labour Market: The Role of Training Systems and Labour Market Regulation.' in W. Müller and M. Gangl (eds.) *Transitions from Education to Work in Europe*, Oxford: Oxford University Press.

Wallin, G. (2005) 'Youth falling at the hurdles of working life.' *Nordic Labour Journal* 10: 14-17.

Wang, R. and Weiss, A. (1998) 'Probation, Layoffs, and Wage-tenure Profiles: A Sorting Explanation.' *Labour Economics* 5: 359–83.

Waters, M. (2001) *Globalization*. London/New York: Routledge.

Werner, H. (1997) ‚Kann Deutschland von den Niederlanden lernen? Arbeitsmarktbilanz mit hohen Beschäftigungsgewinnen und niedrigen Arbeitslosenquoten. Durch Konsens zu Erfolgen in der Reformpolitik.' *IAB-Kurzbericht* 12, Nürnberg: Institut für Arbeitsmarkt- und Berufsforschung.

Werthes, Sascha, Heaven, Corinne and Vollnhals, Sven (2009) *Development, Security and the Contested Usefulness of Human Security: A Human (In-*

)*Security Index (2009)*. APSA 2009 Toronto Meeting Paper, available online at: <http://ssrn.com/abstract=1449319> (accessed 10 February 2010).

Westergaard-Nielsen, N. (2001) 'Danish Labour Market Policy: Is it worth it?' *CLS Working Papers 01-10*, University of Aarhus, Aarhus School of Business, Centre for Labour Market and Social Research.

Westergaard-Nielsen, N. (2008) 'Low-Wage Work in Denmark.' in Westergaard- N. Nielsen (ed.) *Low-Wage Work in Denmark*, New York: Russel Sage Foundation.

Wilthagen, T. (1998) 'Flexicurity: A new Paradigm for Labour Market Policy Reform?' *WZB Discussion Paper* FSI 98–202, Social Science Research Centre Berlin.

Wolbers, M. H. J. (2008) 'Increasing Labor Market Instability Among Young People? Labor Market Entry and Early Career Development Among School-Leavers in the Netherlands since the Mid-1980s.' in H.-P. Blossfeld, S. Buchholz, E. Bukodi and K. Kurz (eds.) *Young Workers, Globalization and the Labor Market. Comparing Early Working Life in Eleven Countries*, Cheltenham, UK/Northampton, MA, USA: Edward Elgar.

Zdrojewski, S., Grelet, Y. and Vallet, L.-A. (2008) 'Increasing Employment Instability in France? Young People's Labor Market Entry and Early Career since the 1990s.' in H.-P. Blossfeld, S. Buchholz, E. Bukodi and K. Kurz (eds.) *Young Workers, Globalization and the Labor Market. Comparing Early Working Life in Eleven Countries*, Cheltenham, UK/Northampton, MA, USA: Edward Elgar.

Zimmermann, K. F. and Hinte, H. (2005) *Zuwanderung und Arbeitsmarkt. Deutschland und Dänemark im Vergleich*. Berlin/Heidelberg/New York: Springer.

Appendix

Figure A.1: Scatterplot of the countries' positions within the four labor market entry regimes, 1997

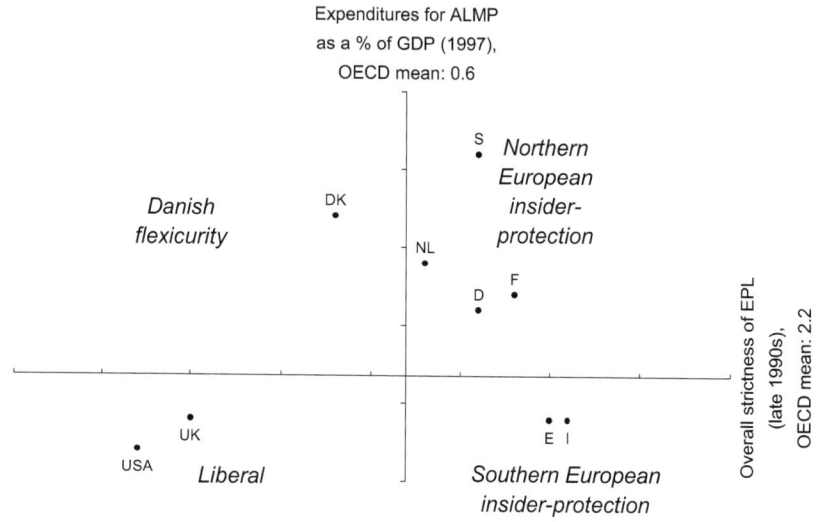

Source: Own illustration, based on OECD 2004a; 2009b.
Notes: The horizontal axis of the figure represents the countries' values on the OECD's composite employment protection legislation (EPL) index for the late 1990s, Version 2 (OECD 2004a): the higher its value, the stricter the country's overall employment protection regulations. The vertical axis denotes the countries' expenditures on active labor market policies (ALMP) as a percentage of their GDP in 1997 (OECD 2009b). Both axes intersect at the means of the respective measures over all OECD countries.

Table A.1: Total unemployment rates of 15- to 24- and 25- to 54-year-olds of both sexes, 1985-2005

	15- to 24-year-olds					25- to 54-year-olds				
	1985	1990	1995	2000	2005	1985	1990	1995	2000	2005
Denmark	11.6	11.6	9.9	6.7	7.9	7.1	8.0	6.2	4.1	4.2
France	25.6	19.2	25.9	20.7	20.2	7.5	8.0	10.5	9.2	7.8
Germany	9.1	4.4	8.0	8.4	14.8	6.3	4.7	7.6	7.1	11.0
Italy	30.8	26.3	32.2	29.9	22.9	4.9	6.5	8.9	8.8	6.5
Netherlands	16.1	10.5	11.7	5.3	8.7	9.2	7.1	6.3	2.3	4.2
Spain	43.8	30.3	40.5	25.3	19.7	15.6	13.2	20.0	12.3	8.0
Sweden	5.7	4.5	19.6	11.9	–	1.9	1.3	7.8	4.9	–
United Kingdom	18.4	10.5	15.9	12.2	11.6	9.7	5.9	7.6	4.6	3.5
United States	13.6	11.2	12.1	9.3	11.3	5.8	4.6	4.5	3.1	4.1

Source: OECD 2009a.

Figure A.2: Schematic representation of the career phase definition

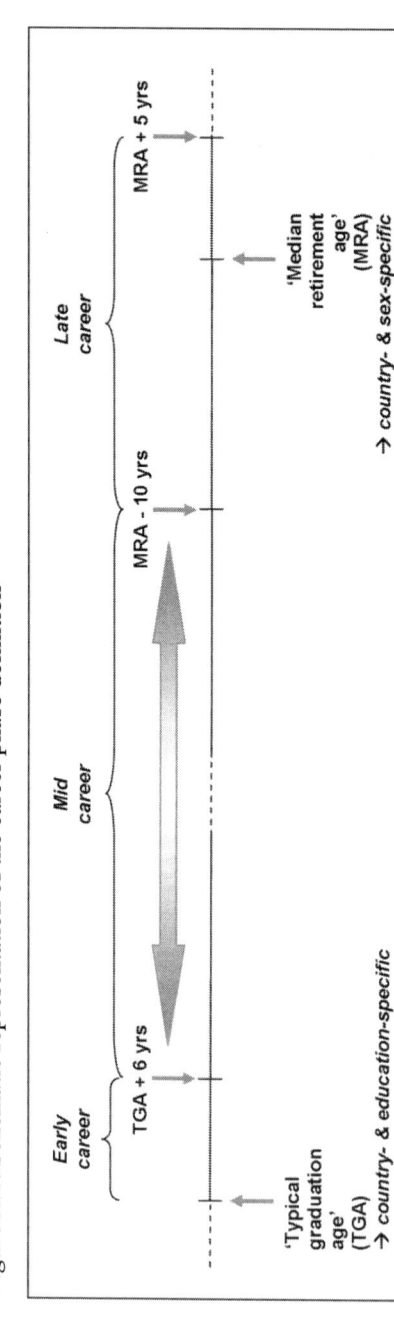

Source: Own illustration.
Notes: See next page.

Figure A.2: continued

Notes: The early career is defined as the phase of labor market establishment during the first 6 years after graduation; the late career, as the phase of labor market withdrawal during the last 10 years before retirement; and the mid career, as the employment phase between the end of the early career and the beginning of the late career.

Early-career employees were identified using education-specific *typical graduation ages* for each country taken from the OECD (1997b; 2002) and the UNESCO Statistics Data Center (for details, see Table A.2). An example: The typical graduation age for Danish university graduates is 27 years; following the above definition, this group is in their early career when they are between 27 and 32 years old.

Late-career employees were identified by using sex-specific median retirement ages for each country taken from EUROSTAT (2007) and (Gendell 2001). The age span defined for late-career employees included not only the last 10 years before but also the 5 years after reaching the respective median retirement age. For example, for men in Denmark, the country-specific median retirement age is 62 years; consequently, male employees from Denmark between 52 and 67 years of age were classified as late career employees.

Finally, mid-career employees were identified using the information underlying the early and late-career definitions: the respective country, educational level, sex, and age. For example, male university graduates from Denmark over 32 years (by definition the last year of this group's early career) and under 52 years (by definition the first year of this group's late career) were classified as mid-career employees.

Table A.2: Typical graduation ages and subsample age ranges used in this study

Coding of the 1997 ISSP variable 'degree'	Coding of the 2005 ISSP variable 'DEGREE'	GB	D	DK	E	F	I	NL	S	USA
2 Incomplete primary[a]		16	18	16	16	16	16	17	16	17
3 Primary completed[a]	1 Lowest formal qualification attainable[a]	16	18	16	16	16	16	17	16	17
4 Incomplete secondary[a]	2 Qualifications which are above the lowest qualification, but below the usual entry requirement for universities (intermediary secondary completed)[a]	16	18	16	16	16	16	17	16	17
5 Secondary completed	3 (Usual) Entry requirement for universities (higher secondary completed; the German *Abitur*, the French *Bac*, English *A-level*, etc.)	18	19	20	17	19	19	19	19	18
6 Incomplete university[b]	4 Qualifications which are above the higher secondary level, but below a full university degree; other education[b]	21	23	24	20	22	23	22	23	22
7 University completed	5 University degree completed	24	26	27	23	25	27	25	27	25
Resulting age ranges for the ISSP sub-samples of early-career employees (individuals in their first 6 years in the labor market)[c]		18-30	18-32	18-33	18-29	18-31	18-33	18-31	18-33	18-31

Sources: OECD (1997b; 2002); UNESCO (2009). (*Notes*: See next page.)

Table A.2: continued

Notes: "The typical graduation age is the age at the end of the last school/academic year of the corresponding level and programme when the degree is obtained. [It] is based on the assumption of full-time attendance in the regular education system without grade repetition" (OECD 1997b: 351).

a The typical graduation ages for respondents with education below completed upper secondary were based on UNESCO's (2009) information on national ending ages of compulsory education. Values for Italy were raised from age 14 to age 16, based on empirical minimum leaving ages observed by Gangl (2003c).

b The typical graduation ages for respondents with incomplete university education (coded as 6 in 1997 and 4 in 2005, respectively) were computed as follows: (typical graduation age for 'university completed' + typical graduation age for 'secondary completed') / 2.

c The lower age threshold was 18 irrespective of different country-specific typical graduation ages for respondents with education below completed upper secondary, because only individuals aged 18 years or older were interviewed in the ISSP surveys. This causes a particular bias: In all countries except for Germany, individuals without completed upper secondary education had only low chances of being included in the sample in their first (NL, USA) or first two (GB, DK, E, F, I, S) employment-career years, respectively. Should this group perceive higher insecurity in the early stages of their career, their insecurity perception has probably been underestimated in this study.

Table A.3: Explanatory variables used in the Danish country study

Education leavers' cohort:	Defined by the general labor market situation in the year when leaving education (see Figure 2.2): – 1981–83 – 1984–87 – 1988–93 – 1994–2003/1994–2002[a]
Time since leaving education:	– Up to 1 year – 1–2 years – 2–3 years – 3 and more years
Duration of first job search:	– Up to 1 year – 1–2 years – 2 and more years
Duration of first employment spell:	– 1–2 years – 2–3 years – 3–4 years – 4–5 years
Yearly average unemployment rate:	Based on figures from Statistics Denmark
Sex:	– Male – Female
Ethnic origin:	– Danish – Non-Danish (immigrants and their descendants)[b]
Qualification:	Highest completed education, time-varying, measured using a 5-point scale similar to CASMIN (see Brauns and Steinmann 1999): 1: lower secondary education without vocational qualification 2: upper secondary education without vocational qualification 3: lower secondary education with vocational qualification in the dual system 4: lower secondary education with short/medium-cycle higher vocational education 5: college/university education and any other long-cycle higher tertiary vocational education

Table A.3: continued

Wage level:	A person's position in the wage distribution of all employees between the ages of 15 and 59, time-varying, based on gross hourly wages, deflated, and summarized in five categories: 1: very low (wages within the lowest 10% of all wages) 2: low (wages above the lowest 10%, but within the lowest 20% of all wages) 3: medium (wages above the lowest 20%, but within the lowest 80% of all wages) 4: high (wages above the lowest 80%, but within the lowest 90% of all wages) 5: very high (wages above the lowest 90% of all wages)
Job quality:	– Low-wage job (time-varying, marks jobs with earnings within the lowest decile of the wage distribution, i.e., within the lowest wage-level category) – Higher paid job
Firm size:	Based on the company's number of employees: – 1–10 employees – 11–50 employees – 51–500 employees – Over 500 employees
Industry:	Coded according to the classification developed by Singelmann (1978): – Extractive sector – Transformative sector – Producer services – Distributive services – Personal services – Social services
Interaction: qualification*cohort:	– Qualification 1*1981–83 – Qualification 2*1981–83 – Qualification 3*1981–83 – Qualification 4*1981–83 – Qualification 5*1981–83 – Qualification 1*1984–87 etc.

Source: Own illustration.
Notes: a As the risk set for the early-career analyses was restricted to school-leavers registered in a first employment before 2003, the youngest cohort for the early-career analyses included individuals who left education between 1994 and 2002, whereas the youngest cohort for the labor market entry analyses included individuals who left education between 1994 and 2003.
b Note that immigrants from Western and non-Western countries were not distinguished and that the immigrants in the subsample were a selective group: foreigners who completed their education in Denmark.

Table A.4: OECD indices on labor market conditions and policies used in the present study

	Average unemployment, past 6 years[a]		Overall EPL strictness[b]		Public spending on ALMP[c]		Public spending on unempl. compensation[d]	
	1997	2005	1997	2005	1997	2005	1997	2005
Flexicurity regime:								
Denmark	7.9	4.8	1.8	1.8	1.7	1.7	2.1	1.3
Liberal regime:								
Great Britain	9.0	4.9	1.0	1.1	0.4	0.5	0.5	0.3
United States	6.1	5.2	0.7	0.7	0.2	0.1	0.3	0.3
Northern European insider-protection regime:								
France	11.6	9.0	2.8	2.9	1.2	0.9	1.4	1.6
Germany	8.3	9.2	2.6	2.5	1.1	1.0	1.4	1.5
Netherlands[e]	6.2	-	2.3	-	1.4	-	2.4	-
Sweden	9.1	6.1	2.6	2.6	2.1	1.3	2.1	1.2
Southern European insider-protection regime:								
Italy[e]	11.3	-	3.1	-	0.4	-	0.4	-
Spain	21.7	11.2	3.0	3.1	0.4	0.8	2.5	2.2

Source: Own illustration.
Notes: a The first measure refers to the OECD's average unemployment rates for men and women between 15 and 65 years of age (OECD 2009a). For 1997, the average unemployment rate was computed for the period from 1992 to 1997; for 2005, for the period from 2000 and 2005.
b The second measure refers to the OECD's summary measure of employment protection legislation strictness. For 1997, the indicator for the late 1990s was taken (Version 2); for 2005, the indicator for 2003 (OECD 2004).
c The third measure refers to the OECD's indicators for public spending on active labor market programs as a percentage of GDP (OECD 2009b; aggregated data).
d The fourth measure refers to the OECD's indicators for unemployment compensation as a percentage of GDP (OECD 2009b; aggregated data).
e There are no data for the Netherlands and Italy in 2005, because these two countries were not included in the 2005 ISSP's *Work Orientations* surveys; that is, the data set used for this study refers only to the 1997 interviews (and indicators) for these countries.

Table A.5: Explanatory variables used in the cross-national study on job-loss worry

Sex:	– Male – Female
Age group:	– 18–24 years – 25–33 years
Education in years:	– Up to 9 years – 10 and more years
Union membership:[a]	– Yes – No
Fixed-term employment:[b]	– Yes – No
Child(ren) living in the household (hh.:)[c]	– Yes – No
Interaction: child(ren)* sex:	– Child(ren) in the hh. * female
Employed spouse:[d]	– Yes – No
Child(ren) living in the household:	– Yes – No
Sector :[a]	– Private sector – Public sector
Average unemployment rate, past 6 years:	Based on figures from the OECD's Employment Statistics Database (OECD 2009a)
National strictness of employment protection:	Based on the OECD's (2004a) summary score for overall employment protection
Government spending on active labor market policies (as % of GDP):	Based on figures from the OECD's Social Expenditures Database (OECD 2009b)
Government spending on unemployment compensation (as % of GDP):	Based on figures from the OECD's Social Expenditures Database (OECD 2009b)
Country dummies	– Denmark – Great Britain – United States – France – Germany – Netherlands[e] – Sweden – Italy[e] – Spain

Source: Own illustration.
Notes: a In 1997, union membership and employment sector were not surveyed in the United States.
b The type of employment contract was not recorded in any of the 1997 surveys.
c In 1997, the number of children living in the respondent's household was not surveyed in Great Britain and in the Netherlands.
d Spousal employment was not a topic of the 1997 surveys in the Netherlands.
e The Netherlands and Italy did not take part in the 2005 surveys.

Unsere Fachzeitschriften auf www.budrich-journals.de

- Einzelbeiträge im Download (Micropayment)

- Kombi-Abos für AbonnentInnen

- IP- und Domain-Zugänge (Mehrplatzlizenzen)

- Großer *open access*-Bereich

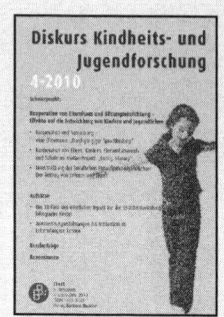

Wir haben unsere Fachzeitschriften für Sie online gestellt. Als AbonnentIn z.B. mit Kombi-Abo bekommen Sie weiterhin Ihr Heft wie gewohnt bequem nach Hause geliefert und Sie haben Zugriff auf das gesamte online-Archiv.

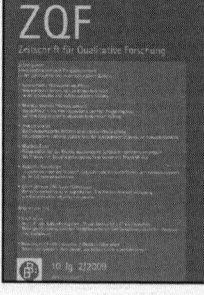

Zu günstigen Preisen. Fragen Sie uns!

**Verlag Barbara Budrich •
Barbara Budrich Publishers**
Stauffenbergstr. 7. D-51379 Leverkusen Opladen
Tel +49 (0)2171.344.594 • Fax +49 (0)2171.344.693 •
info@budrich-verlag.de

www.budrich-verlag.de • www.budrich-journals.de